THE FORGOTTEN FRONTIER

PUBLICATIONS OF THE
CENTER FOR MIDDLE EASTERN STUDIES, NUMBER 10
William R. Polk, General Editor

Publications of the Center for Middle Eastern Studies

THE FORGOTTEN FRONTIER
A History of the Sixteenth-Century Ibero-African Frontier

ANDREW C. HESS

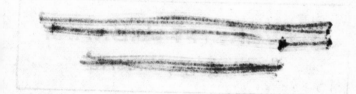

The University of Chicago Press
CHICAGO AND LONDON

THE UNIVERSITY OF CHICAGO PRESS, CHICAGO 60637
THE UNIVERSITY OF CHICAGO PRESS, LTD., LONDON

Printed in the United States of America
82 81 80 79 78   54321

ANDREW C. HESS is associate professor of history at Temple University and the author of many scholarly articles.

Library of Congress Cataloging in Publication Data

Hess, Andrew C
    The forgotten frontier.

    (Publications of the Center for Middle Eastern
Studies)
    Bibliography: p.
    Includes index.
    1. Africa, North—Relations (general) with Spain.
2. Spain—Relations (general) with North Africa.
3. Africa, North—History—1517–1882. 4. Spain—
History—House of Austria, 1516–1700. 5. Western
Mediterranean—History. I. Title. II. Series:
Chicago. University. Center for Middle Eastern
Studies. Publications.
DT197.5.S7H47   301.29'46'062   77–25517

ISBN 0–226–33028–1

To Sue

CONTENTS

ILLUSTRATIONS

ACKNOWLEDGMENTS

While writing this frontier history I have become indebted to a large number of scholars and friends. For a work of this complexity it could not have been otherwise. None of them bears any responsibility for what this book contains; yet without their encouragement it would never have come into being.

Stanford and Ezel Shaw joined Hikmet Sebüktegin in providing me with the inspiration to study Ottoman history. In Turkey, Professor Necat Göyünç taught me the mysteries of Ottoman scripts. He, along with the archivists of the Baş Bakanlık Arşivi, helped me unlock the secrets of the Ottoman archives.

Bruce Craig introduced me to the subject of frontier history. Dennis Hyde, William Cleveland, and Richard Chambers patiently suffered through my initial struggles with this area of history.

I am particularly grateful for the assistance and guidance I have received over the years from Professor Halil Inalcık. His deep knowledge of Ottoman history and his enthusiasm for the field kept the spirit alive. As the references indicate, it is his work that lies at the core of my own interpretation of Ottoman history.

Three men were instrumental in urging me to set my research within a large framework. Norman Itzkowitz of the Near Eastern Center at Princeton University has at one time or another read and criticized nearly everything I have written. Roderick McGrew of Temple University not only encouraged me to move in the direction of comparative history but also expended much of his own time helping me bring this book under control. For the assistance of John Elliott of the Institute for Advanced Study I am deeply grateful. At a time when historians rarely look outside their chosen fields of specialization, he gave willingly of his energies in order that I might cross some scholarly boundaries.

Just as I am indebted to the individuals who have played a major role in shaping the content of my work, so also am I grateful for the institutional aid I have received. Office of Education grants supported a year of study in Istanbul and another year of work in Morocco. At various times, the American Philosophical Society, the American Research Institute in Turkey, the American Council of Learned Societies, the Social Science Research Council, and Temple University have provided grants in aid for summer travel and research. An appointment to the Institute for Advanced Study in 1973–74 gave me the opportunity and the stimulus to put together my ideas.

Without the support of my wife, to whom the book is dedicated, it is unlikely that I would have been able to complete this task. She gladly endured the strains of travel and gave invaluable assistance in the preparation of many drafts.

NOTE ON TRANSLITERATION

The system of transliteration employed in this book for the Middle Eastern languages follows that of the *International Journal of Middle Eastern Studies*, with some exceptions. For Ottoman Turkish I have employed modern Turkish orthography. The Latin letters used in modern Turkish present some problems for the reader of English. They are pronounced nearly like their English equivalents, with the following exceptions:

LETTER	ENGLISH PRONUNCIATION
c	*j*
ç	*ch*
ğ	after *e, i*—like *y* in saying; after *o, ö, u, ü*—like *w* in sowing; after *a, ı*—hardly sounded, but has the effect of lengthening the preceding vowel
ı	like the *a* in serial
j	*zh*
ö	like the German *ö*
ü	like the German *ü*
v	lighter than the English *v*

In modern Turkish the tendency is to change the final Ottoman letters *d* and *b* into *t* and *p*. Thus Murad and Bayezid become Murat and Bayezit. However the final *t* or *p* returns to *d* and *b* when followed by vowels. Since Ottoman personal and place names are not always rendered entirely in the modern Turkish form, readers will find some variation in their spelling.

Arabic names not found in an Ottoman context are given according to the common transliteration for Arabic, with some departures.

Several of the more cumbersome devices have been left out where it helps correlate Latin and Romance versions of the Muslim name. Thus the elision of *al-* with words beginning in *d, dh, n, s, ş, sh, t, ṭ, z,* and *ẓ* has been adopted because the Spanish scribe faithfully reproduced these sounds. In Hispanic situations I have employed the Romance form of Muslim names in order to avoid confusion. In any event, the vagaries of multiple transcription make an etymological reconstitution difficult.

For North African names I have attempted to use the form, either Arabic or French, most familiar to the reader. We have little knowledge of how Arabic was pronounced in the early modern Maghrib. Where necessary I have used the classical system of transliteration.

Arabic terms used in an Ottoman situation have been given their Turkish pronunciations and spellings. In doubtful cases the transliteration comes down on the side of modern usage.

One: THE IBERO-AFRICAN FRONTIER

Santiago of Spain
Killed my Moors,
Scattered my company,
Broke my standard.

Alfonso Oncero

Themes of unity and diversity run like broad bands of contrasting color through the history of the Mediterranean world. Linked together by the sea, the inhabitants of the lands bordering this island-strewn inland body of water long ago developed a set of common cultural traits. A distinctive attitude toward sexual honor, widespread use of certain foods, and a shared pattern of daily life are only a few of these familiar Mediterranean habits. They imply cultural unity. Yet with a perverse irony, Mediterranean peoples rejected the union the sea fostered and divided themselves into well-defined and oftentimes hostile civilizations.

Ideally, the historian of the Mediterranean world should struggle to expose the patterns of both unity and diversity that lie beneath the surface of events. Practically, however, the scale of most ventures into the field of Mediterranean history tends to drive the scholar toward a viewpoint based upon only one of the two themes.

For the sixteenth century, any discussion of this problem must deal with one of the twentieth-century's great historians. Fernand Braudel's monumental study of Mediterranean life in the age of Philip II firmly establishes unity as the vantage point for explaining the history of a period long dominated by narrative accounts of the conflict between Latin Christendom and Islam. Even though Braudel is sensitive to the bitter relations between the great religious

1

communities, his sweeping geohistory of the societies living within the boundaries of the date palm and the olive tree deemphasizes the divisions between Mediterranean civilizations. Over and over again he demonstrates how thoroughly the actions of societies were shaped by the geographical unity the sea imposed upon its peoples. Where possible he marshaled information about those sixteenth-century events that leaped cultural boundaries—monetary movements, climatic changes, population increases, economic fluctuations, technological limits—to describe the rhythms of Mediterranean life. Against such a background, old-fashioned political and diplomatic history lost its cultural cutting edge. Elites no longer made their decisions just on the basis of political and religious values. Policies were selected from a narrow range of alternatives dictated by the day-to-day run of events, by the behavior of phenomena obeying short-run cycles, and by the glacierlike motion of forces whose movement largely escaped the knowledge of statesmen.[1] War, for example, was related more directly to the collisions, conflicts, and limitations created by the interactions of these three waves of historical change—all operating in a common arena—than to the division of the Mediterranean community into mutually antagonistic civilizations.[2]

Cultural lag undoubtedly played its part in the formation of Braudel's unitary vision of the Mediterranean world. By the mid-twentieth century a sophisticated history from the bottom up could be written only for regions of the Mediterranean where sources and methodologies were well developed: the lands of Latin Christendom. Braudel knew he could not assume that what happened within the Habsburg empire also took place within the boundaries of the Ottoman state. And so he made a valiant attempt to include the preliminary results of research among the mountain of documents held within the Ottoman archives. But modern Turkish historians were in no position to accomplish overnight what their European colleagues had taken centuries to do. Limitations imposed by time and sources, then, compelled Braudel to rest his account largely on examples drawn from the experience of Latin Christendom.[3] Thus a geographical framework that was culturally neutral and an archival research that was predominantly European merged with Braudel's concern for cross-cultural economic and social phenomena to attenuate the theme of diversity.

Whatever the problems of the modern historian, travelers with a sense of the Mediterranean's early modern past have little difficulty locating the symbols of cultural division. One can see an early sixteenth-century Roman Catholic chapel set uncomfortably in the middle of the Grand Mosque at Cordoba; or the tourist can attempt to understand why an Italianate pleasure palace of the same vintage seems so out of place next to the quintessence of Moorish architecture, the Alhambra. So raw is the aesthetic conflict between these architectural symbols of the respective civilizations that it suggests a theme, and a pattern of analysis, for Mediterranean history that is much at odds with the synthesis of Braudel. There on the sixteenth-century Hispano-Muslim frontier, the architecture of a cultural collision gives visual proof that the early modern era was a period when the division between Mediterranean civilizations became more important.

To state it baldly, I believe that the separation of the Mediterranean world into different, well-defined cultural spheres is the main theme of its sixteenth-century history. Moreover, this divergence in the internal patterns of Latin Christian and Turko-Muslim civilizations continued long past the death of Philip II in 1598; it retained its momentum during two centuries of decline, to determine the strikingly different responses both civilizations made to the revolutionary events of the late eighteenth century.

If, as I hold here, the process of historical change during the sixteenth century produced a new segregation of Mediterranean life, such a discovery would go a long way toward explaining the special structure of succeeding centuries. To accept the argument that Turko-Muslim civilization had a nontraditional history of successful expansion provides a basis for understanding why European students of Musim decline failed to appreciate the overall cohesion of Islamic society. Second, an understanding of the heightened division between the two great empires in the age of Philip II would help show why European imperialism struck the Ottoman empire with such force much later on: a high level of military conflict in the sixteenth century turned the two civilizations away from each other, while a rapid divergence of institutions made borrowing anything but weapons appear both unnecessary and disloyal. So Western civilization, armed with the sailing ship, encircled Turko-Muslim empires. Unlike Japan, however, the House of Islam did not find the appearance of Western sailors and merchants on its fringes sufficient cause for modifying its society through any substantial acquisition of the foreigner's institutions. Instead, an introverted Islamic civilization suffered a devastating invasion by the armies and merchants of Europe during the nineteenth century. But this forced integration of Turko–Muslim empires into a worldwide political and economic system dominated by the West produced, in modern times, no cultural unification of the Mediterranean world; it merely super-imposed new divisions, phrased in political and economic rather than religious terms, on the old reasons for disunity.

It follows clearly that we need an approach to the sixteenth-century history of the Mediterranean world that would brighten the theme of diversity. How should this be done? To transcend Braudel's emphasis on unity by juxtaposing modern histories of Ottoman and Habsburg empires would certainly yield an indigestible mass of information. Again, Granada's architectural history suggests a solution: would not a study of the zone where the edges of these two sixteenth-century empires met both reduce the scale of analysis and at the same time direct attention toward the diverging paths of the two great traditions?

To be meaningful within the framework of Mediterranean history, such a study should also show how each imperial center dealt with the common periphery.[4] Here the main line of investigation would be directed toward understanding how the representatives of two sharply opposed civilizations changed or failed to change their societies within a region where the two great cultures did not exist in isolation. Once the events of this zone are linked to their respective culture poles, it will be possible to see whether the history of the frontier has anything to say about the relations between Mediterranean civilizations.

One obvious arena for such a frontier history within a larger framework is the wide meeting ground at the western end of the Mediterranean, where Latin Christendom and Islam had comingled since the eighth century. Not only had the region between the coast of North Africa and the Pyrenees become the stage for a running feud between the two civilizations, but by the middle of the sixteenth century it had also achieved the status of a major front in the war between the Ottoman and Habsburg empires.

It is, moreover, an archetypal Mediterranean frontier. Although the cultural line of division between Islam and Latin Christendom settled on the Strait of Gibraltar after 1492, this late location of the border was not determined by the physical division between the Iberian Peninsula and North Africa. Passage over the narrow waterway has always been relatively easy. It also cannot be argued that acute geographical differences conferred special permanency on a border whose chief symbol was, ironically, the Rock of Gibraltar.

Southeastern Iberia and the northeastern edge of the Maghrib share the same topography, climate, flora, and fauna.[5]

Put simply, the Strait of Gibraltar was a convenient spot for two Mediterranean civilizations to bring to a conclusion a long and complex intercultural history. After the Muslim invasion of 711, the changing balance of power between Islam and Iberian Christendom resulted in a sinuous movement of the military border northward to the Pyrenees and then southward to the coasts of Andalusia. Because warriors regularly outran the ability of societies to assimilate the civilization of the conquerors, the boundaries of the no-man's-land rarely matched the location of a much wider region of mixed Muslim and Latin Christian societies. During the medieval centuries, this broad belt in which the social order was neither Christian nor Muslim divided Spain into three zones. Along the foothills of the Pyrenees, solidly Christian kingdoms blocked the northward march of Islam. To the southeast in Andalusia an overwhelmingly Muslim society imported the culture of the eastern Mediterranean. Between the northern and southern regions of the peninsula an intermixing of Muslim and Christian populations formed a zone where religious and social pluralism was the common order. There the interaction of the different communities brought into being a history of social tension that oscillated between poles of cultural flexibility and outright intolerance.[6]

Fostered mostly by Islam's evolutionary view of religion and the sheer necessity to exist, a tradition of religious cohabitation emerged during the three centuries of Umayyad rule. By the late medieval period, however, confessional pluralism became less tolerable. This waning acceptance of multiple cultural order is the key to understanding what made the early modern Hispano-Muslim frontier uniquely Mediterranean. A history like that of China, where nomads plunged across the steppes of inner Asia to conquer dense agricultural societies and to become Sinified, did not take place in Iberia. Nor did the Hispano-Muslim clash create a moving frontier like that of the Americas, where one culture overwhelmed the other. Rather, the relatively high ability of each civilization to organize its populations, to make the task of assimilation either impossible or extremely difficult, is what branded this frontier.[7]

Military history, however, not intractable social conflict, began the discussion about the importance of the Hispano-Muslim frontier to Europeans. How the Arab conquerors crossed the Pyrenees to threaten the heart of Europe until stopped at Poitiers in 732, and how they were gradually driven back into Africa by the champions of Christendom, provided the substance for the epics that lie behind the modern interest in Spain's military history. On a less romantic plane than the narratives spawned by the *Chanson de Roland* or the *Poema de mío Cid*, modern scholars have worried over the degree to which constant warfare with Islam shaped the institutions of Christian Iberia. Was medieval Spanish society a vast military encampment?[8] Did Christian warriors borrow military institutions from the Arabs? Or, more important, did the successful campaign to reconquer the peninsula from the Muslims form the early modern states of Iberia?

If the Hispanic wing of the Islamic conquests established the military reputation of the Iberian frontier, the confrontation of medieval Christian and Islamic civilizations on the edge of Europe also excited cultural historians. Few accepted the hypothesis of Henri Pirenne that the Arab conquests cut Europe off from the heritage of antiquity and the wealth of the Mediterranean world.[9] Exactly the opposite conclusion predominated when scholars recognized the important role of the Iberian frontier in transferring the heritage of Mediterranean antiquity to Europe through the medium of classical Arabic. Going even further, some historians claimed that the intellectual exuberance of Muslim courts in Spain substantially influenced the creative processes at the base of an emerging Western civilization. Here comparative cultural history strongly suggested that the authors of a new European literature were inspired to some unknown degree by the intellectual achievements of Hispano-Muslim writers. All this led only to other studies on how Islamic science, art, and philosophy beat a Spanish path into Europe.[10]

The idea that the jumble of cultures on the medieval frontier of Iberia stimulated creative movements of crucial importance for Latin Christendom soon stirred up a profound argument about the origins of Spanish society. In the same way that Paul Wittek explained the birth of Habsburg Spain's great competitor, the Ottoman empire, Américo Castro located the home of modern Spanish civilization in the mixed culture of the Hispano-Muslim frontier. This departure from the standard historical approach, which laid heavy emphasis on the Christian background of Portuguese and Spanish society, could hardly go unnoticed. Opponents of Castro pointed to the kinglets of northern Spain as the faithful custodians of a pre-Islamic Iberian identity. It was these Old Christians who weathered the Arab conquests and transcended their rivalries to fight for their intense vision of Iberian Christianity.[11] And so began an unfinished debate—a modern version, on the plane of history, of the struggle between Islam and Latin Christendom.

Almost too familiar is the end of Islamic political history in Iberia. Along the Ibero-African frontier a historical triptych unfolded to announce the transformation of Iberian society from its medieval structure: the expulsion of Jews from Iberia, Columbus's discovery of the New World, and the defeat of the last Muslim kingdom in Spain—all in the year 1492. From the viewpoint of Mediterranean frontier history, these three shocks to the old order of life once again affirmed the importance of the western region where Islamic, Jewish, and Latin Christian civilizations intermingled.

If previous interaction between these three great cultures acted as a guide, one would expect a new period of mutual stimulation. Yet the creative ground of the past brought forth not an era of intercultural invention but an age of European oceanic discoveries. Swiftly, intrepid Iberian navigators shrank the space between the world's older societies and the innovative states of early modern Europe. This new framework for global relations in turn gave birth to one of the major themes of modern world history: as the breakthrough in maritime technology created a closer-knit and more dynamic world economy, so also did it intensify the differences between the subsections of an emerging global community. On the Ibero-African frontier this discordant sound of modern history was heard very early; for while European navigators sailed beyond the sight of Andalusian and Moroccan shores, contrasting Mediterranean civilizations separated themselves at the Strait of Gibraltar, ending their history of integration in a little-known exchange of ambassadors and border populations.

Few European historians worried about the conditions under which Spain shook off eight centuries of Islamic civilization or how Iberia detached herself from an ancient entanglement with North Africa. Although warfare between the Iberian states and the Muslim rulers of North Africa continued throughout the sixteenth century, the voyages to the New World and the doubling of the Cape of Good Hope suddenly widened the horizons of Europe. As though a great burden had been lifted from the history of Iberia, scholars brought to an end the old argument between Islam and Christendom over who owned the peninsula and turned their talents to describing the conquests in Asia and the New World, the bloody religious and dynastic wars in Europe, the pageantry of the Spanish Armada, and the play of powerful new economic forces unleashed by the Discoveries. Even the narratives concerning the wars with the Ottoman Turks moved the center of the struggle with Islam away from Spain and North Africa to the east, where the siege of Malta and the spectacular battle of Lepanto claimed much attention.[12]

Muslim historians followed this same general pattern. There was, after all, little merit in dwelling upon the Muslim community's expulsion from Iberia. The warriors of the western frontier did gain some honor when they destroyed the crusading army of the Portuguese at Alcazar in Morocco during the summer of 1578.[13] Yet this battle in which three kings perished made only a light mark upon Islamic history. With the exception of a nineteenth-century North African scholar, Aḥmad ibn Khālid an-Nāṣirī (Es-Salâoui), who saw the Muslim accomplishment as symbolic proof of monotheism's victory over the Trinity, the utter destruction of Iberia's last crusade did not occupy great space in the chronicles of the Islamic community.[14] Far more attention was devoted to the spectacular holy wars of the Ottoman Turks on eastern Mediterranean frontiers.

Outbursts of social and religious violence during the late sixteenth century did attract some attention to the history of the Ibero-African border. After the conquest of Granada, Spain's aggressive frontiersmen pushed the no-man's-land across the Strait of Gibraltar to Africa, where it became stable. Meanwhile, the social perimeter of Latin Christendom continued to lag behind the military frontier, marking off a zone of mixed cultures in the southeast corner of the peninsula. There the increasing intolerance of the Old Christians matched the Muslim determination to resist assimilation. Impatience and social instability followed until the last expulsion of the Hispano-Muslims ended religious cohabitation in 1614. To explain this uprooting of the religious minorities, historians studied—not always with the objective of understanding the history of the peninsula—the rise of religious intolerance in Spain. Other scholars examined the sources to document the non-Christian resistance to assimilation.[15] Whatever the explanation, by the turn of the seventeenth century Iberia was rid of all but Latin Christian civilization. Thereupon the history of the Hispano-Muslim frontier, now an Ibero-African border, attracted much less attention until the European penetration of North Africa in the nineteenth century.

One reason for the near absence of interest in the history of the Ibero-African frontier during almost two hundred years is that it ceased to play a distinctive part in the evolution of either Muslim or

European history. No longer did Muslim leaders like the celebrated Almoravid ruler Yūsuf ibn Tāshufīn threaten the western edge of Europe from North Africa.[16] No longer did Iberians need to maintain a heroic mythology in order to sustain the spirit of the Reconquest. Spaniards, with a touch of sadness that finds its way into the second part of *Don Quixote*, gradually displaced the old bellicosity they felt toward Muslims in favor of a more peaceful indifference.[17]

Other Europeans joined the Iberians in this intellectual and emotional disengagement. Muslim corsairs based in North Africa disturbed the trend somewhat. Yet only so many accounts could be written about the scourge of Christendom, the Barbary corsairs. Educated men sensed that firing moral broadsides at Muslim privateers was an uncomfortable business, especially in light of how often western sailors were involved in the same brutish profession.[18] Besides, it was a minor affair; and in any event the historians of the Oceanic Discoveries found the adventures of European sailors in other exotic corners of the globe vastly more intriguing than the torments suffered by the prisoners of Algiers.

Braudel's masterly account of the Mediterranean world in the age of Philip II did little to remove the cobwebs that gradually obscured the history of Iberia's Muslim frontier after 1492. Philip II's reign was, after all, the period when Spain broke away from imperial warfare with Islam. Only the nasty internal problem of unassimilated Muslim converts to Christianity—the Moriscos—disturbed the tranquility of life along the peninsula's Mediterranean perimeter until the completion of the expulsions in 1614. What nearly finished off the history of the Ibero-African frontier was not this final agony of Islam in Spain, but Braudel's unitary vision of the Mediterranean world. His trinitarian waves of historical movement simply lapped over cultural divisions. Moreover, his analysis of Philip II's reign concerned the outcome of events in Europe far more than it did the movement of inner affairs in North Africa and Asia Minor. Thus did the conclusion of his study, setting the Mediterranean outside the grand arena of history, become a metaphor for the arrival of an unparalleled event: the shift of the center of European civilization from the world of cloudless skies and blue seas to the dark and rainy climate of northern Europe, where a precapitalist order was emerging.[19] Within such a scheme, Spain's final expulsion of the crypto-Muslims in 1614 could only be a concluding act of minor proportions: the history of the Ibero-African frontier could be forgotten.

   If, however, the cruel fates of Iberian Jews and Muslims were not
just failures of assimilation to be studied in isolation but clues to a
wider issue, then the mental framework for that larger problem must
be clearly stated. National or unicultural approaches to the history
of this border are no longer sufficient. Somehow the changing
character of frontier society must be perceived so as to link the course
of events with the actions of the empires representing the Mediterranean's two opposed cultural blocks. This means that the problem
posed herein—What does the history of the Ibero-African frontier
say about the relations between Mediterranean civilizations?—must
be examined with a mind sensitive to cultural difference.
   Approached from such a viewpoint, the history of the Ibero-
African frontier sheds its remoteness. Unlike previous eras, powerful
armies and bureaucracies subjected border populations to unheard-of
controls. Over the course of the sixteenth century, imperial administrations and border societies clashed and together defined the space
of two increasingly different civilizations, so that the wide belt of
cultural pluralism of the late fifteenth century, the zone including
both Hispano-Muslims and the Christian-Muslim military border
in North Africa, shrank to a thin line. Paradoxically this rigidly
delineated boundary virtually eliminated the possibility of cultural
experimentation in the very region where innovation in maritime
technology drew the world's populations closer together. How this
once famous borderland reflected a formalization of relations between two Mediterranean civilizations and thereby attained the
status of a forgotten frontier is the subject of this book.

Two: A MILITARY REVOLUTION

The Arabs of Fez and Marrakech are neither armed with pistols and matchlocks nor are they fond of or accustomed to using these offensive weapons. (Morocco, ca. 1550)

Mármol, *Descripción general de Affrica*

Technological innovation and political change converged during the mid-fifteenth century to revolutionize the art of waging war. More efficient armies, navies, and bureaucracies contributed greatly to the era of expansion that began with the fall of Constantinople (1453) and the rise of Catholic Spain (1469). At first glance the geography of these changes seemed to strike a rough balance between the Mediterranean's two civilizations: the Portuguese and Spanish states organized the manpower of Iberia, while the Ottoman empire tapped the human wealth of Asia Minor. But powder technology was exploited first among these northern states, not by the sultanates of Africa's Islamic rim. No Mediterranean balance at all was visible in the use of early modern naval invention. Only the Portuguese and the Spanish gambled with the maritime technology that led to the European Discoveries.[1] Moreover, the appearance of vigorous empires in the Christian west and the Muslim east took place at a time when Muslim Spain and North Africa were in a state of political decentralization. Thus a new concentration of power in the hands of Iberian ruling classes found the governments of the Muslim west singularly unprepared. The result was a mutation in the history of the Hispano-Muslim frontier.

Behind the exterior manifestations of Iberia's experience with the fifteenth-century military revolution lay a general increase both in Europe's population and in its wealth. Dense human populations

11

provided governments with demographic reservoirs from which men and women could be drawn to fill the ranks of armies, repopulate conquered areas, and fuel overseas expansion. Commercial success reordered the economy, funded the independence of cities, and spurred on the search for new sources of wealth. Concurrently, technological innovations in the fields of warfare and transportation visibly confirmed a departure from the past. Yet new equipment alone did not make soldiers and sailors dance to a different piper. What made the difference was the emergence of a state capable of controlling vast resources for that most expensive imperial luxury, war.[2]

These and multifold other changes in the ways of European life reached Iberia and exerted pressure on the Hispano-Muslim border at different times and in ways that are difficult to measure. If, however, border history is confined to the reign of the Catholic kings (1469–1516), prominent changes in three areas on the Christian but not on the Muslim side of the frontier directly influenced the course of imperial history: the revolution in the technology of naval communication, the employment of powder weapons by ever-larger formations of disciplined foot soldiers, and the centralization of state finances for warfare on a large scale. These three advances in the means of waging war increased the marginal advantage the Portuguese and Spanish regimes already enjoyed in their contests with the Naṣrids of Granada and the Muslim rulers of North Africa. How the Iberians exploited this additional power subsequently determined the path and intensity of their clash with Islam.

Just where the Portuguese would continue their reconquest after they had recovered from fourteenth-century plagues and political upheavals was undoubtedly a subject of much discussion at the court of the Avis dynasty. Portuguese magnates pressed their ruler to open up a new frontier in Africa as a logical extension of the past. Yet to resume the reconquest in the lands across the Strait of Gibraltar created some formidable problems. First, the campaign against African Muslims would cease to be an exclusively terrestrial operation: a fleet would be required to transport men and materials from Portugal. Second, the Lusitanians would enter a relatively well-inhabited region of the Muslim world where the modest demographic resources of Portugal, a million inhabitants perhaps, could not sustain extensive warfare.[3] Tempted, nevertheless, by the strategic position of Ceuta, the Portuguese took the seaport from its Muslim defenders in 1415. Though it is customarily employed as the date for the beginning of Portuguese seaborne imperialism, at the time the arrival of the Christians on the African side of the strait appeared to be no more than an extension of old practices.

The partial encirclement of the Atlantic entry into the Mediterranean, on the other hand, put the Portuguese in a unique geographical position. Off the southern coast of Atlantic Iberia, navigators were forced to borrow each other's techniques to overcome the severe challenges posed by the heavy seas and empty spaces of the Atlantic. There the wind and current patterns were admirably suited for the navigation of the Atlantic by sail.[4] Geography also mingled with economics to favor an exploration of the Atlantic coastline of Morocco. Closer to the gold mines and slave centers of West Africa than other Mediterranean ports, the harbors of southwestern Iberia were well situated for oceanic expeditions aimed at breaking the domination Muslim cameleers exerted over trade with Black Africa. And the short naval voyage to the grain-producing regions of Morocco—the plain of the Gharb and the Sus. valley— was one more reason why Portuguese, Castilian, and Genoese sailors had already expanded their knowledge of the sea spaces west of the Strait of Gibraltar during preceding centuries.[5]

Whether the Portuguese would adopt a terrestrial or a coastal line of advance in the fifteenth century was influenced greatly by the existing state of naval technology. As early as the fourteenth century, European designers married Atlantic and Mediterranean technology to launch a clinker-built ship whose keel-to-beam ratio—3.3. to 3.8— placed it between the long and unstable Mediterranean war galley— 5 to 7—and the ponderous merchant ships of northern Europe—2 to 2.5. Then bigger sails were added to these vessels in another combination of Atlantic and Mediterranean technology to fit out three masts with square and lateen rigs. By 1430 the evolution of the major structural components—the hull, the sails, and the stern-post rudder— of the caravel had been completed.[6] This ship, with its great range and cargo capacity, became available to the Portuguese shortly after the conquest of Ceuta.

Though there is a general agreement upon the outline for the caravel's history, there is no chronological structure for a parallel event, the evolution of Atlantic navigation. Probably the knowledge of how to use the winds and currents off the Atlantic coast of Morocco was consolidated, through practical experience, during the first half of the fifteenth century. An early sixteenth-century history of the Atlantic voyages by the Ottoman cartographer Piri Reis hints at a simultaneous advance in celestial navigation.[7] Certainly, during the time of the Iberian encounter with the Muslim navigators of the Indian Ocean at the end of the fifteenth century, the Christians were ahead of their counterparts in the art of locating one's position on the open sea through the use of the stars.[8]

A conjunction between an evolving naval technology and a desire to open a new border outside Iberia followed. First, the settlement of the Atlantic islands after 1419 gave physical permanency to a young frontier. Then the application of state resources, as well as personal funds, under the direction of Prince Henry the Navigator sanctioned the naval alternative to land war in Africa. By 1434, maritime expeditions along the west coast of Africa yielded enough experience to encourage navigators to sail out on the unknown open sea past Cape Bojador. By 1444, when the island of Arguin was discovered, the new coastal route from Portugal past Islamic North Africa to the edge of the gold and slave regions of West Africa emerged in a raw but clearly distinguished form.[9]

Pausing for some forty years, then exploding with activity after 1482, European sailors traced out on the face of the Atlantic the outlines of the grand routes that were to link Iberia with the New World and Asia. The first of the turning points in this second phase of exploration was the decision in 1487 to erect a trading post at São Jorge de Mina on the Gulf of Guinea. Besides committing merchants to new ventures, the trading post at Mina attached the Iberians to a frontier beyond the Maghrib.[10] Navigators then systematically explored the coast of Africa to the south until Bartolomeu Dias rounded the Cape of Good Hope in 1488. During the ten-year interval between the expeditions of Bartolomeu Dias and Vasco da Gama, Christopher Columbus, the Genoese navigator and servant of the Catholic kings, drew Spain into long-range oceanic imperialism with his successful voyage from Atlantic Andalucia to the New World in 1492. Six years later Vasco da Gama reached Calicut on 20 May 1498, and within three years thereafter Pedro Alvárez Cabral navigated the great figure-eight course through the Atlantic that so many other Portuguese ships would follow on the way to India. These routes then became the highways for a revolutionary extension of the western end of the Ibero-African frontier.[11]

It is commonly held that the arrival of the Atlantic sailing ship not only revolutionized Europe's ability to reach other areas of the world but also rendered the Mediterranean war galley obsolete.[12] If so, Mediterranean states retained oared vessels for an inordinately long period of time. An examination of the tactical relation between the two naval vessels during the first half of the sixteenth century demonstrates that the sailing ship did not overwhelm the galley. The short range—200 to 500 yards depending on the conditions—and unpredictable behavior of cannons, the lack of rigging flexible enough for the light winds of the Mediterranean, and the deep draft of Atlantic vessels all limited their effectiveness against the Mediterranean war galley. The oared vessel's maneuverability in calm weather and shallow water, and its ability to beach, often neutralized the greater fire power and cruising capacity of the Atlantic sailing ship in Mediterranean regions.[13]

Atlantic sailing ships nevertheless gave the European sailors technological superiority over the galley in three areas. The caravel could operate on rough seas where the long, high rolling waves and the fierce southwesterlies would swamp the narrow galleys of the Mediterranean. Greater cargo space and a smaller crew permitted the round ship to sail before the wind throughout the year rather than remaining at dockside during winter months, when the scarcity of food and the severity of the weather usually prevented Mediterranean galleys from operating. By no means the least of the sailing ship's advantages in relation to the oared vessel was that it combined commercial and military potentialities more flexibly than did the galley: the large number of people—144 oarsmen and 30 to 40 soldiers and crew carried on the average early-sixteenth-century galley, compared with about 40 men on Columbus's *Santa María*—absorbed much of its cargo capacity. Adding it all up, the comparative impact of the Atlantic sailing ship, until the last quarter of the sixteenth century, was to award its experimenters with flexibility and especially range rather than with tactical superiority over the galley.[14]

At the Strait of Gibraltar the result was a striking differentiation of naval systems. In terms of space the consequences are well known. Except for the Ottoman naval expedition from the Red Sea to India in 1538, the fleets of the Islamic world remained confined to the Mediterranean, whereas Magellan's voyage of 1519–22 carried the Iberians around the globe. Another expression of this sharp difference between Atlantic and Mediterranean naval systems results from a comparison of the time required for the sixteenth-century maritime ventures sponsored by Iberian and Turkish empires. Roughly, for commercial and conquest convoys the trip from Atlantic Andalucia to the New World and back took fourteen to fifteen months. The trip from Lisbon to India and back, for those who completed the voyage, lasted approximately two years.[15] In the Ottoman world, where all state ventures were military except the convoy carrying the tribute from Egypt to Istanbul, imperial armadas operated within a rigidly circumscribed temporal framework. Fleets left the eastern Mediterranean in April and returned, as in the Malta campaign of 1565, to their home base in September.[16] Considering only the time factor, the Iberians managed naval systems three to five times larger than the Ottomans.

This grand scale upon which the Discoveries were conducted tended to disperse Iberian manpower and thereby discouraged the dense populations needed for conquest and repopulation. On the North African coast the technological advantage the sailing ship conferred was manifested in the tendency of the Portuguese to move away from a terrestrial line of advance. Rather than plunging into the interior of the Rif, they began to leapfrog south along the coast of Morocco, capturing Alcazar el-Saghir in 1458 and Tangier and Arzila in 1471. By the turn of the sixteenth century the Portuguese had emplaced Christian outposts along the Atlantic shore of Morocco at strategic points designed to tap the inner commerce of the western Maghrib. Mazagan (El Jadida) was taken in 1502; Agadir and Safi were seized between 1502 and 1508; and Azammour (northeast of Mazagan) was fortified in 1513. Hitherto a state with contiguous land borders and a southward-bound tradition of conquest and conversion, the realm of the Portuguese king now included a discontinuous Moroccan frontier whose outposts were twisted ninety degrees at odds with the past to take advantage of a new naval technology.[17]

Spain had a more complicated experience with early modern naval technology than did Portugal. When the marriage of Ferdinand and Isabella united Castile and Aragon in 1469, the Catholic kings soon discovered that the acquisition of an eastern frontier embroiled them in Italian politics. In addition, their Aragonese holdings put the boundaries of Catholic Spain close to the eastern borders of an aggressive Ottoman empire. There the short-lived Turkish invasion of Otranto in 1480–81 and the response of Catholic Spain fore-shadowed the beginning of a naval war for control of the Mediterranean's passageways.[18] But the technology that would govern this impending conflict would be the Mediterranean system of galley warfare, not that of the Atlantic sailing ship.

This union of the crowns also brought to Catholic Spain a long history of Catalonia's limited domination of North Africa's Mediterranean coast.[19] When the port of Melilla fell to Castile in 1497, it appeared that this Catalonian heritage would be replaced with a permanent conquest. By 1511, however, the Spanish had emplaced a frontier system in North Africa which, like the Portuguese occupation of Morocco's coastline, was defended by a series of fortified ports whose garrisons were supplied by sea.

It is not so clear what effect the revolution in maritime technology had on how Spain structured its frontier in North Africa.[20] Events suggest one line of explanation. In the year Granada fell (1492), Columbus left on his voyage and found the New World. It is reasonably safe to conclude that the Catholic kings were just as prepared to exploit the technological advantages of the sailing ship as they were to profit from advances in the use of gunpowder. When Columbus returned triumphant, the royal commitment to a new frontier, along with many other factors, rapidly dissolved an old form of peninsular conquest and settlement. Blessed by rapid conquests, the oceanic mode of expansion prepared a revolutionary future in the New World for the old agents of settlement: the aristocracy, the church, and the Christian emigrant.

Certainly one other reason why the Iberian kingdoms built a discontinuous screen of petty fortifications on the coast of the Maghrib, supplied by ship, was their superiority on the seas. Why the Muslim community in North Africa, where the naval challenges were the same as those faced by the Portuguese, did not experiment with new ships is related in part to the geography of the Iberian reconquest. Attached more to the culture of the Mediterranean world than to the Atlantic, the Hispano-Muslims found themselves pushed into the southeast portion of the peninsula. The Mediterranean direction of the Christian advance then drove Hispano-Muslims away from the Strait of Gibraltar toward the regions of the Mediterranean where the galley prevailed. That the naval expression of Muslim opposition to the Latin Christian advance in the Maghrib during the last half of the fifteenth century came in the form of decentralized privateering by light galleys showed how the Muslim community had fallen back upon their Mediterranean naval heritage.[21]

Just as important in explaining the inability of North African Muslims to adopt the technology of the sailing ship or to mobilize galley fleets was the condition of government within fifteenth-century North Africa. Everywhere small in scale, none of the impoverished Maghribian sultanates appeared able to bear the costs

of maintaining a flotilla of any kind. Each of these petty governments feared being overwhelmed by tribesmen, Christians, or local
competitors. Their chronic political instability strengthened a social
conservatism that excluded the innovation demanded by the daring
imperial experiments of the Iberians.

A recovery of Muslim naval power under the Ottomans could
have stimulated maritime experimentation that might have altered
the stark division between the two naval cultures at the Strait of
Gibraltar. Geographically, however, the locus of Turko-Muslim
naval strength could not have been in a less advantageous position
for producing solutions to the nautical problems faced by Atlantic
sailors. To compete with already-established Mediterranean naval
powers, the Turks had married ancient naval practices to their own
warlike ambitions.[22] Given this exclusively Mediterranean framework, Ottoman sultans built ever-larger galley fleets whose use
extended the range of the Turkish army on a distance scale much less
ambitious than that of the Iberian empires. But warfare with oared
vessels did not prevent the Turks from experimenting with ship
designs. Under Bayezit II (1481–1512), the Ottoman captains Kemal
and Burak Reis deployed two large sailing ships in the naval
war with Venice (1499–1503). Still, expansion proceeded very well
with galleys, and the Turks had no reason to adopt the round
ship.[23]

An unequal distribution of the military technology employed in
land warfare also had a hand in the Iberian domination of North
Africa's naval border. Throughout the fifteenth century the states
along the northern rim of the Mediterranean applied firearms on a
large scale to bring on an offensive cycle in the history of war. Here
the paramountcy of the heavily armored horseman was challenged
by the foot soldier who, first with the crossbow and then with the
less-complicated arquebus, finished off his social superiors at
seventy-five yards. This was only the beginning. Firearms eventually
altered the design of fortifications, reshaped the battlefield, changed
the structure of armies, increased the cost of warfare, and recast the
relation of ruling classes to society.

For Hispano-Muslims, the fifteenth-century advance in the use of
gunpowder had deadly implications. Spanish toponyms—Castile for
one example—testify to the weighty place the fort played in the
Hispanic world of the pregunpowder era. What little is known about
the military organization of Islamic Spain in its last centuries points
up how carefully the Naṣrids had combined the mountainous

terrain of Granada and the weapons of defensive warfare to protect themselves.[24]

Methods of waging warfare in the century before the arrival of gunpowder varied little from a standard pattern. During the winter months before the season in which the army was to campaign, the sultan decided on the direction of what normally amounted to a large-scale raid. Because exterior conditions over which the generals had little control often destroyed even the most basic winter assumptions, strategic planning was not carried on to any sophisticated degree. Whatever the objective, the Muslim army assembled in the spring for a quick summer campaign. If an attack on a fortified position was contemplated, a substantial number of foot soldiers would be mustered. Yet the heart—and one might say the soul—of the Muslim force consisted of armed cavalrymen whose striking power depended upon their mobility and their skill with lance and saber. Success in combat rarely was related to the variety of stratagems frontier warfare produced but came directly from the loyalty and proficiency of regular units.[25]

As the progress of the reconquest crowded Spanish Islam into the mountainous southeast corner of Iberia, Muslim warfare gradually became more defensive. Although there is evidence that Naṣrid soldiers employed crossbows and firearms in the fifteenth century, these arms were mainly used to defend fixed positions. Naṣrid elites resolutely clung to cavalry tactics as the best means of warding off Christian attacks short of the walls of their castles.[26] At the same time, the mountainous terrain of Granada and the military abilities of the Muslims reduced the effectiveness of Christian heavy cavalry. Clearly, in the last years of campaigning in Granada the Catholic kings needed a more effective means of penetrating the walls of Muslim castles and of maintaining sieges.

Though still medieval in many respects, the campaigns the Spanish began when Alhama fell in 1482 displayed much that was new. Military expeditions of the Castilian army were now planned with a well-defined goal in mind—the removal of Islamic political authority from Spain. To complete this ejection of the Naṣrids, the Catholic kings reorganized their army to fit the military requirements of their march through the tortuous geography of Granada. Because the terms of warfare—methodical siege operations—demanded troops less dependent upon the casual mobilization of a boisterous military aristocracy, the agents of the crown launched an administrative campaign to detach the army from the old rhythm of border

warfare. This was all the more necessary when the rulers of Spain
learned how far their army lagged behind the innovative methods
being employed in combat by the Swiss and the Turks.[27]

Crucial to the new method of warfare was the substitution of
professional soldiers for the troops who rallied to the standard of a
Castilian magnate or answered the crown's appeal on the eve of a
crusade. After the capture of Alhama in 1482, the Spanish monarchs
relentlessly increased the number of permanent soldiers in their
army. Among the new recruits, the most sought-after were those who
had some technical ability with powder weapons. Just as Spain joined
this fifteenth-century race to command the advanced military
technology, so also did she begin to unseat the horsemen. Between
1482 and 1489 the records of Castilian mobilization for the final wars
of the reconquest show that the number of infantry had risen from
somewhat over 50 percent to 75 percent of the army.[28]

But the great military lesson of the war in Granada was the deadly
advantage cannons gave to the offense. As early as 1430 Spanish
generals learned, as had the Ottomans at Constantinople in 1453,
how artillery could be applied with special effectiveness against both
fortified positions and massed formations of either horsemen or
infantry. Yet only after the Catholic kings finally controlled the
politics of Spain did the army begin to acquire a substantial number
of the new weapons. Hiring foreign casters, the crown increased its
supply of cannons sharply—from 16 in 1480 to 66 in 1482, 77 in
1495, 113 in 1506, and 162 in 1508.[29] During this same era firearms
spread among the foot soldiers as the matchlock began to replace the
crossbow.

What connected the rapid increase in the number of cannons with
the political unity of Catholic Spain was their inordinate expense.
Only a wealthy state could afford this new equipment. By 1488–89,
artillery costs, together with the salaries of military men, became the
most important charge against royal income.[30]

Did the new equipment and professional units justify the expense?
Whatever the wider answer to that question might be, the effectiveness of the Castilian army against the Muslims of Granada was
brutal. From 1482 to the fall of the Alhambra ten years later,
Spanish artillery ripped through the Muslim defenses. In these
campaigns professional soldiers worked out the tactics and formations
that made Spanish foot soldiers among the world's most efficient
military men.

This unique combination of firepower, mobility, and political unity explains, to a degree, the rapid enclosure of the North African coast between the Portuguese occupation of Santa-Cruz do Cabo de Gué (Agadir) in 1505 and the emplacement of Spanish troops in Tripoli five years later.[31] But the opposition, or lack of it, of the Muslim states of the Maghrib had as much bearing upon the ease with which the Iberians ran along the coasts of North Africa as did the Christian use of firearms, sailing ships, and infantry formations.

Travel accounts from the early sixteenth century give some sense of how North African society prevented the frontier sultanates from bearing the heavy burdens that warfare with early modern military technology implied. Both Leo the African's survey of North Africa and Mármol's history of the same region draw a vivid picture of embattled peasants and city dwellers challenged by powerful tribesmen. Their observations reflect a shift in the military and political relations between the two subcommunities of the Maghribian social order. There in late-fifteenth-century North Africa, a large number of cohesive kin groups with no political center—the tribes—severely reduced the military efficiency of urban governments. Sultans were unable to impose their bureaucracy over great chunks of countryside and therefore could afford neither large standing armies or great cannon parks. So often had the nomads come like a whirlwind to shatter the fragile defenses of urban society that they dominated the sociology of warfare. To descend from a horse, to fight in serried ranks, to give up tribal freedoms for the disciplined life of a professional soldier as an urban ruler might wish was not only unthinkable, it was unmanly.[32]

Just what made the Maghribian city-states particularly unable to hold off the tribesmen at the time Granada fell awaits a detailed history of the post-Almohad era. No doubt the more healthful life of the Bedouin and the military abilities of the nomads in this period before the introduction of powder weapons had a tendency, over time, to increase the number of warriors intent upon harrying settled communities. Because the Bedouin economy is naturally buoyant— animals reproduce themselves but land does not—it was also possible that the kinsmen had increased their power through an accumulation of wealth. Yet this scattered society that depended upon elaborate structures of mutual support had a natural tendency to break down into small units and thus usually offered even weak sultans the opportunity of dividing the tribal threat. And animal disease and bad weather frequently checked the power of the nomads by suddenly erasing much of their capital. Whatever the explanation for the

growing strength of the tribesmen, it seems probable that it was the
shrunken power of urban governments unable to find some religious
and political magic to unify rural and urban regions that made both
the Bedouin and Iberian aggressors seem so formidable during the
quarter-century after the fall of Granada.[33]

When the Christian armies invaded North Africa, they encountered
a military culture that mirrored this fluctuating balance between
tribal and urban society. Armies formed in the petty successor states
of the Unitarian empire—the Marīnids of Fez, the Zayānids of
Tlemsen, the Ḥafṣids of Tunis—were composed of men drawn mainly
from tribes friendly to the policies of ruling dynasties, whose family
origin was tribal but whose political center had become urban.
Always available for war, tribesmen made recruiting an army
relatively easy for a strong state; but their failure to remain loyal to
institutions outside their tribal structures ruled out a stable military
organization of the countryside. Maghribian sultans, like most
Muslim rulers, tried to establish their right to control force by
arranging these fickle allies around a fixed core of elite troops who
were not connected with tribal society. Alien recruits—Muslims
from Andalucia, Christian mercenaries from Iberia, black slaves
from sub-Saharan Africa, and Turkish archers from the lands of the
eastern Mediterranean—gave Muslim armies what seemed to the
Spanish an amorphous cast.[34]

Military administration reflected the generalized distribution of
military power in Maghribian society. For the tribes who recognized
the authority of the sultans, pay usually came in the form of tax
concessions, grants of certain pasturelands, or outright distributions
of pay. However, the chronic instability of a society made up of
small units, each of which derived its inner cohesion from opposition
to a changing exterior threat, constantly forced renegotiations of
previous agreements. The supply of warriors therefore fluctuated
greatly, making it impossible to calculate the number of effective
troops before the assembly of the army. Tribesmen, moreover,
fought only during the spring and summer, then returned to their
tribal areas, often without the permission of the sultan. In addition,
what influence urban government did have over the kinsmen tended
to decline over long periods of time. A shrinking periphery usually
meant a decreased ability to control rural wealth and therefore to
attach the tribesmen to the causes of urban government.

Yet if instability characterized the relations between the tribes and
the sultans, some degree of stability marked the agreements between

the rulers of the cities and the warriors of nontribal origins.[35] Garrisoned in cities near agricultural regions whose taxes paid their salaries, the small groups of professional soldiers—often Christian mercenaries—usually showed greater loyalty to sultans' objectives than did the vast majority of the tribesmen.[36]

A lack of an elaborate military hierarchy also exposed the kinship orientation of fifteenth-century North African armies. Field commanders and adminstrative officers were appointed for each summer expedition, and no pyramidal chain of command between generals and tribesmen embraced the sultan's appointees and the kinsmen. Before the campaign, messengers carried orders to friendly tribesmen and to the dispersed units of the sultan's guard, directing them to assemble their men at a designated spot near the capital. Once formed, the Maghribian armies, which rarely exceeded 10,000 men, marched against the sultan's opponent without further complication.[37] Tribesmen took their orders from the leaders of their kin groups, and the sultan's militia obeyed the instructions of its own officers. Overall responsibility for the behavior of the army remained in the hands of a general who hoped for a quick victory before his army dissolved. When the fighting began, or even before, tribal leaders made their own estimates about the course of the conflict. If the sheiks judged that the combat would go badly, the kinsmen simply abandoned the field, leaving the sultan's loyal guard naked in front of the enemy.

Combat under such conditions involved few complicated maneuvers and no elaborate technology. Siege warfare in North Africa did not develop into a sophisticated art, because most cities preferred to negotiate rather than undergo a lengthy blockade. Maneuvering the army therefore consisted merely of marching toward the enemy until they were found. On the eve of battle Maghribian generals drew up their forces in a formation that placed the heavy cavalry and foot soldiers in the center while light horsemen covered the wings or attacked the opponent's forward positions. Armed with sabers, lances, or short javelins, the light cavalry began the battle by skirmishing with enemy horsemen. If they found a hole or weak spot in their opponent's massed formation, then the attacking general committed his heavy cavalry and infantry to the fray. Equipped with lances or crossbows, the core units of the attacking army attempted to break through the enemy's front lines. Even though North African generals understood the advantages of mass, which made them eager to recruit heavy cavalry and crossbowmen from Christian lands, none

of the Maghribian sultans attempted to displace the light horsemen
from their dominant position in the military culture of North Africa.
So strong was the prestige of the cavalry that when powder weapons
appeared in North Africa in the latter part of the fifteenth century
the military elite, like the Mamluk emirs of Syria and Egypt, were
very slow to restructure their armies to fit the new technology.[38]

Though Maghribian sultans were not able to organize the power
of firearms, other Muslim rulers were. Already the Ottoman Turks
had demonstrated in their conquest of Constantinople (1453) and
their defeat of Venetian seapower (1503) that they possessed the
infantry, the large cannons, and the galleys to wage warfare on a
scale altogether different from that of their coreligionists in Africa.
Their participation in the age of powder empires depended in part
on their capacity to centralize the collection of taxes. Abundant
resources enabled the Ottomans to draft men without regard to the
social criteria of the times, building the famous slave regiments that
were loyal to the sultan throughout most of the sixteenth century. In
the same manner the fluid social conditions of an expanding Muslim
frontier allowed the Ottomans not only to mingle gunpowder
technology with the military culture of the mounted archer but also
to expand unhesitatingly the taxing authority of central government.
But kinsmen did not give up their independence without a struggle,
and even Mehmet the Conqueror had to defeat strong challenges to
the social and financial forms of early modern warfare within the
House of Islam.

Castile's political evolution yields this same experience within a
different institutional matrix. From the middle of the thirteenth
century, Castilian monarchs strove to create a centralized state.
Gradually taxes and taxing procedures were improved to fashion a
new system by the reign of Henry II (1393–1406). At mid-century,
however, an aristocratic reaction against this centralizing trend
delayed but did not destroy the momentum of the crown's bureaucratic appropriation of Castile's wealth. When the Catholic kings
came to power in 1469, they promptly restored monarchial superiority in fiscal matters.[39] It was not at all coincidental that this
administrative victory was followed by an encouragement of naval
exploration, a vigorous expansion of the professional army, a costly
expenditure of royal funds on firearms, and an increase in the scale of
warfare against Islam.

The central government's assertion of its fiscal superiority within
both Spanish and Ottoman empires and the absence of a similar
event in North Africa became another reason for the Maghrib's

technological backwardness. It was not that the Maghribian sultanates lacked a tax system, but rather that their control over the wealth of the countryside was receding at the time when other states expanded dramatically. Political difficulties with a multitude of tribes simply accelerated the momentum of internal and external decline. Independent tribesmen captured more economic resources and entrenched the military culture of the horse and camel. Linked to the ecology of the steppe and the mountains, the kinsmen, if they had any contact at all with early modern technology, were contemptuous of the sweaty work of cannon casters and indifferent to the naval inventiveness of the Iberians.[40]

How rampant tribalism weakened the Maghribian community at a time of military innovation can be vividly illustrated by the divergent history of the herding economies of Castile and the Maghrib. Although the tribesman had, as Ibn Khaldun noted, disappeared in Spain, the geography of the Spanish plateau favored sheepherding.[41] But in contrast to the management of the herding economy in North Africa by the largely independent tribes, the monarchs of Castile unified the wool industry under their control. They then conferred the power to regulate vast sheep herds upon an institution known as the Mesta.[42] Its control of some three million sheep yielded for the crown the famous *servicio y montazgo* and other taxes that made sheep a primary source of royal income.[43] In North Africa, on the other hand, tribes hostile or indifferent to the problems of declining urban governments dominated the herding economy and harassed the peasantry at the time when the costs of early modern military technology skyrocketed.

If the collection of taxes and the mobilization of the newest technology of warfare and communication was any measure of state power, the Iberians held startling advantages over the petty governments of the western Islamic community during the last quarter of the fifteenth century. Surely no Muslim power offered any competition. The Mamluk empire of Egypt, in the throes of its own decline, made empty threats against Christian possessions in the Holy Lands on the eve of Granada's conquest, and the Ottoman Turks under Bayezit II (1481–1512) confined themselves to the eastern Mediterranean.[44] With little resistance, the Iberians moved the military frontier from Iberia to North Africa, where geography, society, and recent history converged to create a bias in Muslim areas against the political unity and military specialization the new style of warfare demanded. The way seemed to be open for a great Christian crusade in Africa, one that would reach even to Jerusalem.

Three: NORTH AFRICA AND THE ATLANTIC

> *In consequence of the representation of Columbus, the council of Castile determined to take possession of countries of which the inhabitants were plainly incapable of defending themselves. The pious purpose of converting them to Christianity sanctified the injustice of the project. But the hope of finding treasures of gold there, was the sole motive which prompted to undertake it.*
>
> Adam Smith, *The Wealth of Nations*

The question why Spain and Portugal did not employ their military superiority to continue the Iberian reconquest in North Africa has generated little excitement. Speculation on the motives behind the Atlantic Voyages, rather than on the failure to plant the standards of Christendom in the Maghrib, has dominated the historical discourse. But it is not difficult to sum up what is known about this less popular side of Iberian history. Both crowns made the decision to do away with the old form of peninsular expansion in North Africa because the cost of absorbing the Muslim sultanates was too high relative to the cost of imperial activities elsewhere. Yet this is too simple an explanation; for the change did not occur overnight upon the whim of some imperial adviser. It resulted in part from a slow resolution of conflicts that altered the social and political balances at the very core of the Iberian states. Between 1415 and 1514 the outcome of these inner wars—the birth pangs of the early modern state—directly affected the structure of the frontier in North Africa. First, the Iberian occupation appeared to be a continuation of the reconquest; second, the Maghribian periphery became a limited holding of the seacoast for commercial purposes; and, finally, the entire border system faded into a defensive operation aimed at protecting Atlantic naval routes and the shoreline of Latin Christendom. All this took place in conjunction with the mobilization of imperial energies to monopolize the revenues from more distant peripheries. Very early in the sixteenth century the history of Iberia's frontier in North Africa could no longer be written in terms of religious and chivalric passions.

Europe's march along the coast of Africa began with Portugal's acceptance of a political order whose central feature was a steady rise in the power of the monarchy. Toward the end of the fourteenth century, John I (1385–1433) exploited the economic and social distresses of the times to found a new dynasty, the Avis.[1] What differentiated this political upheaval from others was that support for the revolution came from a new alignment of social elements. Put crudely, urban social units heretofore not present in grand politics in any magnitude joined nobles who backed the rebel cause because they were pinched by the economic dislocation of the seigneurial regime.[2] When the violence of the foundation period subsided, the monarch profited substantially from the new complexion of politics. Urban groups, conscious of their own weakness, sought the support of the new ruling family as a check against the unruly behaviour of the nobles.[3] The monarch, who was also the guarantor of the aristocratic structure of society, then found himself in a better position to control a treacherous and violent nobility. Swiftly, this nascent absolute monarchy entrenched its political supremacy by expanding the powers of a royal bureaucracy.

All this history is well known. What is not sufficiently appreciated is the general instability of the monarchial system in its early period. The history of the aristocracy in particular is largely underplayed in favor of a description of an emerging middle class. Yet though John I profited from the rise of an urban self-consciousness, at the same time he had to contend with a powerful nobility.[4] Economic conditions, religious passions, and political ambitions conjoined to make this class particularly dangerous.[5] This was all the more so since the reconquest in Portugal had ended long ago and the war with the Castilians had resulted in a peace treaty (1385) that, for the moment, excluded the possibility of peninsular expansion.[6] What to do with an unemployed and financially ill at ease aristocracy was, with little doubt, the chief problem facing John I as Portugal entered the second decade of the fifteenth century.

To preserve the loyalty of the aristocracy through a crusade against the nearest Muslim city, Ceuta, represented a traditional

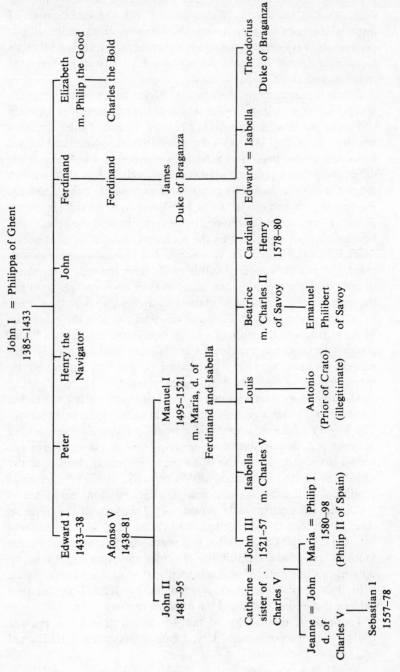

THE AVIS DYNASTY TO THE SPANISH SUCCESSION (1580)

John I = Philippa of Ghent
1385–1433

Edward I 1433–38
Peter
Henry the Navigator
John
Ferdinand
Elizabeth m. Philip the Good
Charles the Bold

Afonso V 1438–81

Ferdinand
James Duke of Braganza

Edward = Isabella
Beatrice m. Charles II of Savoy
Cardinal Henry 1578–80
Theodorius Duke of Braganza

Emanuel Philibert of Savoy

John II 1481–95

Manuel I 1495–1521 m. Maria, d. of Ferdinand and Isabella

Louis
Antonio (Prior of Crato) (illegitimate)

Isabella m. Charles V

Catherine = John III 1521–57 sister of . Charles V

Jeanne = John d. of Charles V

Maria = Philip I 1580–98 (Philip II of Spain)

Sebastian I 1557–78

solution to an old problem.[7] On the surface, the campaign to take
the Moroccan port aimed to capture the usual spoils: land, agricultural and animal products, and peasants. Yet the conquest of Ceuta
in 1415 also serves as the historical benchmark for the evolution of
an Iberian frontier system that eschewed large territorial acquisitions.
Much energy has therefore been spent analyzing the commercial
advantages that possession of Ceuta conferred. Lisbon's merchants,
both Portuguese and Genovese, certainly recognized the value of
the Muslim city and willingly provided the financial backing for the
expedition.[8] This first campaign into Africa by the Avis dynasty
arose, therefore, out of the converging interests of two different
social groups whose political relationships had recently changed, not
as a resumption of the medieval crusade.[9]

Nobles joyfully enlisted in an expedition that seemed to promise
personal gain.[10] Merchants settled in behind the army with the
expectation of wresting a portion of North African commerce,
especially the Saharan gold trade, from the Muslims.[11] Although the
effort to take Ceuta did not require great exertion, the Portuguese
were not able to attain any of their longer-range goals in northwest
Africa. When it became clear that the campaign had failed, a political
dispute quickly surfaced in Portugal over what the future course of
action ought to be. A party favoring further land conquests emerged
under the leadership of Prince Henry. Meanwhile, Prince Pedro
organized a counterfaction that opposed large-scale invasion of
Africa. This clash over the definition of Portugal's African periphery
disturbed the unity of the Portuguese ruling class until the death of
John I in 1433, reflecting the differing orientations of the landed
aristocracy and the commercial classes. And failure to achieve a
consensus on what to do in North Africa put the exploitation of
frontier advantages into the hands of border entrepreneurs.[12]

Portugal's most famous fifteenth-century frontiersman, Prince
Henry the Navigator, mixed in his career those feudal and early
modern elements that characterized the fifteenth-century history of
the Portuguese. An advocate of further land conquests in the
Maghrib, he also subsidized those numerous Atlantic explorations
that eventually made territorial imperialism economically un-
attractive.[13] During his lifetime, Atlantic navigators entered the
first stage of open-sea navigation. Then Portuguese seamen took
control of Morocco's fisheries, and, with the help of Genoese
merchants, settlers from the homeland began the argicultural
exploitation of the Azores.[14] More important in the long run,

the establishment of a trading post on the island of Arguin initiated a commerce in African gold and slaves in which Prince Henry himself participated. Not totally indifferent to the possibilities of taxing the oceanic commerce, the crown founded the Casa de Ceuta in 1434 to handle these Moroccan exchanges. In the same manner, the state granted the first monopoly over African trade in 1443 as the sale of gold and slaves rose on the island of Arguin.[15]

Despite these indications that commerce with North Africa might yield as much as conquest, enthusiasm for terrestrial warfare was far from dead. Duarte's reign (1433–38) opened up nearly half a century of aristocratic ascendency, during which the energies of the state were directed away from the naval frontier. In 1437 Portuguese troops marched off to a spectacular failure when they attempted to take Tangier. Chastened by the consequences of their campaign, the aristocracy confined themselves to internal politics until Afonso V, the African, took full control of Portugal in 1449.[16] An ally of the magnates, he approved an attack on Alcazar el-Saghir, which fell to the Christians in 1458. Although this victory boosted the prestige of the king, Portuguese warriors were again unable to add to their African conquests. Two expeditions in 1460 and 1463–64 failed to extend their toehold on the northern tip of Morocco. Only in 1471, when Arzila fell and its sister city, Tangier, was abandoned by its population, were the Portuguese able to creep past their enclaves at Ceuta and Alcazar el-Saghir. Thereupon, the imperial effort in North Africa languished as the Lusitanians invaded Castile during 1475 in an outburst of feudal politics.[17]

Much of significance happened on the African naval frontier during the long aristocratic resurgence. Navigators pushed their explorations ever southward from the mouth of the Senegal River to the Congo. There the naval technology of the oceanic frontiersmen opened up new worlds faster than the Portuguese aristocracy could dream of controlling them, even with the aid of the firearms then becoming available. Yet probably the most important development for the African frontier was the joint involvement of the state and major Lisbon merchants in the commercial trade that began to link the sub-Saharan territories with Portugal. In 1463 the crown gained control over the commercial post at Arguin. Six years later the entire trading operation with sub-Saharan Africa was sold to the merchant Fernão Gomes as a tax farm. Increasingly concerned, yet not directly involved, the monarchy remained in touch with a naval frontier more than ever shaped by commercial success.[18]

Portugal was nonetheless still a state in which the politics of the aristocracy would, to a great degree, determine the direction and character of expansion. When Afonso V hastened to take advantage of Castile's internal divisions in 1475, he raised the expectations of the aristocracy that internal expansion in an ancient manner would bring them benefits. This overestimation of Portugal's military abilities in Iberia lasted for a very short time. In 1476 Afonso suffered a defeat at Toro that discredited both his policy and his authority.[19] Quickly he shored up the monarchy by bringing his son, the future John II (1481–95), into the councils of government and by beginning negotiations with Catholic Spain. One result of the deliberations at Alcaçovas and Toledo (1479–80) was that Spain conceded to Portugal a position of supremacy in the exploration and conquest of the Atlantic coast of Africa. Specifically, Castile acknowledged Portugal's monopoly over exploration and trade south of the Canaries, south of Cape Bojador.[20]

On the death of Afonso V in 1481, Portugal experienced a second social revolution designed to break the political ascendency of the nobility. Ruthlessly, John II stripped the aristocracy of their estates and titles while tilting the balance of power within Portugal in favor of the urban classes. In this same violent period, the king directed the course of state expansion into an area ill suited for medieval warfare.[21]

Not merely a commitment of the moment, the monarch's firm decision to adopt oceanic over terrestrial imperialism was well planned. During 1474 a state decree established a monopoly over the African trade for the crown that grew in importance under the royal administration of the Casa da Guiné.[22] A year before the Portuguese defeat in Castile, Afonso V displayed the crown's determination to supervise the African frontier more closely when he placed his son in charge of naval affairs. After John II secured control of Portugal, closely guarded plans for the discovery of the route to India were implemented. Thus in 1482 Diogo Cão left on the first of many scrupulously organized naval expeditions.

Some indication of Portuguese ambitions at this time was revealed in the series of diplomatic compromises worked out with Castile in 1494. Known collectively as the Treaty of Tordesillas, these agreements not only clarified which portion of northwest Africa fell to the Portuguese but also divided up the rest of the non-Christian world.[23] Shortly before his death in 1495, John II confirmed Portugal's seaborne imperialism when he added "Lord of Guinea" to his

official titles. The reality behind this imperial statement rested
not solely upon the acquisition of land in West Africa but rather
on the accelerating commercial yield of the naval frontier.

Quantitative sources for the Portuguese trade with the coastal
populations of West Africa exist only in part for the last quarter of
the fifteenth century. Nonetheless, these fragmentary accounts, these
memoirs of merchant sailors, leave no doubt of the exhilarating
advantages the caravel made available to Portuguese entrepreneurs.
Most outstanding among the ventures of the time was the founding
of the Portuguese trading factory at La Mina. Farmed out to
Fernão Gomes, the commerce through La Mina became so productive that the crown ennobled Gomes and placed the entire trade with
West Africa under a royal monopoly.[24]

African gold lay behind the spectacular social advance of Fernão
Gomes. Exchanging clothing and metal articles for the products
of Africa—slaves, gold, ivory, and spices—Portugal sparked a
commercial revolution that drew West African trade away from the
Muslim interior toward the periphery of Christian Europe's emerging
oceanic economy. By the turn of the sixteenth century this commerce
sustained a system of exchanges that sent an annual average of
twelve ships from La Mina to Lisbon. Each year these vessels placed
approximately 410 kilograms of gold worth 100,000 cruzados in the
hands of the crown. If the acquisition of precious metal from other
regions of Africa is added, the estimated annual contribution of
gold to royal coffers reached 700 kilograms, worth 200,000 cruzados,
during the first two decades of the sixteenth century.[25]

Gold was not the only valuable product Portuguese merchants
brought back to Lisbon. Previously sold by the merchants of Muslim
North Africa, slaves and spices now reached Portugal by an Atlantic
route. In 1506 this commerce attained a figure of 11,000 cruzados
for the state, indicating that the level of Portuguese trade in these
commodities vastly exceeded that in North African ports.[26]

By 1521 the galloping success of the commerce with West Africa
had provoked competition from both Muslims and Christians. One
consequence was a sudden decline in the yield of the gold trade at
La Mina. No matter, other opportunities opened up along the fringe
of Portugal's gigantic oceanic frontier. Between 1500 and 1520 the
spice route to India began to yield its riches. With an annual haul
of between 9,500 and 10,500 metric tons of spices, the crown achieved
an income that grew from 135,000 cruzados in 1506 to 300,000 in
1518–19.[27]

TABLE 1   *Royal Income in Cruzados*

Origin	1506	1518–19
Crown income	173,000	245,000
Customs (Lisbon)	24,000	40,000
Gold (La Mina)	120,000	120,000
Slaves and African spice (Grains of Paradise)	11,000	?
Sugar (Madeira)	27,000	50,000
Azores	2,500	17,500
Cape Verde Islands	3,000	?
Brazil wood	5,000	?
Asiatic spices	135,000	300,000
Antwerp and other commercial houses	?	?
Total	500,500 (+)	772,500 (+)

Summarized from the table given by Vitorino Magalhães-Godinho, *L'économie de l'empire portugais aux xve et xvie siècles* (Paris, 1969), p. 830.

Clearly, the contribution the gold and spice trade made to royal revenues is the major reason the Portuguese monarchy committed itself to a commercial naval empire. By the death of John II in 1495 the collection of gold at La Mina alone had doubled state resources. Approximately ten years later in 1507 the sum the royal treasury realized from the spice trade with Asia began to pass the amount of income produced by La Mina. Taken together, the maritime commerce in gold and spices rose to one-half the state revenues. To this amount should be added the income from the Atlantic islands, which reached 67,500 cruzados in 1518–19.[28] From these data alone it is clear that the dynamics of Portuguese expansion had carried the state far away from the terrestrial mode of imperialism.

Since the potential yield of the vast oceanic frontier so clearly favored commercial imperialism, the old military elite found it difficult to defend a policy of land conquests for which the population resources of Portugal were overwhelmingly insufficient. Already aware of how the sailing ship extended the range of opportunity, the aristocratic party also faced the revolutionary social implications of powder weaponry. These changes and the spirit of an age of expansion shook the nobility loose from their old cultural moorings persuading them to risk their lives not so much for God and land as for commercial advantage.[29]

Warrior merchants, then, descended upon the Atlantic coast of North Africa between the capture of Agadir (1505) and the fortification of Mazagan (1514) with devastating efficiency. Coastal fortifications locked Muslims within Morocco and secured the oceanic routes leading to India and beyond. On land the jolting superiority of Portuguese arms threw back Muslim warriors and permitted Christian merchants to tap the economic resources of Morocco's rich plains.[30] Soon a three-cornered commerce sprang up to link Guinea, Morocco, and Portugal. Yet the success of this trade and the local military advantages the Portuguese enjoyed did not tempt the Christians to engage in great land conquests: the commercial frontier had arrived in the western Maghrib.[31]

Even as the Portuguese established the nodal points of their seaborne empire along Morocco's Atlantic coast, the extraordinary yield of the oceanic frontier beyond Agadir lessened the importance of this Muslim border. Meanwhile, Muslim opponents of the Portuguese regrouped in Morocco under the militant Saʿdian dynasty. Now armed with powder weapons, the holy warriors initiated a new period in the history of the frontier when they captured the Portuguese fort at Agadir in 1541. Yet so much had Portugal changed in the years since the capture of Ceuta that the crown responded to this disaster not by avenging the loss of Christian territories but by abandoning two Moroccan forts at Safi and Azemmour. Atlantic considerations were behind this decision, for the Portuguese maintained their garrisons at Mazagan and along the Muslim lip of the Strait of Gibraltar only to protect their oceanic routes. When the tricornered trade between West Africa, Brazil, and Portugal began during the last quarter of the sixteenth century, it merely assisted in the final metamorphosis of the Portuguese frontier in North Africa.[32]

If the formation of a dynamic, nearly global economy lay behind this restless history of the Portuguese in North Africa, the creation of a huge land-based empire led the Spanish to a similar Maghribian policy. Not only did they transform their moving medieval frontier from one of inclusion to one of exclusion, they also accomplished this imperial pirouette in approximately one-third the time it took the Portuguese monarchy to divest itself of the old form of imperialism.

Much of the explanation for the chronological brevity of Spain's frontier history in North Africa rests upon her late achievement of political cohesion. Until the last quarter of the fifteenth century, the

The House of Castile from the Reign of Henry II of Trastámara to the Habsburg Succession

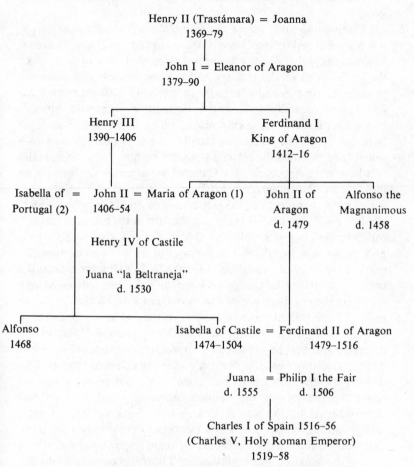

Henry II (Trastámara) = Joanna
1369–79

John I = Eleanor of Aragon
1379–90

Henry III
1390–1406

Ferdinand I
King of Aragon
1412–16

Isabella of = John II = Maria of Aragon (1)
Portugal (2)   1406–54

John II of
Aragon
d. 1479

Alfonso the
Magnanimous
d. 1458

Henry IV of Castile

Juana "la Beltraneja"
d. 1530

Alfonso
1468

Isabella of Castile = Ferdinand II of Aragon
1474–1504   1479–1516

Juana = Philip I the Fair
d. 1555   d. 1506

Charles I of Spain 1516–56
(Charles V, Holy Roman Emperor)
1519–58

union of Castile and Aragon under the Catholic kings had not resolved the clash of interests between the crown and the magnates into any new balance of political groups in which the urban classes played a more important role. Castile maintained the traditions of a conquering aristocracy more than did Aragon. In the thirteenth century the Kingdom of Aragon had embarked upon a course of maritime expansion within the Mediterranean that produced a wealthy urban patriciate capable of checking the landed nobility. Castile, on the other hand, continued to be entangled in the land-bound politics of the unresolved conflict with Islam. Only in 1479, ten years after the marriage of Ferdinand and Isabella, were the Catholic kings able to tame the nobility, to create an early modern state.

Championing royal power, the Catholic kings created a monarch- ical regime based on a mixture of Castilian and Aragonese interests. In Castile as well as Aragon, the crown associated the aristocracy with the government of the country and the war against Islam. At the same time, the monarchs forged a strong bond between themselves and the municipalities. Like the Portuguese monarchs, Spanish rulers also fortified their centralizing effort by opening the royal bureaucracy to men from the middle ranges of society, who pre- sumably represented the crown's position. To this scribal class, many of whom were Aragonese, the Catholic kings gave over the task of molding an efficient government.[33]

Granada's conquest in 1492 blessed this union of the two crowns.[34] Yet like the Portuguese monarchy at the turn of the fifteenth century, the Catholic kings were left with the problem of what to do with a militant society in which a still-powerful aristocracy customarily enjoyed the fruits of expansion.[35] Fernando de Zafra, the official the crown had placed in charge of Granada's defense, advanced one solution: the continuation of the reconquest into North Africa. In making his proposal, he restated one of the oldest positions taken by self-serving frontiersmen. Security along Granada's shores, he argued, could best be obtained by appropriating the coast of North Africa. The time was ripe. Not only were the rulers of the Maghrib divided among themselves, but none of the sultanates possessed either the firearms or the military organizations that Spain had developed during the war in Granada. A quick conquest would, moreover, place the Spanish in a position to exploit the gold trade that reached the nearby oases of the Tafilalt region on the northern edge of the Sahara.[36] Pope Alexander VI heartily concurred with this proposal to cross into North Africa. In 1494 he gave his blessing to an African crusade and continued the extraordinary tax, the *cruzada*, that would defray the expenses of such an expedition.[37] One dissen- ter, however, warned in 1495 that the crown might have difficulty maintaining a garrison in a region where the surrounding population was hostile.[38]

While the Catholic kings listened to this advice, they had already reached an accord with the Genoese navigator, Christopher Columbus, on 17 April 1492, to open up a frontier far away from the natural line of advance into North Africa. Moreover, there was plenty of evidence that the crown had thought carefully about oceanic expansion. Mariners from Huelva and Cadiz, or Genoese merchants in Seville, probably passed on intelligence concerning the Portuguese gold trade with West Africa. To discover the extent of this commerce, the Catholic kings licensed privateers to prey on the Atlantic shipping of the Portuguese.[39] In 1478 a Spanish squadron left Seville to occupy the Canary Islands, then the subject of negotiations between Portugal and Spain. The Luso-Iberian treaty of 1479 delivered these islands to the Spanish monarchy, and between 1492 and 1496 the Catholic kings concentrated their attention on settling them. Thereafter the Canaries became the jumping-off spot for the territorial conquests of the New World in the first quarter of the sixteenth century.

Though the value of the discovery of the New World could hardly be assessed at the time of Columbus's first voyages, the worth of Spain's Italian possessions was known. French ambitions in Italy, which led to their invasion of 1495, precipitated a long war with the Valois dynasty and sidetracked any appeal to conquer the Maghrib.[40] Here the dispatch of a Spanish army to defend Italy against the advances of another Christian state was a harbinger of a much deeper involvement by Spain in European affairs.

It was when the war in Italy subsided that the Catholic kings gave their approval in 1497 for a resumption of the crusade against Islam. Spanish troops experienced little difficulty in taking the port of Melilla in September of that year. Part of the explanation for this is suggested by the "modern" composition of the garrison they left in place on the Maghribian shore. Melilla's defense force consisted of 700 foot soldiers, 50 cavalrymen, 150 laborers, 300 crossbowmen, 100 arquebusiers, 20 artillerymen, 35 clerks, 2 clergymen, a doctor, a surgeon, and an apothecary.[41]

This easy victory at Melilla only increased the pressure for a deeper penetration of the Maghrib. Again frontiersmen advanced familiar reasons for crossing the no-man's-land. An increasing number of corsair raids on Spanish shores, probably brought on by the migration of upper-class Muslim families to the Maghrib, could be halted only if the enemy bases were taken. In 1499 the first revolt of the Alpujarras played into the hands of the Castilian imperialists when it opened an unbridgeable gap between the Christian and Muslim populations of southeastern Spain while at the same time injecting a new batch of angry Hispano-Muslims into Africa. Revolt was now a constant possibility in Granada, and therefore the imperialists could play upon the fear that Iberia was again vulnerable to another invasion from Africa.[42] Ferdinand, however, temporized and sent his best soldier, Gonsalo de Córdoba, off to Turkish territories before resuming the war with France in Italy.

On 26 November 1504, the death of Isabella raised the question whether the crown ought to adopt a forward policy in North Africa. Isabella's famous testament certainly left no doubt about what should be done: Castilians should devote themselves unremittingly to the conquest of Africa and the war against Islam. Castilian grandees agreed and did not hesitate at all to use this issue and the succession crisis Isabella's death caused to reduce the authority of Ferdinand and thereby the influence of Aragon upon Castile.[43]

With civil war brewing in Spain, Castilians seized the initiative on the Maghribian border. The object of their plan was to capture the port of Mers el-Kebir, the outlet for the commercial and agricultural products of the interior region dominated by the city of Tlemsen. In the spring of 1505 Cardinal Jiménez de Cisneros agreed to finance a major portion of a Castilian expedition that left Malaga in September of that year. Once more the military superiority of the Christian soldiers and the power of their cannons dispersed Muslim cavalry and brought down the thin walls of the Mers el-Kebir fortifications. Ferdinand, in no position to resist what the Castilians had accomplished, attempted to assert a measure of control over the frontier by appointing Diego Fernández de Córdoba captain general for the conquest of Barbary. The crown also granted him authority over the cities of Oran and Tlemsen, even though they had not yet been brought under Spanish sovereignty. In any event, a lull in border warfare ensued and the Spanish detachment at Mers el-Kebir found itself ringed by Muslim warriors and forced to depend upon food shipments from Spain.[44]

Three years after the capture of Mers el-Kebir, Ferdinand had restored his authority over the Castilian grandees but had not regained control over the North African periphery. Bowing once again to the Castilian penchant for the old mode of expansion, he accepted another proposal for the continuation of the Maghribian campaign. At this point, the crown was strong enough to appoint its own man as the military commander of the African army, and Pedro Navarro, a former corsair, was elevated to the rank of captain general for the military campaign in North Africa.[45]

Still, Castile retained a good deal more influence over Maghriban policy than the appointment of Pedro Navarro indicated. Drained of financial resources by war in Italy and politics in Castile, Ferdinand agreed to extraordinary conditions for the management of the Maghribian campaign. In return for his pledge to defray the initial expenses of the Spanish force, the warrior priest Cardinal Cisneros obtained overall command of this minor crusade. He was also assured that the conquests of the Christian army would be attached not to the crown but to the diocese of Toledo. On the basis of these terms, troops were raised from Castile in the spring of 1509. During May of that year, an army of 10,000 men, more than fifteen times the size of the force Cortés used to conquer Mexico a decade later, left for North Africa.[46]

One of the most complex personalities of early modern Spain, Cardinal Cisneros commanded an expedition whose history epitomized the last hours of the medieval crusade. The seventy-three-year-old priest rode a mule among his troops before the walls of Oran, displaying the silver cross of Castile's most Catholic city, Toledo, and exhorting all to fight for God and the crown. Cannons once more gave the Christian army an easy victory. Elated by the fall of the city, Cisneros mustered all the pageantry of medieval Christendom to celebrate the conversion of Oran, with the hope that the crusading ardor of the African army would be preserved.

Oran, however, was on the edge of becoming one of Spain's monuments to a bygone era. From the beginning of the campaign, the cardinal and Pedro Navarro had violently disagreed over military policy. When the captain general brashly announced that the lands taken in the course of the conquest belonged not to the bishop of Toledo but to the crown, the larger political issues surrounding war in North Africa were joined. Just as this dispute turned on the question of who would direct the expansion of Spain, the refusal of Navarro to invade the interior of the Maghrib also provoked a controversy over what form the imperial effort should take in Africa. Here the cardinal displayed his dedication to the ideals of fifteenth-century Castile when he accused Pedro Navarro of wanting to raid the coastal cities of North Africa with no other objective than booty.[47] Backed by Ferdinand, Navarro won control of military policy, and Cisneros retired, with some speed, to the university of Alcalá.

Without hesitation Ferdinand imposed his own policy for the North African frontier. During the fall of 1509 Pedro Navarro made plans for implanting a Spanish outpost at Bougie, which would give the crown access to a port serving the commercial and agricultural networks of the eastern Maghrib. Meanwhile, in 1510 Ferdinand

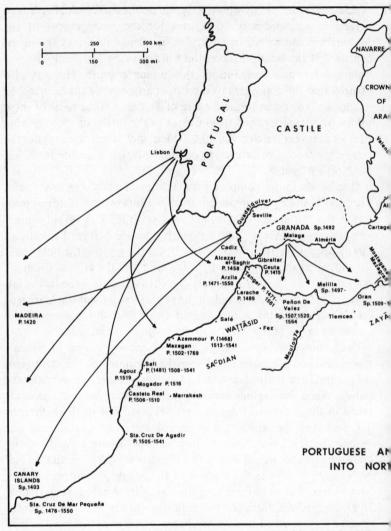

Fig. 1. Portuguese and Spanish expansion into North Africa, 1415–1510

SPANISH EXPANSION
AFRICA 1415-1510

Barcelona

CORSICA

Rome

Naples

MINORCA

MAJORCA

SARDINIA

IBIZA

SICILY

Cherchel   Algiers   Bougie Sp.1510-1555   Bône   Tunis
Sp.1510-1529   Sp.1535-
1574

MALTA

H A F Ṣ I D

Mahdia
Sp.1550-1554

KERKENNAH

JARBA

Tripoli
Sp.1510-1551

secured the consent of the pope and the Aragonese oligarchy to
create along the coast of North Africa an imperial system that
resembled the structure established by the Catalans during the
heyday of their expansion.[48] In a final burst of violence Pedro
Navarro completed Ferdinand's design when he established Christian
garrisons at Bougie and Tripoli in 1510.

Like the forts Castilian warriors used to raid Muslim lands in
Iberia, the *presidios* of North Africa sat on the edge of hostile territories. Yet this line of fortifications that the Spanish dug into the
shoreline of the Maghrib was not intended to move. Instead, Ferdinand's orders to his border commanders clearly directed them to
maintain these posts as defensive bastions where only Christians
resided while allied Muslim tribes provided a shield against the
hostile confederations of the outer frontier. Thus the primary responsibilities of Spanish frontiersmen were static: to turn the inner
barbarian against the outer in the manner of the Chinese governors
responsible for the defense of the Great Wall, and to protect the
coastline and commerce of Latin Christendom. Finally, the African
generals were encouraged to stimulate trade and to make their outposts self-supporting.

One of the great mirages of Spanish frontier policy, this attempt
to make the African forts self-sufficient was a dismal failure. Divided
by water from the Iberian Peninsula, the Christian posts in the
Maghrib appeared much less secure to Old Christian settlers than
did the territories in southwestern Spain or, later on, the lands in the
New World. Ordinary dangers of frontier life were compounded
because the population of the Maghrib was solidly Islamic and the
Moriscos of southeastern Spain were still Muslim despite the forced
conversions of 1502. Moreover, the growth of a strong Muslim
opposition, which began to be armed with powder weapons, made
the future of the Maghribian outposts look ominous; for after 1513
seamen from the borders of the Ottoman empire formed an alliance
with exiles from Spain to begin a Muslim cycle of offensive warfare.
By 1529, when the Spanish fort at Algiers fell to the cannon fire of
these Muslim frontiersmen, the *presidios* had become isolated
enclaves whose only reason for existence was their defensive role.[49]

No doubt the explanation for the hasty transformation of the
frontier rested on far more solid grounds than the political disputes
between the crown, the magnates, and the church militant. A clue
to one other reason can be found in the crown's heightened concern
for its own financial strength.[50] After the reorganization of the fairs

at Medina del Campo in 1483, the Catholic kings decreed that all commercial activities with Barbary were to pass through the city of Cadiz.[51] Yet the growth of Spain's power in the first quarter of the sixteenth century seems to have gone hand-in-hand with a precipitous decline in the trade with North Africa. At the end of Ferdinand's reign in 1516, the crown considered Maghribian commerce insignificant enough that it issued orders forbidding its subjects to carry on business with any part of North Africa.[52] At mid-century Charles V observed in a letter to his son, the future Philip II, that trade with Barbary yielded only 25,000 ducats a year in taxes.[53] In 1559 this figure amounted to less than half the amount—59,272 ducats—paid out in salaries to the Spanish soldiers at Oran.[54]

What happened on the New World frontier during this half-century contrasted strongly with Spain's waning involvement in North Africa. With breathtaking swiftness the conquerors gained control over huge territories. After 1519 their penetration of America's plateaus added more than two million square kilometers to the domains of Charles V. Even though these conquests were essentially private affairs, the state did benefit financially as Spanish warriors brought down the Aztec and Inca empires. From 1511 to 1520, 9,153 kilograms of gold arrived at the Casa de la Contratación in Seville. During the next decade only 4,889 kilograms of gold crossed the Atlantic; yet in this same span of time a flow of silver began, bringing the crown an average of 200,000 to 300,000 ducats a year until after 1561, when the flow of silver became a flood.[55] In a much less spectacular manner the merchants of Seville slipped in behind the conquerors to sponsor a burgeoning trade between Seville and the new frontier. Both state officials and ambitious *hidalgos* had learned rather early that the frontier of opportunity lay in the New World, not in Africa.[56]

European politics more than New World adventures sealed Spain's negative judgment on the attractiveness of expansion in North Africa. Old and sick, Ferdinand died in Madrigalejo on 23 January 1516, with the knowledge that the union of Castile and Aragon would, through royal marriages, fall into the hands of northern Europeans. When the Habsburg family imposed its rule, not only did the political center of Spain shift northward but the unity of the new regime cracked. Popular anger based upon a variety of troublesome internal issues exploded into widespread violence in 1520. The revolt of the Comuneros and its aftermath then restricted the possibility of further conquests in North Africa through the unsettled first five years of Charles V's reign.[57]

Even when authority was restored, the Maghribian margin of
Spain remained frozen in a defensive posture.[58] While the spirit of
the crusade against Islam would remain very much alive in Castile,
the attachment of most Spaniards to the more consequential interests
of the Habsburg empire in Europe carried Spain away from North
Africa. This was especially so after 1517, when checking the Protestant Reformation, conquering the New World's plateaus, and
containing the Turks made arguments for continuing the war against
Islam in Africa seem not only irrelevant but dangerous. Already the
Habsburg empire suffered from an old imperial complaint now
sharpened by the economic revolutions of the sixteenth century. A
helter-skelter growth of the state had overextended the ability of
the imperial bureaucracy to control the margins of an empire whose
territories were scattered like windblown seeds over Europe and the
New World. Under such conditions proposals to invade the Maghrib
carried little weight in imperial councils. North Africa became the
only extremity to be rejected as a political and financial burden far
exceeding whatever value its conquest might produce.

Four: ISLAM RESURGENT

Süleyman is the sultan of the fisherman because the Turks are masters of fleets and make war on the sea.

Muḥammad ash-Shaikh

Mehmet the Conqueror united in his person the highest qualities of a World Conqueror and a Sultan.

Tursun Bey, *Tarih-i Ebul Feth*

Between the fourteenth and the sixteenth centuries Islamic religious organizations spread throughout North Africa. Known to French historians as the maraboutic crisis, this three-century-long growth of popular piety coincided with the failure of post-Almohad states to maintain the cohesion of society. Internal dislocation and external defeat weakened the political legitimacy of Muslim rulers at the very time the countryside definitively converted to Islam. Beset by the tensions arising from these two broad and contrary trends, the North African community entered the sixteenth century in search of leadership.

Ottoman and Saᶜdian sultans advanced two widely different claims for the right to represent the faithful. A combination of local and communal legitimation emboldened the Saᶜdian family to attempt great acts from the tribal fringe of Morocco. For the central Maghrib, the Ottoman dynasty based its right to rule upon the communal and imperial achievements of nearly a century of eastern Mediterranean conquests. How each ruling class promoted its cause in a Muslim environment that was permeated by tribalism and confronted by a triumphant Christendom determined the typology of politics along the Muslim face of the frontier.

At the turn of the sixteenth century three ruling families—the
Waṭṭāsids of Fez, the Zayānids of Tlemsen, and the Ḥafṣids of
Tunis—claimed to rule the lands of North Africa. Located in cities
that were centers of trade and religious learning, these sultanates
projected their authority into rural areas through the legitimacy the
men of religion provided them, through the commercial and cultural
position of the cities, and, more directly, through the power of
their military organizations. Yet these urban dynasties of fifteenth-
century North Africa commanded no great swaths of agricultural
lands worked by submissive peasants whose taxes might finance
grand armies. Constrained by the divisive politics of the age, the
weak governments of the post-Almohad era (thirteenth century)
defended limited agricultural holdings not only against rival dynasties
and the infidel but also against the repeated challenges to stable
urban rule that Maghribian tribesmen launched.[1]

Though nomads had long ago ceased to be a threat to both urban
and rural society in Iberia, this was not true of North Africa at the
beginning of the sixteenth century. The appearance of extraordinary
leaders in rural areas or the inner dynamics of tribal alliances increasingly produced war bands whose military strength often exceeded that of the post-Almohad sultanates. Each year expeditions
sallied forth from the main cities to discipline refractory nomads and
mountaineers and to extend the range of the sultans' authority
against the outer, dissident tribes. Yet the cut-up geography of the
mountains, the vastness of the steppe, the weakness of the post-
Almohad dynasties, and the sultans' own use of tribal divisions
preserved these tribes and ultimately restricted the power of urban
government. Pockmarked by zones of dissidence, which were the
political consequence of a tension between tribal and urban ways of
life, the Maghribian community possessed an internal frontier whose
vicissitudes affected the ability of the Islamic rulers to wage war
against the infidel.[2]

Unlike the more independent cities and towns of Europe, the
urbanized regions of North Africa held tightly to their connection
with the ruling dynasties. In constant fear of being overrun by tribesmen, the city populations relied directly on the sultans for the defense
of the nearby agricultural regions upon which the life of the urban
areas depended. Rulers reinforced this bond by residing in the
cities and quartering the most powerful and trustworthy elements of
the army in the capitals rather than in rural zones. Since politics in
this age of weak dynasties and strong tribes came to be stated in

terms of a constantly changing pattern of alliances between the
sultans and the tribes, there could be little notion of the state's
territorial status.[3] This concentration of life in the cities, moreover,
created a significant cultural division between urban and rural
regions that was bridged only by a common allegiance to Islam and
by economic needs.

Beyond the range of urban armies and tax collectors, the independent tribes of North Africa evolved a highly organized way of
life that, although preserving the cohesiveness of their own social
structures, inhibited the formation of great states. Rather than
giving up to some exterior institution the right to apply sanctions
for maintaining law and order, as was increasingly done in early
modern Europe, the tribes set themselves against each other as a
means of obtaining social discipline. Orderliness of life was preserved, in this particularistic world of the tribesmen, by the threat
other tribes could pose from the outside.[4] Yet the life of mountaineers and herdsmen changed so often, in so many circumstances,
that a simple balance of power between one tribal unit and another
could hardly be maintained for any period of time. When presented
with a serious external challenge, tribesmen often formed themselves
into an interlocking series of concentric kinship alliances known as
leagues, or *liffs*.[5] From time to time an exceptional man might build
up a network of personal loyalties among kinsmen through which
he manipulated the dynamics of these tribal groupings, but rarely
could the personal strength of a chief restrain for long the underlying separatist tendencies of a society that lacked the institutional
means for a rich cultural life.

Between the eleventh and twelfth centuries the short but brilliant
histories of the Almoravid and Almohad empires demonstrated how
effectively religious revivalism could transcend the particularisms
of North African society. Yet at the moment when the reformers of
Western Islam established a central tradition that would draw the
community together, a kaleidoscopic response to Islam on local
levels reversed the drift toward religious unity. Missionaries for this
personal rather than abstract brand of religion found willing converts
among the near-pagan tribes of North Africa, just as they did in the
eastern regions of the House of Islam. This autonomous and varie-
gated growth of religion in the Maghrib merged with the segmented
social order of the rural world to bring forth a multitude of religious
lodges and fragmented saint cults. Within North Africa popular
Islam had a dual impact. It tended to diffuse authority, since the

bearers of Sufism were thought to possess the highest form of knowledge: they were close to God. On the other hand, the victory of the marabouts tightened the tribesmen's attachment to the world of Islam.[6]

Although the pattern of religious history after the eleventh century seemed to intensify the decentralization of cultural life, a political tradition for the formation of large states on the tribal periphery of Maghribian society survived. Schematized by Ibn Khaldun, the process of creating a new dynasty in the Islamic West involved a circulation of elites from the brutal life of the steppe to the cities. In this process the Maghribian historian assumed that the constant struggle between tribes imbued the steppe warriors with a military strength and a political cohesion superior to those of urban society. The formation of group solidarity, ʿaṣabīya, among victorious tribesmen became, for Ibn Khaldun, the fundamental act calling into being kingdoms and empires. But as the political movement on the steppe expanded from a tribal chieftainship to the government of cities, the cohesion of the original organization was no longer sufficient. Rule over large populations required a regular army, a bureaucracy, and a religious legitimation. Once these institutions were established, the founder of the new regime then delineated the frontiers of his empire up to the point where the internal cohesion of his state could no longer maintain itself. Then, somewhere on the border, a new combination of political and military talent would appear to challenge an imperial core weakened over time by the fatal incompatability between the hard life of the steppe, the soft existence in the cities, the authoritarian tendencies of urban government, and the dissident behavior of a society infused with tribal mores. Thus the old order would pass and a new cycle would begin.[7]

The Islamic community of the western Maghrib entered the second half of the fifteenth century in the midst of a complex struggle for power that had all the earmarks of Ibn Khaldun's last stage of urban decline. In Fez, the Marīnids had given way to a collateral branch of their family, the Waṭṭāsids, in a welter of tribal infighting. Even before the new sultan could install himself, a mob assassinated the last Marīnid sovereign, ʿAbd al-Ḥakk, in 1465 and pledged its loyalty to the head of the Idrisid family. This popular selection of the family that not only founded the first Muslim dynasty in Morocco but also bore a relation to the Prophet Muḥammad and therefore could carry the prestigious title Sharīf was clearly an attempt to establish a wider religious legitimacy in place of the purely political claims of the Waṭṭāsids.[8]

Although the Waṭṭāsids were able to put down the revolt of the Sharīfs in 1472, the movement to exploit the religious prestige of members of the Prophet's family continued to gather strength. In the Rif region of northern Morocco the Sharīfs of Jabal ʿAlam— southeast of Tetuan—founded the independent principality of Chechaouen (Ar. Shafshāwin) at the end of the fifteenth century with the help of Muslim exiles from Spain.[9] Claiming descent from the Idrisids as well as the Sufi saint Ibn Mashīsh, the rulers of the border city added another element to the prestige of the Sharīfian families and thereby broadened the social and religious base of their appeal.[10] This frontier city state, along with Tetuan, also built up its military reputation by mounting attacks upon the African garrisons of the Portuguese and Spanish. Like the Idrisids of Fez, however, the Rifian Sharīfs did not find the right mixture of policies and politics to attract a widespread following throughout the western Maghrib.

In rural regions of southwest Morocco, the Jazūlī sect displayed a mixture of religious and political elements similar to the Sharīfian movement in the north. Early in the fifteenth century, the Sufi scholar Muḥammad al-Jazūlī, a member of the Jazūla tribe from the Anti Atlas, acted out the Islamic drama that was required of Muslim saints who wished to attract a following. To acquire a full measure of religious charisma, the future Sufi leader immersed himself in the study of the doctrines propounded by the Shādhiliyya order, then made the pilgrimage to the holy cities of Islam. Thereupon he moved to the coastal city of Safi, where his fame as a holy man began to attract numerous disciples. In the manner of other Sufi masters, al-Jazūlī organized his following. Near the mid-fifteenth century, Jazūlī adepts began to claim a Sharīfian descent for their founder. Since the growth of the sect probably threatened the authority of the government in Fez, al-Jazūlī soon took up a secret residence in the village of Afughāl (near Essaouira-Mogador), where he died, allegedly poisoned, in 1465. His chief lieutenant, al-Sayyāf, then embarked on a political pilgrimage through the countryside, carrying the remains of the Sufi leader with him and exhorting those who revered the master to rebel against the government in Fez. But soon al-Sayyāf was killed (1488), and the corpse of al-Jazūlī ended its odyssey, being buried in the village of Afughāl. Other disciples maintained the organization of the fraternity, which for the time being sought no political objective.[11]

Tribal violence, ineffective urban government, and Christian incursions were the stuff of Leo the African's grim description of southern Morocco at the turn of the sixteenth century. Yet the weakness of urban government and the presence of the Christians in the cultivated regions of the south also created an incentive for the formation of a new political organization.[12] Long free of the control of northern sultans, the plains and mountains of southern Morocco stood well away from the centers of either Iberian or Waṭṭāsid strength. Moreover, the trade caravans that passed through southern Morocco yielded intelligence and transit taxes for those who controlled the Saharan routes that crossed the Wadi Draʿa on the way to the Atlantic plains of Morocco.[13] The dry and rocky surface of the southern steppe provided rough warriors for a fledgling state; and the nearby plain of the Sus produced the populations and agricultural resources necessary to sustain a large political movement.[14] For whatever immeasurable advantage it conferred, history blessed new dynasties born in the south, where both the Almoravid and Almohad empires had emerged.

A foundation myth attached the birth of the Saʿdian dynasty at Tidsi near Taroudant in 1510 to its participation in the holy war. In all probability the Saʿdians had reached a position of political importance among confederated tribesmen—such as those belonging to the Arab confederation known as the Maʿḳil—long before they were anointed with a militant religious role.[15] If their detractors are to be believed, they descended from one of the Arabian tribes that had migrated westward after the Arab conquests rather than from the Prophet's family. Once in Morocco, they settled in the village of Tagmadart within the valley of the Draʿa. There the Saʿdians became tribal strongmen. When sustained political success raised their authority to a level at which they could control the *liffs* in the Anti Atlas region, they offered the religious leaders of the south some hope of creating a larger and more cohesive Muslim community.

According to tradition, the rise of the Saʿdian dynasty began when ʿAbdallāh ibn Mubārak, the Sufi master who had preached the doctrines of al-Jazūlī, selected the Sharīf Muḥammad al-Ḳāʾim as commander of the faithful in the holy war against the infidels.[16] Although the Portuguese threat gave meaning to the holy war as an element in the legitimation of this new dynasty, the public acceptance of the Saʿdian genealogy by Sufi leaders had more importance at the time than did the jihadist appeal. This acquisition of inherited

THE SAʿDIAN DYNASTY

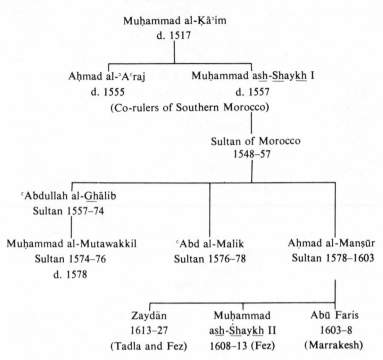

Muḥammad al-Ḳāʾim
d. 1517

Aḥmad al-ʾAʿraj   Muḥammad ash-Shaykh I
d. 1555   d. 1557
(Co-rulers of Southern Morocco)

Sultan of Morocco
1548–57

ʿAbdullah al-Ghālib
Sultan 1557–74

Muḥammad al-Mutawakkil   ʿAbd al-Malik   Aḥmad al-Manṣūr
Sultan 1574–76   Sultan 1576–78   Sultan 1578–1603
d. 1578

Zaydān   Muḥammad   Abū Faris
1613–27   ash-Shaykh II   1603–8
(Tadla and Fez)   1608–13 (Fez)   (Marrakesh)

charisma connected the Saʿdians to a Maghribian religious and social network that transcended the tribal background out of which the southern dynasty was born.

Between 1511 and 1524 the Saʿdians sought to transform their tribal confederation into a traditional agrarian state ruled by a stable dynasty. Hoping to avoid the tendency of kinship societies for succession conflicts, al-Ḳāʾim established the ranking procedure among his male offspring when he assigned the rights of rule to his oldest son, al- ʾAʿraj.[17] To widen the scope of his political appeal, the Sharīf moved his headquarters to Afughāl, where the proximity of al-Jazūlī's tomb permitted the Saʿdians to profit from Moroccan saint worship.[18] Meanwhile, Saʿdian tax collectors, themselves a sure sign of an attempt to create a territorial state, extracted revenues from the inhabitants of the Sus in order to resume the holy war against the Portuguese.[19] Saʿdians, however, avoided a direct attack upon the Christians, perhaps because they still lacked the unity and the military equipment to defeat them.[20]

In 1517 al-Ḳāʾim died and his son al-ʾAʿraj succeeded without any political difficulties. At approximately the same time the leader of the tribal opposition to the Saʿdians and main ally of the Portuguese, Yaḥyā, also perished.[21] Again the Saʿdians refrained from assaulting the Christians. Instead they turned their energies toward acquiring an urban center. This structural transformation occurred when the troops of the new dynasty captured Marrakesh in 1524.[22]

Although the paucity of the sources prevents a detailed analysis of internal events, the conquest of Marrakesh provoked the nominal rulers of Morocco, the Waṭṭāsids, into two unsuccessful attacks upon the Saʿdians between 1527 and 1529.[23] In each campaign the southerners gained the upper hand, decisively defeating the army of Fez in 1529. Fearing that further bloodshed between Muslims might undermine their position as holy warriors, the Saʿdians employed religious leaders to negotiate a peace with the Waṭṭāsids. The arbitrators then forced the Waṭṭāsids to recognize the Saʿdians by dividing Morocco between the two sultanates at the headwaters of the Oum err-Rbia near Tadla.[24] Six years after the establishment of this boundary the Saʿdians resumed warfare when they crushed Waṭṭāsid columns at Bu ʿAqba on 24 July 1536.[25]

Throughout this early period of Saʿdian growth, the Portuguese showed little interest in Moroccan politics. Short of men, money, and supplies, the governors of the coastal fortresses merely watched the Moroccan drama unfold from behind their ramparts.[26] But peace masked a significant change in the military history of the Maghrib. In Morocco, as in the other regions of North Africa, the impact of firearms and new military formations altered the means of waging large-scale warfare.

Iberian soldiers who served in North Africa during the first half of the sixteenth century uniformly commented upon the lightness of Muslim armament and the absence of powder weapons. Keeping the weight and size of their harness and saddle to a minimum, the light cavalry-men of the Muslim West went to war with short lances. For close combat they used daggers or swords, preferably of European make, since those manufactured in North Africa were not properly tempered. Some warriors went into battle with a handful of short javelins; others shot the crossbow from horseback. Moreover, light cavalrymen refused to employ firearms because they allegedly killed a man before he could display his valor. War, according to the Maghribian military aristocracy, ought to be fought on horseback; so foot soldiers were of little use and therefore were provided with few weapons.[27]

Despite the cavalryman's exalted hold upon the military life of North Africa, the Saᶜdians sought to modernize their army by acquiring new arms from Europe. As early as 1500, Portuguese frontiersmen reported to Lisbon on the attempt of the Muslim ruler at Safi to buy European-made arms.[28] By 1510 the crown learned that Spanish and French merchants had exchanged artillery balls, powder, and contraband weapons for the agricultural products of the southern Moroccan plains. In 1517 the king of Portugal stated bluntly that firearms were not to be sold to Muslims and that merchants who performed such an act against the good of Christendom would be exiled to the island of São Tomé in the Gulf of Guinea.[29] Yet the trade in arms attracted an ever-larger number of European merchants. In 1529 Spanish merchants sold arms to the Sharīf and to the Turkish corsairs operating in the Strait of Gibraltar.[30] By the 1540s the trade in weapons reached a peak as the variety of items sold—pikes, lances, coats of mail, wood, oars—and the regularity of the exchanges for French-made artillery carried the Moroccans beyond the stage of acquiring armaments piecemeal.[31]

Even then, the Spanish historian Mármol noted that Moroccans looked with disdain upon the work associated with the new technology. Unwilling or unable to change the equestrian orientation of their army, the Saᶜdian sultans were compelled to comb the ranks of French and English renegades for cannon casters and armorers.[32] Not until the campaigns of the 1530s did the Moroccan armies deploy, in any effective manner, units with powder weapons. What happened in the south of Morocco also took place in the north, so that by the 1540s the sultans of both Fez and Marrakesh could field an artillery train and an infantry unit capable of employing handguns.[33]

During September 1540, a Saᶜdian truce with the Portuguese expired. Shortly thereafter the brother of the Sharīf, Muḥammad ash-Shaykh, dispatched troops to take the heights above the Portuguese fort at Agadir. On 16 February 1541, the Muslims began their siege of the Christian position with a large number of cannons. Before the Portuguese could react to this unexpected display of Muslim firepower, the Saᶜdians breached the defense and the fort was taken in March.[34]

Among the faithful the victory confirmed the belief that the Saᶜdians were divinely supported. A less supernatural explanation holds that this success was due to their ability to afford new troops and equipment. Regular collections of taxes from the agricultural economy of the Sus valley surely financed the new army. Peasants, however, did not carry the entire burden; for the transformation of the army coincided with the declining gold trade at La Mina.[35] This suggests that between 1521 and 1541 the Saharan economy had recovered from whatever damage the Portuguese seagoing commerce had inflicted upon it. A Muslim riposte, the fall of Agadir, filled the arsenal of the Sharīf with new weapons and increased his treasure through the ransoms paid by the Portuguese. Suddenly, however, the good fortune brought on a dynastic crisis.

When internal warfare broke out in 1542, it appeared that factionalism would bring down the Saᶜdian attempt to unify Morocco. The energetic Muḥammad ash-Shaykh, however, grasped the leadership of the dynasty and temporarily reconciled family differences by agreeing on a complicated succession plan that would pass on the rule of the state among brothers or even cousins rather than in the European mode of father to eldest son. On the basis of this political agreement, Muḥammad ash-Shaykh resumed the war with the outside. Once more military operations began not with a charge against the Christians but with a march upon the center of Moroccan opposition in Fez.[36]

This time the internal expansion of the Saᶜdians was much better organized. The defeat of the Portuguese at Agadir persuaded John III to abandon two other outposts, Safi and Azemmour, during 1541. While the Christians retreated, Muḥammad ash-Shaykh spent his time remodeling his army, with the experience of the Turks as a guide. When the Saᶜdian and Waṭṭāsid armies clashed during the summer of 1545 near the river Derna, the Saᶜdian drew up his men in the crescent-shaped formation employed by the Ottomans.[37] His coordinated use of cavalry, arquebusiers, and cannoneers overwhelmed the Waṭṭāsid force. News of the Saᶜdian victory encouraged political division in Fez; and when the legal scholar and Saᶜdian opponent Aḥmad al-Wansharīsī was assassinated, the southerners took Fez on 31 January 1549.[38]

Though at the zenith of his power in Morocco, Muḥammad ash-Shaykh knew that he presided over an expansive movement whose ideological themes—holy war and unity under the charismatic leadership of the Saᶜdian family—masked an ever-present tendency toward decentralization. A continuation of successful warfare was one way to avoid an erosion of tribal backing. Hostile tribes in the Rif needed pacification; but the terrain gobbled up armies. To the east the oases of the Tafilalt, where ambitious members of the Saᶜdian family might be collecting gold and troops, seemed the most logical avenue of expansion. Without a navy, without an army comparable to that of either of the Iberian states, the Saʿdian sultan elected this eastward-bound line of advance.[39] Before ong, however, the conquest of the eastern oases encouraged the Moroccan cavalry to raid the territories of the Ottoman Turks, who, since the second decade of the sixteenth century, had gradually extended their administration westward into the region of Tlemsen.[40]

Contact with the Ottomans at Tlemsen initiated an unequal contest for political predominance in the Maghrib between a dynasty only recently emerged from the tribal periphery of Morocco and a sultanate whose century-old military record made it the acknowledged leader of Mediterranean Islam. Perhaps unaware of the true strength of the Ottomans, perhaps unable to restrain the exuberance of a conquering army whose ranks were filled with tribesmen, the Saʿdians crossed into Ottoman territories and took Tlemsen in May 1550. By the end of the summer of that year, the Turks managed to blunt the Moroccan penetration. Then in the winter of 1551 the Ottomans expelled the Saʿdians and reestablished their authority in Tlemsen. Muḥammad ash-Shaykh had, in the meantime, deployed his army in the High Atlas, where a revolt by the Maṣmūda Berbers raised the specter of tribal dissidence.[41]

Before this mid-sixteenth-century border incident, the Ottomans had shown little interest in the Muslim regimes of the western Maghrib. Selim the Grim may have received an envoy from the Waṭṭāsids shortly before his conquest of Egypt in 1517.[42] During 1528 the court at Istanbul entertained an ambassador from Fez.[43] By all accounts, however, Ottoman viziers preferred to make their strategic moves on Balkan and Asian fields rather than on the distant North African frontier.[44]

Even after the border skirmishes over the possession of Tlemsen in 1550–51, the Ottomans elected to negotiate rather than to make war when they dispatched the imam Muḥammad al-Kharrūbī to Morocco in 1552. However, the price of good relations with the eastern empire was acceptance of a client-state status, and neither Moroccan history nor the dynamics of the Saʿdian movement prepared Muḥammad ash-Shaykh to agree to such a proposal. In a meeting whose stormy overtones underlined the clash between competing legitimacies, the Moroccan sultan provided an insight into the terrestrial ethos of his state when he mocked the Ottomans, calling them fishermen.[45]

Frontier warfare between the eastern and western Muslim states was only a matter of time. Within two years the Ottomans found a candidate for the Moroccan sultanate and provided him with sufficient military aid to drive the Saʿdians from Fez in 1554.[46] Defeated, the Saʿdians regrouped their forces and waited until the population of Fez tired of the Ottoman occupation. By the fall of 1554 the Turks departed and Muḥammad ash-Shaykh was again able to take Fez. Although his final conquest of the northern city ended the civil war within Morocco and to a degree restored the prestige of the Saʿdian family, the climate of politics in the Maghrib had changed; for in the Ottomans the southern dynasty confronted a formidable Muslim opponent.

Once more master of the western Maghrib, Muḥammad ash-Shaykh retreated from the Ottoman border to strengthen his position within Morocco. In 1556 he turned to the holy war, mounting an unsuccessful assault on the Portuguese fort at Mazagan (El Jadida). Meanwhile the Saʿdian leader had driven his tax collectors ever deeper into the countryside in search of revenues with which he could purchase the military power of the powder age. But society was beginning to set limits to the internal ambitions of the Moroccan government. In 1557 another tribal rebellion required the dispatch of the Saʿdian army to the High Atlas.

Part of the Sharīf's plan to improve his army included hiring infantrymen who could use firearms. This preoccupation, which the tribal resources of the Saʿdian state could not or would not satisfy, allowed Ottoman agents to infiltrate the Moroccan army disguised as deserters. On 23 October 1557 the Turkish soldiers did their work, sending the head of the assassinated Muḥammad ash-Shaykh to Algiers, where it was repacked and dispatched to Istanbul.[47] For a dynasty still highly dependent on personal loyalties, the death of the hard-driving Moroccan sultan had a profound impact on Saʿdian politics. Members of the royal family concluded that aims had exceeded abilities and that the policy of the state should therefore be turned toward peace. Between 1557 and 1576 the pendulum of Moroccan history began to swing back toward localism.

Judged against the patterns of state formation in previous eras of expansion, the appearance of the Saʿdians represented a conservative use of Maghribian traditions. Rising above the tribal elites by combining a personal religious prestige—their alleged relation to the house of the Prophet—with political and military ability, the Saʿdians allied themselves with southern tribesmen and with religious brotherhoods whose base lay outside the capital cities of Morocco. When the core of their new state was formed, the southerners advanced along internal lines that led from the southern steppe of Morocco to the Atlantic plains and to the major cities in a manner not markedly different from the outline the historian Ibn Khaldun had drawn up for the formation of previous North African states.

Yet exterior conditions rendered a Moroccan state constructed on the Khaldunian pattern obsolete long before the Saʿdians finally captured Fez. Powder technology and political competition in the early modern era demanded a greater separation between state and society than the Saʿdians were able to attain. In military matters, they were unable to transform the social basis of their army to a degree that would allow them to compete with either the Iberian or the Ottoman empire. Similarly, imperial warfare in the sixteenth century demanded high levels of financial support. Saʿdians, however, did not control large agricultural tracts through a highly centralized bureaucracy like that of the Ottomans, nor was there a cohesive commercial class ready to incite their rulers to engage in an institutional form of early modern state capitalism like that in Iberia.[48] It was true that the widespread support of Sufi lodges provided the Saʿdians with the kindling for a great religious fire. Yet they were unable to organize the marabouts, with whom they shared legitimacy, into a religious bureaucracy acting in support of their cause. Moreover, the Moroccan dynasty proclaimed its legitimacy at a time when the Ottomans had already established a creditable claim to leadership in the Muslim world.[49]

Often viewed as a militant response to an Iberian challenge, the holy war record of the Saʿdians was not impressive. Since the restrained imperialism of the Iberian states did not threaten the heart of the Moroccan polity, the weaker Saʿdian regime made little effort to build a navy, to invade Iberia, or to compete with the Christians in the new commercial arenas. During the first half of the sixteenth century only one major attempt was made to expand beyond the geographic boundaries of Morocco. The result of the Tlemsen campaign, however, ended the hope of external growth in the direction of Egypt and, disastrously for a jihadist state, drove it into an alliance with the Spanish.[50] By the mid-sixteenth century, the Saʿdian sultanate had become a local reply to an age of expansion and attenuated external challenge.

If this abridged expansion of the Saʿdians preserved the symmetry of North African history, the near-simultaneous extension of

Ottoman sovereignty over the tribes and cities of the central Maghrib broke decisively with old political traditions. More comparable to the Byzantine acquisition of North African lands than to the advance of tribal confederations from desert or mountain peripheries, the Ottoman conquerors came from the urban heart of the eastern Mediterranean and reached North Africa by sea.[51] Of all the distinguishing elements between the Saᶜdians and the Ottomans, the different social base of the eastern ruling class was the most striking: their origins were not local, and their political cohesion did not rest upon kinship alignments.

A phase ahead of the Saᶜdian movement, the Ottoman conquest reached North Africa when the imperial core had already acquired the equipment and institutions of a Muslim gunpowder empire.[52] This meant that the Ottoman border warriors could draw upon the powerful technological and bureaucratic resources of a great state.[53] They therefore could carry on the holy war against the Iberians with far more vigor than could the Saᶜdians. This urban, orthodox, and militant cast of Ottoman expansion allowed the Turks to exploit the consequences of the collapse of Islam in Spain; to form an alliance with the refugees from Iberia; and to use their military and agricultural talents to accomplish the aims of the Turko-Muslim empire in North Africa. Taken all together, the abilities and advantages of the Ottoman frontiersmen explain why the eastern conquerors entered the Maghrib through the cities.

A half-century before the rise of the Saᶜdians, the initial acts that led to the Ottoman conquest of North Africa were performed. The fall of Constantinople in 1453 bore witness to the effectiveness of a Turko-Muslim army equipped with powder weapons and at the same time announced the appearance of an Ottoman navy. Mehmet the Conqueror hesitated not at all in using the millenarian expectations this victory awakened among Muslims to adopt an internal policy of vigorous centralization and an external plan of vast, imperial proportions. By 1503 the effort at creating a great empire had succeeded on the naval border to the degree the Ottoman navy had defeated the Venetian fleet and opened the maritime lanes leading to the western basin of the Mediterranean. But it was the sudden conquest of the Arab lands by Selim the Grim in 1516–17 that catapulted the Ottomans to political supremacy among Muslims.[54] Protector of the holy places of Islam, defender of vast Muslim lands, hammerer of the infidels in the Balkans, the Ottoman sultan cast an imperial shadow over territories wherever, as in Spain and North Africa, Muslims might be in trouble.

The Ottoman Dynasty in Its Golden Age 1453-1622

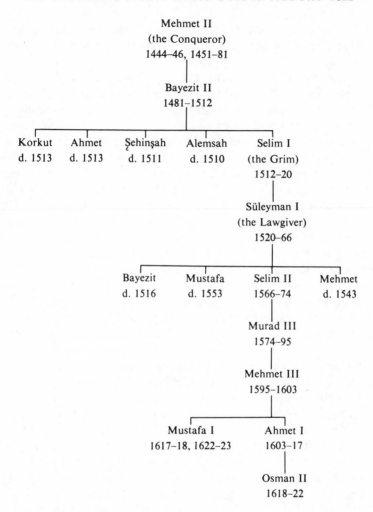

When Ottoman frontiersmen began their migration from the shores of the eastern Mediterranean to North Africa during the reign of Bayezit II (1481-1512), the event came as no surprise to Catholic Spain. Already in July 1480 a unit of the Ottoman army under Gedik Ahmet Paşa had landed in southern Italy and taken the city of Otranto. This occupation of lands so close to the main altar of Christendom drove both Portugal and Catholic Spain to dispatch naval units to assist the Christian counterattack. Before much military action took place, Mehmet the Conqueror's death in 1481

brought on a succession crisis and compelled the Turks to give up
their foothold on the Italian mainland. This fleeting contact between
Spain and the Ottomans nevertheless became the first event in a long
parade of frontier movements that would bring warfare on a much
larger scale.

Three years later the rumor that the Ottomans had gathered a
large fleet caused sufficient concern at the Spanish court to provoke a
flurry of orders for the fortification of Sicilian ports. In 1488 a small-
scale attack on Malta by Turkish corsairs stimulated anxiety in Spain
over the strength of Sicily's defenses and prompted a halfhearted
attempt to work out some sort of an alliance with Mamluk Egypt.[55]
But all the energies of the Catholic kings were absorbed by the
reconquest, and little effort was made to deal with the rise of the
Turko-Muslim empire in the east.

Even as the Catholic kings prepared for their final assault on
Granada, the Ottoman sultan displayed some interest in the fate of
the Hispano-Muslims. By 1487 a poetical appeal for aid from
Muslims in Granada reached both Mamluk and Ottoman courts.[56]
A desire for more information about the perilous situation of the
community in the west prompted Bayezit II to call upon the services
of a corsair. Provided with ships and equipment, the privateer
Kemal Reis sailed into the western basin of the Mediterranean on a
mission of reconnaissance.[57]

Somewhere along the southeastern shore of Spain, Kemal Reis's
raiders made the first direct contact between Ottoman sailors and
the Hispano-Muslims of Granada. Since the privateers began their
activities during the last hours of the Naṣrid sultanate, the Ottomans
learned how weak their Spanish coreligionists had become.

Successful raiding then encouraged the corsairs to select bases on
the North African coast where galleys could be careened, prizes sold,
and winter endured in relative safety. At Bougie, the Ottoman freebooters were welcomed by the patron saint of the city, Sayyid
Muḥammad Tuwallī, who according to a local myth had magical
powers that would protect the port against the Spanish.[58] This
meeting provided early evidence of an important link between the
Ottomans, the popular religious leaders of the Maghrib, and those
who were committed to the holy war.

Alternating between the island of Gerba and the ports of Bône and
Bougie, Kemal Reis continued his raids upon Christian shores and
shipping until the year 1495, when Bayezit II recalled the experienced
sailor to Istanbul to strengthen the imperial fleet. The absorption of

these corsairs brought the Ottoman court the news the privateers had gained in the course of their western raids. While Ottoman viziers digested this intelligence and the imperial fleet warred with the Venetians between 1499 and 1503, local Muslim corsairs carried on the holy war along the coasts of Spain and North Africa until a new wave of eastern Mediterranean sailors migrated to those same ports used by Kemal Reis.

Sailors, not tribesmen, were responsible for the first stage of Ottoman expansion in North Africa.[59] Although sixteenth-century sources list various ethnic and religious origins for the most famous of these maritime vagabonds, the Barbarossa brothers, there is agreement that they came from the island of Mytilene, engaged in coastal trade, and made contact with the different cultures of the eastern Mediterranean world.[60] It is also clear that the Barbarossas were involved in the Ottoman political struggles of the early sixteenth century. According to the holy war account of Hayreddin Barbarossa, Oruç, the elder of the brothers, survived captivity by the Knights of Saint John at Rhodes to become the protégé of the Ottoman prince Korkut. When Korkut lost out in the succession struggle with Selim the Grim in 1512, the Barbarossa brothers fled westward toward Tunis rather than face the penalties a sultan as fierce as Selim the Grim applied to those who backed the wrong candidate. At Tunis the corsairs worked out a border arrangement, probably in 1513, with the Ḥafṣid sultan Muḥammad V that allowed them to use the small port of La Goletta. In return for a guarantee not to raid ships sailing under the protection of the Tunisian ruler and to pay a percentage of the booty taken in the war with the infidel, the corsairs acquired a refuge close to the shipping lanes that passed the island of Sicily.[61]

As the military reputation of corsairs grew, the Muslim elders of the coastal cities the Iberians had besieged began to look upon the Turks as a possible source of help. In the summer of 1514 the Barbarossas, acting on an appeal for help from the Muslim elders of Bougie, descended upon the stronghold the Spanish had erected at the mouth of the port after its conquest by Pedro Navarro in 1510. No cavalry charge, the corsair's investment of the Spanish outpost was accomplished with firearms. A bombardment opened a hole in the outer wall, and the Turks attacked only to be driven back when their leader, Oruç, was wounded in the left arm. Unnerved by this event, or more probably by the exhaustion of their powder, the corsairs retreated to Tunis.[62]

Failure at this first siege operation forced the corsairs to seek greater access to advanced military technology. Again the privateers resumed their attacks upon Christian shipping. At the same time the Barbarossas sent the nephew of Kemal Reis, the geographer Piri Reis, to Istanbul with presents for the Ottoman sultan. All past errors were apparently forgotten as the sultan welcomed the corsairs' representatives with enthusiasm, granting them the usual honors reserved for successful frontiersmen—pay, titles, caftans, and jeweled swords. Selim the Grim also ordered the imperial dockyard to resupply the galleys Piri Reis had brought to Istanbul. In addition, the sultan awarded the now-favored Barbarossas two war galleys.[63] Transcending the immediate importance of the new equipment, the mission of Piri Reis wedded the Maghribian privateers to an urban center where the corsairs could obtain powder technology, trained foot soldiers, and the support of an empire with a celebrated reputation in the prosecution of the holy war.

Without local allies, however, the Ottoman frontiersmen would be just as isolated on the North African coast as the Spanish increasingly came to be in their *presidios*. The corsairs recognized this and set off on a search for those elements of the frontier society that would favor war against the Christians. As in Morocco, a vigorous pursuit of the jihad appealed to the religious in both urban and rural areas.[64] Yet the Muslims most exposed to the pressure of Latin Christendom were the best candidates for the war party the corsairs hoped to form. Accordingly, the Barbarossas sent eight ships to Granada to rescue the faithful from Iberia and transplant them to North Africa.[65] There, according to the propaganda of the holy war account, the Hispano-Muslims would be able to build mosques, pay taxes in accordance with the holy law, pray openly, teach their children how to read the Koran, and marry freely: to live within the boundaries of Islamic society as defined in its urban form. Although it is difficult to find evidence of the connections between the Hispano-Muslims and the Turks at this early period, there was an obvious conjunction of interests between the Hispano-Muslims of the first wave of immigrants from Granada, the urban populations of North Africa who were enclosed by the Spanish, and the corsairs, who, as their growing ties with Istanbul indicated, did not represent a tribal-based regime.[66]

Nonetheless, the small band of corsairs had to create a link between themselves and the kinship-oriented society of North Africa. In the spring of 1515 the sailors received a letter from a

sheik, calling upon them to wage holy war once again with the
Christians at Bougie. Assembling their forces, the Barbarossas began
a second siege of the port in August 1515. Once more the Muslims
broke through the outer defenses of the Spanish fort only to be
confronted by a well-defended inner fortress. A resumption of their
cannonade again depleted the attackers' powder supply without
breaching the Spanish wall. Promptly the corsairs petitioned the
Ḥafṣid sultan at Tunis for more gunpowder. Now, however, the
connection between the sailors and the Ottoman empire, which was
on the verge of conquering the Mamluk empire of Syria and Egypt,
awakened a political opposition on the Muslim side of the frontier,
for the Ḥafṣid sultan feared that the frontier clients of the Ottomans
would eventually become the means for his own displacement. Thus
he denied the frontiersmen's request. Thereupon the momentum of
the attack on the Spanish position faltered and the Turks withdrew
to the port of Jijilli (Djidjelli), where Oruç worked out an alliance
with the leaders—the Banū ᶜAbbās—of the tribes inhabiting the
Lesser Kabylia.[67]

Shortly after the failure of the second siege of Bougie, the Muslim
ruler of Algiers, Sālim al-Thaᶜālibī, chief of the Thaᶜāliba tribe,
approached the corsairs with a proposal related to the imbalance of
military power in the central Maghrib. After Pedro Navarro's campaign in 1510, the Spanish had constructed a fort upon a rocky island
just outside the harbor of Algiers—the Peñón. Cannon fire from this
Christian outpost compelled the Muslims of Algiers to pay tribute
to Spain. Oruç agreed to help the Algerians eject the Spanish. During
the spring of 1516 the border warrior loaded his ships with war
supplies and sent his foot soldiers overland to Algiers. First, however, Oruç secured his position in the central Maghrib when he took
the port of Cherchel, where Hispano-Muslim exiles had settled and
repaired the local castle.[68] Then the commander of the corsairs
emplaced his artillery in front of the Christian fort at Algiers. Once
more the power of the corsair cannonade was unequal to the task.
This time, however, the failure of the attack did not cause the Turks
to abandon the city, but instead provoked an internal struggle for
the mastery of Algiers. Accusing Sālim al-Thaᶜālibī of opposing
the holy war, in 1516 Oruç executed the tribal leader and took
control of the port. From a social viewpoint, this brutal act was
the first sign that the corsairs intended to establish an urban foothold
independent of the tribal hinterland.[69]

Spain, in contrast to Portugal, felt compelled to respond to a

frontier aggression indirectly backed by a Muslim empire. Consequently the crown authorized a campaign against the Turkish
position at Algiers. In the same interval the Christians unsuccessfully
attempted to stir both the tribesmen and the rulers of the cities and
towns against the corsairs. On 30 September 1516, Don Diego de
Vera landed 8,000 troops near Algiers and engaged the corsairs, who
managed to hold off their attackers. Weather then took a hand in the
battle as a north wind dashed the unprotected Spanish fleet against
the rocky coast of the Maghrib. No mere border skirmish, the victory
of the corsairs entrenched them in a coastal city with an agricultural
hinterland and a geographical position far away from the centers of
Muslim and Christian opposition. All that remained to be done
before Algiers could become a border port for Muslim war galleys
was to remove the Spanish fort whose cannons overlooked the main
anchorage.[70]

To profit from the victory, the corsairs attempted to take the old
capital city of the central Maghrib, Tlemsen. With an army of foot
soldiers—his own men and Andalusians—Oruç began the campaign
by securing the town of Ténès, to the west of Algiers, in 1517. During
that same year a succession dispute inflamed the politics of Tlemsen's
ruling family, the Zayānids, and thereby presented the Turks with the
opportunity to enter the city. But there were other reasons why the
Turks would be welcomed: the merchants of Tlemsen were compelled
to pay taxes to the Spanish at the ports for their city—Mers el-Kebir
and Oran—and the religious leaders of the Zayānid capital sympa-
thized with the holy war initiative of the Turks. With little difficulty
Oruç succeeded in deposing the Zayānid sultan, Abū Hammū III.
This invasion of Tlemsen and the dethronement of the Zayānid
sultan showed that the Turks intended to conquer the interior of the
Maghrib.[71]

Two major changes in the world of Mediterranean politics during
1517 gave the fall of Tlemsen greater importance than it might
otherwise have had. The rapid maneuvers of the corsairs, which were
now both coastal and internal, occurred at the same time as Selim
the Grim completed his conquest of Syria and Egypt in 1516–17.
Sensitive to events in the east, the western frontiersmen lost no time in
reporting their accomplishments to the Ottoman ruler when the
naval captain, Kurdzade Muslihiddin, met the fleet of Selim the
Grim during the naval campaigns against the Mamluks in 1516–17.[72]
At approximately the same time, the Spanish governor of Oran, Don
Diego Hernández de Córdoba, explained the deteriorating situation

in North Africa to the new sovereign of Spain, Charles I, who now authorized his first campaign against the Turks in North Africa. This decision to counter the growing Muslim threat on the outer frontier of Spain, rather than simply to hold the coastal fortifications as the Portuguese did in Morocco, was another measure of how much the Spanish feared an imperial connection between the hub of the Ottoman empire and North Africa.[73]

Early in 1518, Spanish troops cut the supply route over which aid from Algiers would normally move to the west. Then Iberian troops blockaded the Turks within the walls of Tlemsen. Without supplies and low on men, Oruç Barbarossa decided to break out of the siege at night. Eluding their Spanish guards at first, the Turks marched eastward toward Algiers, but they were surrounded on the bank of the river Salado near the *Zāwiya* of Sīdī-Mūsā, the lodge of a religious organization. The corsairs were defeated and their leader, Oruç, was killed in the summer of 1518.[74]

The small size of the corsair band was now exposed, and Hayreddin, Oruç's successor, found himself without enough power to meet the challenges raised by the Spanish, the old ruling families, and the tribesmen.[75] How to obtain new equipment and men and how to underpin the political authority of corsair rule became the border chieftain's paramount concerns. Turning eastward, Hayreddin sent another delegation to the Ottoman sultan. In Istanbul the envoy of the frontiersmen requested that the territories the corsairs had taken be included within the boundaries of the lands protected by the Ottoman sultan.

Selim the Grim accepted the corsair's gift and extended the charismatic qualities attributed to the Ottoman family into the western basin of the Mediterranean shortly before his death. In accordance with Ottoman traditions, the sultan appointed Hayreddin governor of Cezayir-i Arab, the Algeria of the Arabs. Sometime thereafter, between 1517 and 1520, the Ottoman commander performed in Algeria those symbolic acts that announce the arrival of a new Muslim dynasty; the name of the Turkish sultan was read in the Friday prayer and placed upon the coinage.[76]

This outright expansion of the Ottoman periphery into the central Maghrib cramped the weak Ḥafṣid sultanate between the Spanish and Ottoman empires. Although separated by great distance from Egypt and Istanbul, the ruler of Tunis understood the language of Turko-Muslim imperialism. Like the Christians, the Tunisian sultan tried to form an anti-Turkish coalition composed of tribesmen and old ruling families. But the Ḥafṣid plan was discovered by Barbarossa, who quashed the revolt by executing a number of the plotters.[77]

No sooner had Hayreddin driven off his internal competitors than the Spanish attacked again. On 18 August 1519, late in the Mediterranean naval season, the Spanish disembarked their troops to the west of Algiers and waited for the arrival of North African allies. When the rulers of Tlemsen failed to appear, the Spanish began their attack alone. Unable to penetrate the defenses of Algiers, the Christians were dispersed by another Mediterranean storm that sank most of their ships.[78]

Despite the defeat of the Spanish, the corsairs were still not strong enough to bring the internal politics of the central Maghrib under their control. Moreover, by 1520 the turmoil produced by the three-cornered competition for predominance along the frontier had caused the tribes to coalesce about their leaders. Quick to take advantage of the new situation, the Ḥafṣid sultan convinced Aḥmad ibn al-Ķāḍī, the sheik of the Berber tribesmen from the principality of Kūko, the Greater Kabylia mountains just east of Algiers, of the need to expel the Turks.[79] Encircling Algiers from the land side, the Berber chieftain imposed a tight blockade on the city. Hayreddin fought back by dispatching a unit of foot soldiers armed with powder weapons against the Berbers. The tribal leader not only defeated the Turkish counterattack but also enlisted one of Hayreddin's commanders, Ḳara Hasan, in his own army.[80] Aware that the inhabitants of the city were also of doubtful loyalty, the Ottoman commander decided to preserve the unity of his forces rather than risk a long and debilitating siege in Algiers. Hence the corsair abandoned his capital to return to Jijilli, the port for the Lesser Kabylia.[81]

The mountains behind Jijilli were ruled by the sometime allies of the Turks, the Banū ʿAbbās, who were also enemies of the Berbers of the Greater Kabylia. Too weak to overcome the kinsmen even with the aid of the Hispano-Muslim exiles, Hayreddin now fell back upon an alliance with a portion of North Africa's segmented society. Thus, the first decade of frontier history for the Turks ended with the corsairs confined to a small foothold on the rocky shoreline of the central Maghrib, where only their ability as holy warriors gave them some hope that they would be able to lift themselves above the tribal environment into which they had descended.

Even though the position of the corsairs had deteriorated, neither Charles V nor Süleyman the Lawgiver displayed much interest in the

North African frontier during the third decade of the sixteenth century. In 1520 the emperor sent a substantial army of 13,000 men under Hugo de Moncada and Diego de Vera to destroy the Muslim corsair nest on the island of Gerba. Although the campaign was a success, the Spanish did not consolidate their conquest, being distracted by the French invasion of Navarra in 1521 and the upheavals in Spain associated with the revolt of the Comuneros (May 1520 to April 1521).[82] Charles V also approved an action designed to retake the privateers' lair at Peñón de Velez, south of Malaga on the Rifian coast, which the Muslims had taken by stealth in 1522. But the naval force under Hurtado de Mendoza lost the advantage of surprise when they arrived in front of the Peñón on 13 September 1523 and were compelled to withdraw.[83] During the same period, the Ottoman sultan was fully engaged on other frontiers. Between 1520 and 1529 the armies of Süleyman took Belgrade in 1521, seized the island of Rhodes in 1522–23, launched the Hungarian campaign in 1526, and mounted the siege of Vienna in 1529. North Africa was clearly one of the empire's back doors.

While the great powers were absorbed with European matters, Hayreddin redoubled his efforts to win the political contest within the central Maghrib. He equipped another army at Jijilli and tightened his alliance with the Banū ʿAbbās of the Lesser Kabylia.[84] Throughout this period, the continued migration of Hispano-Muslims into North Africa also added to the military ranks of the pro-Turkish and anti-Christian coalition.[85] Settling for the most part in the coastal cities of the Maghrib, the refugees from southeastern Spain invariably sided with the eastern frontiersmen who, from their point of view, were the most capable defenders of Islamic society. Hayreddin also profited from the social divisions that separated, in varying degrees, the mountain and steppe peoples from urban society. In Algiers the rule of Ibn al-Ḳāḍī and his Berber followers alienated the population of the city to the point where some wished for the return of Turkish rule. At the appropriate moment, Hayreddin launched an attack upon his Berber enemy. Two victories in the Kabylia mountains and the desertion to the Ottoman of the unit of soldiers under the command of the turncoat Kara Hasan gave Hayreddin control of Algiers in 1525.[86]

As soon as he had reestablished his authority in the central Maghribian city, Hayreddin carried his administration to the interior. Driving out the men who had usurped control of the regions the Turks had previously conquered, he expanded the boundaries of his province in 1528 to include the coastline from Jijilli to Cherchel and the interior of the central Maghrib from the plain of Mitidja to the high tablelands of Constantine. Berbers of the Greater Kabylia now acknowledged Ottoman authority by paying tribute. For the frontiersmen, however, the final and most pressing task was to eliminate the Spanish fort at Algiers.[87]

At the beginning of May 1529, Hayreddin offered the Christian garrison the opportunity to surrender. After the Iberians rejected the Ottoman terms, the Turks, who now had enough cannon and powder, mounted a continuous artillery bombardment of the fort that lasted for more than twenty days. When enough gaps had been blown in the defenses of the fort, on 27 May 1529 a rush succeeded in overwhelming the Spanish resistance. Twelve years before the Saʿdians drove the Portuguese from Agadir, the destruction of this Iberian strongpoint confirmed the Ottoman position in Algiers and in the central Maghrib: the Turks demonstrated that they could take a fortified position; the corsairs obtained the use of a port; and naval communication between the western frontier and Istanbul became a bit less dangerous.[88]

No sooner had the Ottomans reconstructed their harbor at Algiers than Hayreddin dispatched a squadron of galleys under Aydın Reis to search the Strait of Gibraltar for prizes and to transport Andalusians to Algiers.[89] In the interior the Ottomans marched upon Tlemsen. Again playing upon the political divisions among the members of the Zayānid family, the Ottomans established in Tlemsen their candidate, ʿAbdallāh, who agreed to acknowledge the sovereignty of Süleyman the Lawgiver by using his name in the Friday prayer and on the coinage. Within a short period of time, however, the Spanish in Oran forced the Tlemsen sultan to shed his allegiance to the Ottomans; nevertheless the wobbly behavior of the Zayānid sultan heralded the end of the dynasty and the transfer of politics in the central Maghrib to Algiers.[90]

From 1529 to 1532 warfare along the Ibero-African frontier featured a series of naval campaigns by Christians against the bases of the North African corsairs. Prodded by injured subjects, Charles V ordered his new Mediterranean naval ally, Andrea Doria, to rid the North African shores of this naval pestilence. During the summer of 1530 the Christian admiral landed his troops at Cherchel with the purpose of leveling the corsair base and rescuing the numerous prisoners held there by the Turks. Although the initial stage of the Christian attack went well, the looting of the city disorganized the Christian forces and permitted the Turks to mount a successful counterattack. The next year, Alvaro de Bazán, the Spanish admiral, carried off a more effective assault on the port of Honain, to the west of Oran.[91]

The limited, almost entirely coastal nature of these Spanish counterattacks implied a Christian acceptance of an Ottoman conquest won not by the slave armies of Süleyman the Lawgiver but by eastern Mediterranean sailors. With a great deal of derring-do, these seamen, who were thrown out upon Mediterranean frontiers by the violence attending the downfall of the Byzantine empire and the rise of the Ottoman sultanate, secured a foothold upon the coast of the Maghrib. Once established, the freebooters employed their familiarity with powder technology and their access to the resources of a highly centralized Muslim empire to carry on the holy war with painful results for the Christians. Within the Maghrib, the naval vagabonds exploited their margins of military and political superiority to defeat the weak post-Almohad sultanates and to differentiate the state from a divided Maghribian society by imposing an alien ruling class.

At the beginning the Ottoman frontiersmen were motivated by personal aims that cannot have differed much from the objectives of their Iberian counterparts. It was true that in the early stages of their expansion both operated as predatory warriors. Iberians, however, soon passed beyond a capricious looting of the frontier to favor a commercial form of imperialism, except in the New World, where the Spanish also began a territorial expansion and an organized extraction of minerals. The difference between the Ottoman and Iberian modes of imperialism where they met on the North African frontier was that nowhere in the Muslim case was there evidence of an institutionalized form of state capitalism or an aggressive merchant group driving the eastern Mediterranean sailors to acquire commercial rather than territorial advantages. It was not that the Ottomans were unaware of the economic implications of the oceanic voyages. In 1517 Piri Reis had informed the sultan of the Christian commercial ventures along the rim of Africa. Yet aside from the profits of freebooting, the Ottomans did not push the objectives of their maritime expansion into the Maghrib beyond imposing an agriculturally based tax system in an area where rich lands and a submissive peasantry were not abundant.[92] More than the conquest of new territories, what drew the Ottomans into North Africa was their imperial legitimacy.

Everywhere in Muslim lands the Ottoman appeal was based upon an ability to defend Muslim territories and to advance the cause of high Islamic society. In both these areas the western community was in trouble. When eastern Mediterranean sailors began to stiffen the front line of the House of Islam, the Ottoman sultan could hardly refrain from supporting their efforts. Yet the commitment of this empire of holy warriors was far from overwhelming. No better evidence of this limited dedication to the cause of urban society in the west can be found than the history of the Hispano-Muslim exiles. Hayreddin makes this point quite clear in his memoirs when he describes how his galleys rescued the Andalusians from Granada and settled them in Algiers. There the Hispano-Muslims became loyal supporters of the Ottoman regime, some serving in the army and navy, and others making the province prosperous through agriculture.[93] Nonetheless, this connection between a militant Turko-Muslim civilization and the Maghribian community was a dynamic event of major proportions. It caused Spain to commit many lives and resources to prevent the growth of another threat to Christian Iberia from Muslim North Africa.

Five: THE CLASH OF EMPIRES

The Ottoman state is so powerful, if an order was issued to cast anchors from silver, to make rigging from silk, and to cut sails from satin, it could be carried out for the entire fleet.

The grand vizier Mehmet Sokollu

During the half-century preceding the Hispano-Ottoman truce of 1580, the widening Mediterranean conflict between Turko-Muslim and Latin Christian empires went hand-in-hand with an increase in military activity along the Ibero-African border. Yet, even as the level of combat on the Maghribian frontier rose, long-term trends were already shaping a conclusion to this era of imperial warfare. For Habsburg Spain, discontinuous boundaries and exterior challenges demanded that the crown adopt a strategy that would concentrate the state's energies on one frontier. For the more cohesive Ottoman empire, distance and a more determined opposition made spectacular victories difficult after the first siege of Vienna in 1529. As the area of military operations expanded and the early modern technologies of powder weaponry and defensive warfare spread, a rough balance of power came into being between the two empires. On all fronts this increased the cost of warfare while decreasing the yield from expansion. Toward the end of the century, rising prices generated by a heated Mediterranean economy thoroughly undermined the use of expensive armadas. By 1565 the Mediterranean system of galley warfare had reached a standoff. Costly naval victories at Lepanto (1571) and Tunis (1574), merely provided the proper ceremonial exits for empires that wished to confirm an early modern line of division between two civilizations.

The imperial phase of Ibero-African frontier history began when Charles V ordered an assault on the Ottoman port at Koron (Koróni) in the Morea during 1532. Designed to relieve the pressure Süleyman the Lawgiver's campaigns had placed on the Austrian branch of the Habsburg empire, the Morean campaign was also intended to stir the Orthodox Christians of Greece into revolt against their Ottoman overlords. But the Greek population failed to live up to the hopes of their Latin coreligionists. This flank attack of the Habsburgs, along with the resistance of the Germans did compel the Ottomans to abandon the Balkan expedition of that year. Moreover, the Spanish jab at the Greek frontier placed the Latins in a strategic position from which they could control the trade routes to the Adriatic. When a hastily assembled Ottoman armada challenged the Hapsburg force, the Christians defeated the Ottoman navy, which, according to the historian Lutfi Paşa, was under the direction of the incompetent wine-drinker Kemankeş Ahmet Paşa.[1]

Shocked into action, Süleyman the Lawgiver decided to reverse the decline that had afflicted the Ottoman navy. Sometime in 1533 a messenger left Istanbul for North Africa with an imperial order for Hayreddin Barbarossa. The corsair, who had just returned from another raid against the coast of Spain, learned that the sultan wished him to appear in Istanbul. Leaving Algiers under the command of Hadim Hasan Ağa, Hayreddin set sail for the Ottoman capital, carrying with him Rashīd, the brother of the Ḥafṣid sultan at Tunis. When he arrived in Istanbul, the sultan appointed Hayreddin commander of the Ottoman fleet that was to assemble in the spring of 1534.[2]

This tightening of the bonds between the western corsairs and the administration in Istanbul was a clear sign that the empire wished to strengthen its position in North Africa. Early in the naval season of 1534, the Ottoman admiral sailed past the Morea, where the Spanish had abandoned their foothold, and landed his troops at Bizerte on 15 August 1534. Three days later the soldiers of Hayreddin occupied Tunis, the capital of the Ḥafṣid dynasty. Mulay Ḥasan, the reigning sultan, fled the city and collected tribesmen near Qairouan, much in the manner of previous rulers. When the cavalry units of the Ḥafṣid forces finally charged the Ottoman army outside Tunis, the military superiority of firearms and disciplined foot soldiers again scattered the horsemen of the Ḥafṣids' archaic military organization.[3]

The conquest of northeastern Tunisia moved the weather vane of Mediterranean warfare sharply. Control over one side of the Sicilian channel would allow the Ottomans to sail between the eastern and western basins of the Mediterranean much more easily.

Quick action took place within Charles V's war council. Plans were made for a military campaign to deny the eastern Turko-Muslim empire access to the Sicilian channel. First the emperor wanted to learn whether the former Ḥafṣid sultan, Mulay Ḥasan, could be restored to his throne in place of Hayreddin. If it was not possible to divide the Muslim opposition between the old Maghribian ruling families and the Ottomans, then the emperor's agents were to play upon the always-ambivalent loyalties of frontiersmen to see if Hayreddin would break his ties with Istanbul. Although the negotiations with the Ottoman admiral proved unfruitful, Mulay Ḥasan's response to the Spanish proposals was favorable.[4]

Assured of some support inside Tunisia, Charles V gathered an army that left no doubt that imperial warfare had reached North Africa. A fleet of more than 400 ships embarked an army of approximately 26,000 men and 2,000 horses. To meet the Iberians, Hayreddin probably mustered somewhere near 8,000 men. It was a hopeless contest for the Ottomans. The size of the Christian army and the wavering loyalty of the Muslim population in Tunis persuaded Hayreddin to abandon the city and sail to Algiers in the summer of 1535.[5]

Whether the ensuing sack of Tunis was justified by the Muslim resistance or by the military customs of the time, it was clear Charles V did not plan on rebuilding this old and highly civilized region of North Africa as an outpost of an expanding Latin Christendom. Instead, on 8 August 1535 he signed a pact with Mulay Ḥasan that restored the Ḥafṣid ruler to his throne under terms of a tributary relationship but rigidly segregated the Christian garrison at La Goletta from the Muslim community in Africa.[6] North Africa was still a no-man's-land.

For the next six years the center of imperial conflict in the Mediterranean shifted eastward, away from the Maghrib. An enervating struggle with the French, who counted on the Ottomans as allies, placed the emperor in the strange position of having to deal with a political union of Christian and Islamic enemies. When, in the summer of 1536, information reached Charles V of an Ottoman and French plot to mount a simultaneous attack on Habsburg domains, the emperor called for the formation of a holy league against the Turk, with the hope that the French might be religiously embarrassed into deserting their Muslim ally.

Much effort was also expended upon another attempt to detach Algeria from Istanbul by playing upon the ambitions of the corsairs. In Istanbul the agents of Charles V tried to seduce Hayreddin with the gift of Tunis. On the frontier itself, Count Alcaudète, the Spanish governor at Oran, offered to reward Hadim Hasan Ağa, the man Hayreddin left in Algiers, if he would surrender the city to the Spanish. Both these tests of the cultural hold of Istanbul were won by the Ottomans.[7] Again the emperor was left with no alternative but a naval expedition if he wished to reduce the Ottoman position in North Africa.

Charles V decided upon just such a plan when he mustered a force to attack Algiers late in the spring of 1541. Given the system of Mediterranean naval warfare, the Spanish gambled that their rendezvous at the Balearic Islands on 13 October 1541 would be late enough to avoid an Ottoman counterattack and too early to run afoul of winter weather. Ten days after the fleet assembled, troops disembarked southeast of Algiers. According to Christian sources, the 65 galleys and 450 support ships of the Spanish fleet carried 12,000 sailors and some 24,000 foot soldiers. Since the number of men commanded by the defender of Algiers, Hadim Hasan Ağa, probably did not exceed 6,000, the Christian army seemed ready to end the history of this Ottoman stronghold.

Late that evening, however, the Spanish lost their gamble with the weather. Heavy rains pelted the besiegers, and a northwest wind sprang up. By morning the storm had increased to a gale, breaking the discipline of the army and offering the defenders in Algiers the opportunity to counterattack. Although the Spanish beat back the Ottoman sorties, the rain had soaked through the Christians' powder supplies, depriving them of their main weapons. But it was the condition of the fleet that pushed the Christians to retreat. Some 140 ships were dashed against the rocky coast of North Africa. Under the orders of Andrea Doria, the remainder of the Christian armada withdrew to the east to seek the protection of Cape Matifou. On 26 October Charles V ordered his wet and hungry army to fall back. In an angry council of war, Hernán Cortés, the conqueror of Mexico, and Count Alcaudète, the governor of Oran, called for a return to action against the Muslims. But cooler heads prevailed and a shattered army was evacuated.[8]

No minor affair, the retreat from the Maghribian coast cost the emperor 150 ships, 12,000 men, and an important amount of military equipment. When the news of this military and financial catastrophe spread throughout the Mediterranean, Charles V's enemies took prompt advantage of an emperor without a fleet. The French resumed the Habsburg-Valois wars in 1542-44, and on 23 April 1543 Süleyman marched out of Istanbul toward Hungary. During the same year, the sultan sent Hayreddin into the western basin of the Mediterranean, where he not only assisted the French in an attack on Nice but also had the audacity to winter his flotilla in the Christian port of Toulon.[9]

At this point Charles V made a decision that the unity of Europe was more important than success against the Ottomans. In 1545 he dispatched Gerard Veltwyck to Istanbul on a mission to forestall another Ottoman attack on the Danube regions. His ambassador was also charged with neutralizing the North African corsairs as well as preserving the position of the Ḥafṣid sultan in Tunis.[10] But on 4 July 1546 the negotiations concerning the Maghrib collapsed when Hayreddin Barbarossa died and was replaced by the future grand vizier, Mehmet Sokollu. Nonetheless, a letter from Algiers, dated 1549 and written in the chancery style employed by the Ottoman bureaucracy in Istanbul, assured the emperor that the sultan's commander on the African frontier was observing the five-year peace Süleyman had signed with Charles V on the eve of the second Persian campaign of 1548.[11] No longer an autonomous region of the Ottoman empire or a training ground for Spanish troops, the Ibero-African border at mid-century had become an imperial frontier whose life depended more and more upon decisions being made at the heart of huge Christian and Muslim empires.

In the central Maghrib, the Spanish calamity at Algiers gave the Ottomans the opportunity to reinforce their grip on the countryside. Additional prestige and captured weapons helped the Algerian garrison reduce the Berber sultan of Kūko to tax-paying subservience during the summer of 1542. To the west of Algiers, the Ottomans tightened the Muslim blockade of the Spanish outpost at Oran until the treaty of 1548 brought a temporary peace. Two years later the firepower and discipline of the Ottomans not only repelled the Saʿdian invasion but also brought the city of Tlemsen within the boundaries of the eastern sultanate.[12]

Slightly behind events in the central Maghrib, the imperial action that marked the arrival of the Ottomans in Tunisia was the fall of Tripoli (1551). In 1510 Pedro Navarro had left behind at this port a small garrison that had come under the administration of the viceroy of Sicily. As elsewhere in North Africa, Muslim notables in

Tripolitania sought to oust these Christian troops, with the aid of the Ottoman frontiersmen.[13] Hence this frontier engagement was fought by Turgut Reis, a Muslim corsair and client of Heyreddin Barbarossa. Like his mentor, Turgut Reis secured a series of bases on the eastern coast of Tunisia and engaged in raiding Christian shores and shipping with enough success to attract a large band of corsairs.[14] When he became bothersome, Andrea Doria, Charles V's naval condottiere, mounted an assault on the privateers' ports in the summer of 1551. Turgut responded by seeking the assistance of the Ottoman fleet. When he caught up with the sultan's armada, he persuaded the admiral, Sinan Paşa, to besiege the Christian fort at Tripoli, which fell to the Ottomans on 16 August.[15]

This conquest reversed the drift of frontier warfare for Tunisia.[16] Offered the city of al-Mahdiye after their African defeat, the Knights of Saint John wisely refused to station their order on the coast of the Maghrib. Soon thereafter, in 1554, the Christian troops that had been garrisoned at al-Mahdiye in 1550 were withdrawn, and the eastern coast of Tunisia passed into the hands of the Ottomans.[17]

Far from being a coastal offensive, the Ottoman conquest reached deep into the Maghribian interior. When Salih Paşa, another member of Hayreddin Barbarossa's corsair band, arrived in Algiers as governor during the spring of 1552, he turned his attention to internal matters. Soon foot soldiers armed with powder weapons marched south into the Sahara. There they easily dispersed Saharan camel nomads and imposed the taxing power of Algiers over the oases of Touggourt and Ouargla, which were important termini for the gold and slave trade from sub-Saharan regions.[18] Two years later, Salih Paşa undertook an expedition against the Saʿdians. This time the Ottomans opposed a Muslim army that had assimilated firearms but was still based upon the military contributions of tribesmen. Superior tactics won the day for the Ottomans as Salih Paşa massed his firepower against Saʿdian cavalry and employed a night attack to defeat the less-disciplined Moroccans. Thereupon the Ottomans occupied Fez for approximately half a year, retreating to Algiers only after they had enthroned an ally. Muḥammad ash-Shaykh in turn reorganized his army, reoccupied Fez, killed off his Ottoman-sponsored opposition, and sought the aid of the Spanish.[19]

Whether the Spanish would be good allies was tested in the summer of 1555 when Salih Paşa besieged the Spanish fort at Bougie. The commander of the *presidio*, however, took advantage of what appeared to be generous terms and surrendered the fort to the Turko-

Muslims.[20] Only the Spanish garrison at Oran now stood in the way of an almost total Ottoman control of the central Maghrib. For this more difficult task, Salih Paşa requested aid from Istanbul. Normally obsessed with land campaigns in the east, Süleyman this time displayed a slightly greater interest in his naval flank by sending 40 galleys and 6,000 Janissaries to Algiers. It was all for nothing, since the plague, a not-infrequent terminator of military events, took the life of Salih Paşa in the summer of 1556 and stalled the land campaign. Meanwhile, the Christian galley operations in the archipelago caused the sultan to recall his imperial squadron.[21] Slightly too far away to be easily exploited by the center, the North African frontier looked a bit more attractive as Habsburg difficulties mounted on the eve of the empire's bankruptcy in 1557.

If the plague and Andrea Doria's raids in the eastern Mediterranean relieved the pressure on the Spanish border in North Africa during 1556, a political challenge to Istanbul's control of its western frontier slowed the Ottoman advance even more in 1557: Upon the death of Salih Paşa, the Janissary corps in Algiers rebelled against the sultan's new governor. Mehmet Paşa, however, found allies among the province's corsairs and was able to restore the authority of the central government. The underlying issue was the foot soldiers' desire to share in one of the two major sources of income on the frontier: the corsair ventures. Naval men resisted this encroachment by the landsmen, arguing that the soldiers' salary, taken from the agricultural and herding economies, was sufficient. But the limited internal resources of the province, the prestige of the Janissary corps, and the lucrative privateering operations of the less formally organized corsairs stimulated a factional conflict between Ottoman frontiersmen that ran through the entire sixteenth-century history of the province.[22]

In the spring of 1557 the Janissaries killed Mehmet Paşa and threw the entire province into political disorder. Since the central Maghrib had been conquered by Hayreddin Barbarossa, the sultan calculated that, as the new governor, the son of the famous sailor would be able to play upon the frontiersmen's respect for the corsair's family to discipline the provincial garrison. Hasan Paşa, moreover, had the additional advantage of being related by birth to the sultan of Kūko, the ruler of the Berber highlands to the east of Algiers. When he entered Algiers in June 1557 both elements of the provincial military elite accepted him as governor.[23] It was none too soon; for Muḥammad ash-Shaykh had sent an army to take Tlemsen, and the Spanish at Oran had begun to collect men and war materials. Anticipating these challenges, the central administration had backed up this new governor by sending a unit from the imperial fleet to Bizerte in the summer of 1557.[24]

By fall of 1558 the Ottomans not only had demolished the Spanish frontier system in North Africa but also had threatened the Mediterranean coastline of Iberia. The assassination of Muḥammad ash-Shaykh in October of 1557 had diffused Moroccan politics, opening up the possibility that the Ottomans might reach the Strait of Gibraltar. During the summer of the next year Hasan Paşa dealt the Spanish a heavy blow when he all but wiped out 6,000 to 12,000 Christian troops at Mosteganum, a coastal town east of Oran.[25] The news of this serious defeat reached Castile at the same time as imperial officials learned that Piyale Paşa, the Ottoman naval commander, had raided the island of Minorca, sacking the city of Cuidadela with a fleet of 150 galleys.[26] These military events rarely brought together in later studies offer some proof of how dangerous the war with Islam had become.

What Philip II would do to stem the alarming Ottoman advance along the Maghribian border depended upon how the new Habsburg monarch would allocate the already overstrained resources of his empire among the various imperial frontiers. At Cateau-Cambrésis on 3 April 1559, the peace treaty with the French temporarily lifted the most pressing of the European problems. In September 1559, Philip II reached Spain. A month later, on 8 October, the Christian monarch announced his official presence with a spectacular auto de fé in front of the Church of San Francisco in Valladolid. It appeared that this symbolic restatement of Spain's duty to defend the faith in its Latin Christian form would precede an ambitious effort to contain a resurgent Islam.

Symbol and reality were never further apart. Philip II began his reign at a time when the crown's credit was at its nadir and when the cost of maintaining galleys was increasing steeply. Moreover, Mediterranean combat no longer featured the jab and parry of border warfare, but involved a frontal clash with a Muslim empire that was technologically equal in terms of the Mediterranean galley system. To face this Turko-Muslim aggressor whose imperial appeal unified Sunni Muslims, Philip II commanded widely scattered European territories wherein the imperial ideal had failed. On top of those considerations, the mounting value of the frontier in the New World added another imperial complication. Between 1516 and 1555 the evolution of a complex Atlantic communications system tripled the volume of exchanges between Seville and the New World. In this same period the flow of precious metals into a financially troubled Spain not only quintupled but also showed every sign of increasing still further. Thus, the impact of America's contribution to the empire's resources at that time must have been great.[27] Whatever the weight of the New World's importance, it helped set the stage for an argument that would profoundly reduce the value of Spain's Mediterranean frontier.

While the unacceptable costs of maintaining an imperial dream caused the Spanish to reassess their military priorities, the resistance to centralization slowed Ottoman imperialism. In May 1559 warfare broke out in Anatolia between the followers of Süleyman's sons Bayezit and Selim. Far more serious than an opening move in a succession struggle, the battle at Konya on 30 May 1559 exposed again the dangerous social antagonisms between the groups who supported a centralized empire based on merit and those who advocated a decentralized government that would give a greater voice to the kinship units of rural areas and to older elements of Ottoman society.[28]

While the Ottoman leaders were preoccupied with Anatolian affairs, Philip II's admiral, Gian Andrea Doria, again tried to isolate North Africa from the center of the Ottoman empire by removing Turko-Muslim bases in Tunisia. His subsequent defeat at the island of Gerba in May 1560 underlined three themes in the history of Mediterranean naval warfare at mid-century. First, imperial conflict now involved two large flotillas, each of which, as Guilmartin has shown, tended to use larger and more expensive galleys. Second, the Christians continued to believe that the distance between the main Ottoman staging area and the North African frontier would limit the effectiveness of the Turko-Muslim navy.[29] Third, Philip II either did not possess sufficient reserves to mount a counterattack, or he did not wish to commit his forces to combat with the Ottomans unless he had a clear superiority of men and ships.[30]

The return of the victorious fleet to Istanbul on 27 September 1560 became a spectacular demonstration of the Ottoman commitment to the holy war. Witnessed by the Holy Roman Emperor's ambassador, Busbecq, Turkish galleys towed one captured vessel after another past the sultan's reviewing stand while columns of Christian prisoners were paraded through the streets of the Ottoman capital.[31] In North Africa the Muslim victory strengthened the tie between Turgut Paşa and Istanbul, encouraging him to petition the sultan to send the imperial fleet westward for the conquest of La Goletta.[32] On the fringe of Ottoman power, the news of the Christian defeat

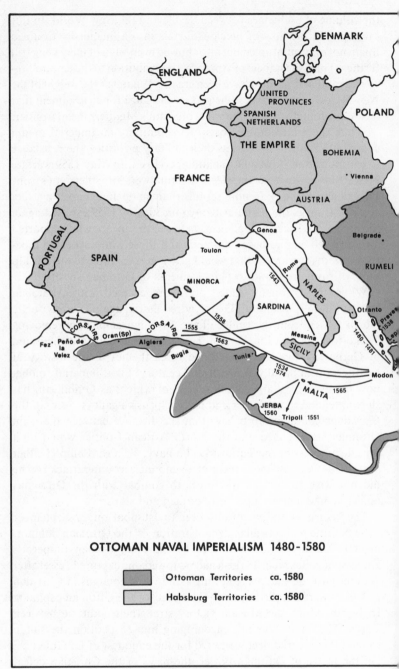

Fig. 2. Ottoman naval imperialism, 1480–1580

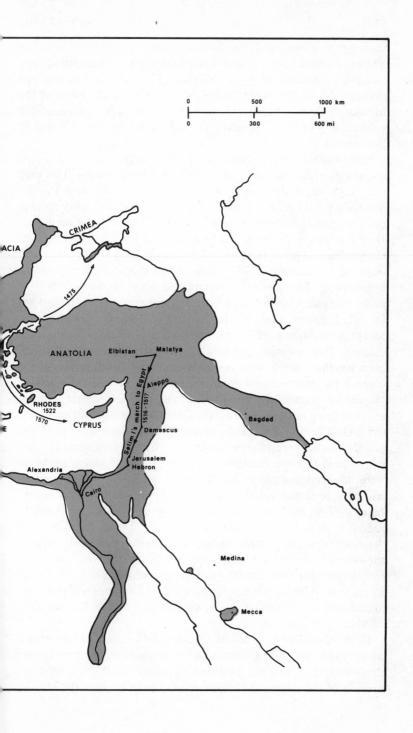

thoroughly discouraged the Saᶜdians, causing them to abandon whatever designs they and the Spanish garrison at Oran might have had upon the shape of the rough internal border that had emerged between the central Maghrib and Morocco along the basin of the Moulouya River.[33] Finally, the loss of so many galleys increased the vulnerability of Christian shipping and shores to the little war of the corsairs.

Paradoxically, the victory at Gerba encouraged centrifugal tendencies within the ranks of the Ottoman frontiersmen. This time the danger came not from local families or the tribesmen. Powder technology, Ottoman military organization, and an ability to play upon the divisions between the tribes kept the old opposition in line. Here the tendency toward localism emerged from within the Ottoman military organization, from the Janissary corps. The governor's response was to arm with firearms the Berbers to whom he was related by marriage. Janissaries, in turn, played upon the sultan's fear of peripheral independence movements to force the recall of Hasan Paşa in 1562. However, when his replacement died a year later Süleyman reappointed Barbarossa's son for a third term as governor.[34]

Hasan Paşa promptly adopted an old policy for solving disputes over whether march warriors or the central bureaucracy would control the frontier. Allowing no time for division, the son of Hayreddin opened his final years as the ruler of Algeria with an effort to conquer Oran. Because the Christian garrison was small and the fleet of Philip II had hardly recovered from the disaster at Gerba and the loss of twenty-five galleys in a storm at La Herradura in 1562, it appeared that the battle would be short. But Spanish engineers were now constructing in North Africa the new fortifications that had been perfected in Italy. This more sophisticated defense system based on low, thick walls and bastions, made it nearly impossible to reduce Spanish forts by battery and assault. Thus a small band of defenders was able to hold out under an intense bombardment that the Ottomans mounted in the spring of 1563. A relief force of thirty-four galleys then took the Ottoman naval squadron blockading Oran by surprise. Without supplies for his cannons and troops, Hasan Paşa abandoned the attack on Oran in what became a prelude to the siege of Malta two years later.[35]

Philip II decided to follow the victory at Oran not with an attack upon Algiers but with a limited naval campaign designed to bolster Spain's control over the Strait of Gibraltar. In August 1564, an armada of 150 ships and 16,000 men set out to conquer the Muslim

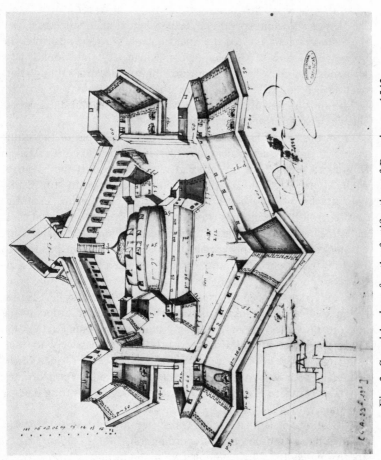

Fig. 3. Spanish plans for the fortification of Bougie, ca. 1543

corsair base at Peñón de Velez near the old port of Badis, on the coast of the Rif just opposite Malaga. When the defenders of Velez, probably no more than 200 men, saw the size of the Christian flotilla they fled, and Spain took possession of a rocky islet. During the next year, the Spanish secured their hold on the Strait of Gibraltar when they blocked the mouth of the river—the Wadi Martin—that the Hispano-Muslim corsairs at Tetuan had used. At the same time the Saʿdian sultan assisted the Spanish cause when he absorbed the holy war emirate of Chechaouen, a Rifian city state founded by Hispano-Muslim exiles.[36] Humdrum military operations though they may have been, these border skirmishes had everything to do with Seville and the Atlantic trade and were the first manifestations of a change in Spain's Mediterranean politics.

From the end of October 1564 well into December of that same year, Süleyman issued orders to his governors on the North African frontier to prepare for an imperial campaign against the island of Malta. Formal reasons for the expedition were two: to stop Christian attacks on the shores and commerce of Muslim territories and to protect the pilgrims traveling to and from the holy cities of Palestine and Arabia.[37] One strategic goal left unstated in the court chronicles was the improvement of the Turko-Muslim position in North Africa, where Ottoman ambitions extended as far west as Morocco.[38]

By the spring of 1565 all arrangements had been made. The Ḥafṣid sultan assured Süleyman of his friendship.[39] Repeated orders to the corsairs in Algiers to stop taking French ships implied that the Ottomans expected the French court to react passively to their campaign.[40] Already the viceroy of Sicily had been informed of the Ottoman objective by the ubiquitous Habsburg spies. Yet his frantic efforts to convince Philip II of the need to prepare a strong defense were met with silence.

The Ottoman siege of Malta, which began on 19 May 1565, was plagued by an unusual lack of coordination. Even though a fleet of approximately 180 ships assembled without difficulty to carry between 30,000 and 36,000 soldiers to the island, the Ottomans were unable to bring the North African corsairs into the fray until midsummer. On Malta itself the battle began with the decision to force the strong defenses of Saint Elmo. Unfortunately for the Ottomans, the reduction of the Christian fort took thirty-one days, and this stout resistance gave the viceroy of Sicily time to collect a relief force. Estimating that the Turks were ready to retreat when the island had not fallen to them by mid-August, Philip II gave his consent on the twentieth of that month for the fleet to move the reserves from Messina to Malta. On 7 September, the Spanish put 9,600 men on Malta without much opposition. Discouraged by heavy casualties, the lack of supplies, the death of the corsair captain Turgut Reis, and the impenetrable Christian defenses, Mustafa Paşa evacuated what remained of his army on 12 September 1565.

Spanish sailors were right. Ultimately the logistic requirements of mid-sixteenth-century galley warfare restricted the range of Ottoman naval warefare. True, the inability of the Ottomans to close off Malta from the outside and the lack of a coordinated plan for the conquest of the island were important reasons for their setback.[41] Yet the improvement of fortifications, the increased size of fleets and armies, and the greater availability of cannons made military operations during the second half of the century more time-consuming and expensive. During the naval season from mid-April to the beginning of October, admirals had to assemble their men, ships, and supplies, reach their objective, accomplish their mission, and then return to their home bases before winter storms destroyed the fragile war galleys. Valiant defenses of vast star-shaped fortifications, which became more resistant to cannon fire during the mid-sixteenth century, left less and less time for decisive action.[42]

Yet the decline in the effectiveness of offensive weapons cannot fully explain why both empires displayed such a lack of determination at Malta. For the Ottomans, the failing health of Süleyman, soon to die in 1566 on his thirteenth campaign, contributed in some way to their indecisiveness. But no such explanation can account for the lukewarm response of the Spanish. Here the reason for Philip II's calculated hesitation lay not in his character but in the outcome of a climatic struggle at the Habsburg court that pitted political factions against each other over the formulation of Spanish policy toward the Low Countries. Reduced to its essentials, the competition between the parties led by the Duke of Alba and the Prince of Eboli involved a decision on whether the European or the Mediterranean frontier should have first call upon the resources of the state. In 1565, the year of the Malta campaign, the Alba faction, which favored both a rigid position against the claims of the Netherlands nobility and a reduction of imperial activity in the Mediterranean, won the battle to direct the foreign policy of Spain.[43] This conjunction of the Spanish decision to begin the long and debilitating war in the Low Countries with the Ottoman realization that naval warfare in the center of the Mediterranean would be difficult prepared the political ground for a Hispano-Ottoman disengagement.

Other events intervened to weaken whatever ability great state leaders had to control events. Early in the 1560s both empires shared a common experience when a wave of internal revolts swept over Europe and the Mediterranean world. This turmoil resulted in part from the spread of imperial authority into regions that had previously maintained some independence, from the imposition in those same areas of new social and religious requirements, and from the political conflicts stimulated by a new phase of economic change.

As though the times produce the men, the election of a militant pope, Pius V, and a warrior sultan, Selim II, intensified the stormy politics of the third quarter of the century. Committed to the preservation of Latin Christendom's unity and the authority of the papacy, Pius V injected new energy into the struggle against both Islam and Protestantism. On the other side of the Mediterranean's cultural division, Selim II (1566–74) inherited from his illustrious father not only a huge empire but also a strong challenge to the authority of the sultan.

Like the governor in Algiers, Selim II found that the threat to the political primacy of the sultanate came not from rural segments of society but from once-loyal elements of the Ottoman ruling class. From the conquest of Istanbul to the death of Süleyman, the extraordinary growth of the empire had increased the number and power of men who were concerned with the operation of the central government. By 1566, for reasons that are not clear, this element of the Ottoman elite had divided into factions more absorbed with preserving their place in imperial society than with unswerving devotion to the sultan's interests. The ascendant faction, led by the grand vizier Mehmet Sokollu, wished to confirm its hold over the government of the empire upon the accession of Selim II in 1566. When the new sultan rejected the Janissary corps' request for an increase in pay, which the grand vizier favored, the most disciplined corps in the Ottoman army rebelled and forced the sultan to pay them out of his own treasury. A second rebellion over wages in 1566 made it very clear that there had been no resolution of an internal political conflict that set the elite military corps and a segment of the bureaucracy against the sultanate.[44] Selim had to occupy his army with some project that would turn the energies of the Janissaries away from raids upon the sultan's purse. The solution was the traditional one—the holy war. But where should the battle be fought?

Between the winter of 1566 and the spring of 1570 the Ottomans hesitated over the location of their next major campaign. Far from Istanbul, Ottoman soldiers secured Yemen, for a while.[45] In that same year, Hızır Bey left the Red Sea with a squadron of twenty-two vessels loaded with firearms and cannon casters, all for the Muslim ruler of the Malacca straits.[46] During the fall of 1569 an Ottoman expedition to Central Asia tried unsuccessfully to secure the routes between the city of Astrakan and the Ottoman empire.[47] These modest efforts, compared with the expeditions of Süleyman, reflected a policy conflict over whether to exploit the Asian or the Mediterranean frontier. Sometime late in 1569 Selim II brought the indecision to an end when he overrode the objections of his grand vizier, Mehmet Sokollu, and redirected Ottoman imperialism along eastern Mediterranean trade routes. On 15 May 1570, an Ottoman fleet set sail for the island of Cyprus.

A romantic interpretation of Ottoman history holds that the quality of Cypriot wines inspired Selim II to invade this island. A more realistic viewpoint is that it was a conservative decision aimed at promoting Ottoman control over the trade routes and shores of the eastern Mediterranean.[48] The invasion of the island also acted as a catalyst for a much larger Mediterranean war, because it coincided with political movements in the western basin of the Mediterranean, which drew the Spanish into this conflict against their will.

First among these events was the continued effort of the Ottomans to undermine the independence of the Moroccan sultanate. When the Saʿdian ruler ʿAbdallāh al-Ghālib (1557–76) came to the throne after his father's assassination, two of his brothers took refuge in Algeria. Süleyman directed his governor in Algiers to support these exiles. In November 1568 Selim II decided to play upon the divisions within the Saʿdian family. Commanded by the sultan to find which of the brothers had the most support in Morocco, the governor of Algiers nominated ʿAbd al-Malik and sent him to Istanbul.[49] At the same time the Ottoman administration granted the two Saʿdians lands from the treasury of Algiers worth 1,000 gold pieces a month in taxes.[50] Selim II then wrote a letter to the emir of Fez, Seyyid ʿAbdallāh, calling upon him to remove discord among Muslims by restoring to ʿAbd al-Malik a rightful share of the lands in Morocco.[51] In the rank-conscious world of Near Eastern politics, the titles employed in this letter announced, as much as the contents of the documents, a forthcoming conflict between the Ottoman and the

Sa'dian sultanates. Against this giant empire from the east, 'Abdallāh could do nothing but search for aid from the Spanish.[52]

In June 1568 Selim II appointed a naval captain, Uluç Ali Paşa, to govern the province of Algeria. A particularly sharp thorn in the side of Christendom, the Calabrian renegade had earned his reputation under Hayreddin Barbarossa. What counted here was that this man's presence in Algiers foreshadowed no diminution of border warfare.

Even before Uluç Ali Paşa entered Algiers, Philip II had set in motion a policy that would stir the population of the Ibero-African frontier into action. On 1 January 1567, an edict devised to blot out the last traces of Islam in southern Spain was published by Philip II's officials. Although some of the restrictions placed upon the Moriscos—Hispano-Muslims who had officially been converted to Christianity—were not enforced immediately, a strong attempt was made to forbid many of the Islamic customs still practiced in Granada.[53] This effort to compel the Moriscos to assimilate came at a time when economic conditions associated with the silk trade also disturbed the communities of southeastern Spain.[54] Pushed into revolt, the leaders of the Moriscos sought the assistance of the Ottomans.[55]

While their agents petitioned for aid from North Africa, the Hispano-Muslims of Granada made the decision to strike during the year 1568. A planned initial uprising on Holy Thursday—15 April—failed to take place. The Muslims then moved the date of their revolt to Christmas of that same year. Rising in Granada, the Moriscos spread their movement throughout the countryside, killing their enemies and desecrating churches with a ferocity born of the mutual intolerance of two civilizations. As the new year began, Philip II faced a dangerous situation that drove him to weaken his garrisons in Italy in order to put down a revolt in Spain while at the same time his northern frontier was showing signs of unrest.

The European slant of Spain's early modern history is largely responsible for the local framework in which the second rebellion of the Alpujarras (1568–70) is analyzed. Philip II believed that the Granadan violence was part of a much larger attack upon church and state. Although neither Selim II nor his Maghribian frontiersmen caused the Hispano-Muslim revolt, they certainly confirmed Philip II's belief in their effort to exploit Spain's internal problems on a scale that exceeded the geographic boundaries of the Mediterranean world. In the spring of 1570 Selim II responded to a Morisco appeal for assistance by approving the dispatch of men and arms from Algiers. This same correspondence noted with approval that the

Morisco rebellion had taken place at the time when a "Lutheran sect"—the Ottoman terminology for Protestants in general—had collected an army and defeated the Spanish.[56]

Although Selim expended his empire's military energies on the eastern Mediterranean objective, Cyprus, his frontiersmen in North Africa did not hesitate to inflame the Granadan revolt. In Algiers, Uluç Ali Paşa openly displayed his interest in the rebellion, collecting arms and ammunition for the rebels in a mosque within the city. He also permitted the Moriscos to recruit Ottoman infantry for service in Spain.[57] Sometime during the first two months of 1570 a company of these soldiers—perhaps 200 men—landed on the southeastern coast of Spain north of Almería. To keep such assistance flowing, the leader of the Moriscos, Aben Humeya, sent his brother to Algiers early in the course of the revolt to press the Turks for more soldiers and arms and to announce the willingness of the Spanish Muslims to accept the rule of the Ottoman sultan. By fall of 1569 the pleas of the Morisco ambassador produced a reaction from the Ottomans, but again only a small force of some 400 arquebusiers under Hüseyn Ağa reached Spain. In Granada the Turks demonstrated their usefulness; but the war went against the Hispano-Muslims. When Galera fell in 1570, the defeat of the Moriscos seemed only a matter of time, and the flow of soldiers and arms from North Africa dried up.[58]

Nowhere in the correspondence between the sultan and Uluç Ali Paşa or the Moriscos did the Ottoman ruler bring up the subject of Tunis. Yet the existence of the Ḥafṣid sultanate as a vassal of the Spanish continued to grow in importance for the Ottomans as they organized and fortified more of North African society. Situated between the provinces of Tripolitania and Algeria, the small patch of territory controlled by the Ḥafṣids not only divided Algeria from its imperial capital, Istanbul, but also reminded North African elites of a local alternative to Ottoman rule.

Uluç Ali Paşa thought carefully about the future of Tunis and the Ḥafṣid family. Observing closely the course of the Morisco revolt during 1569, the Ottoman governor waited until the Spanish had reinforced Don Juan with soldiers drawn from Italy and the naval season had passed. Late in 1569 one of Uluç Ali Paşa's servants, Mami Korso, led an army of Ottoman foot soldiers and tribesmen eastward toward Tunis. At Beja, west of Tunis, the Turko-Muslim army met the Ḥafṣid sultan in a battle that the Ottomans won without great losses.[59] Tunis was the prize; and all that remained before the Ottomans could claim control over North Africa from

Tripoli to Tlemsen was the reduction of the Spanish fort at La Goletta.

Viziers may have applauded the initiative of Uluç Ali Paşa, but the capture of Cyprus remained far more important for the empire than the reduction of La Goletta. By 1570 the cohesive growth of the state from an interior hub had given the empire an eastern Mediterranean size and an agricultural, as opposed to maritime, orientation. Of all the conquests associated with Ottoman growth, clearly the most outstanding from the financial point of view was Egypt: the annual remittance from this province after 1525 started at 400,000 ducats and went up dramatically. Its importance for the Ottomans explains why Cyprus, which overlooked eastern Mediterranean trade routes, was conquered and why Spanish officials regarded the ships carrying the tax yield of Egypt to Istanbul as similar to their own silver-laden convoys from the New World. But the most compelling reason for this cautious naval operation rather than a more daring adventure in the western basin of the Mediterranean was that the fiscal health of the state rested overwhelmingly upon taxes extracted from an agricultural heartland whose major axis ran from the Hungarian plain to the mouth of the Red Sea and the Persian Gulf.[60]

This Ottoman consolidation of an eastern Mediterranean empire that was political as well as economic coincided roughly with the rebellion and defeat of the Moriscos in Spain (1568–70), the capture of Tunis (1569), the elevation of a crusading pope, Pius V (1566), and the temporary pacification of the Protestant rebellion in the Low Countries (1567). Encouraged by the defeat of the Morisco and Dutch uprisings, Spain, Venice, and the pope overcame their differences to confront the Ottomans with a new holy league and a new fleet.

In the famous galley battle fought at Lepanto during the fall of 1571, the Christians decisively defeated the Ottomans. Ironically, however, the results of military operations between 1569 and 1571 improved the strategic position of the Muslim empire. Ottoman soldiers cleared the southeastern Mediterranean of the Christian stronghold at Cyprus, consolidating their control over the sea routes that joined the wealthiest of the Arab lands—Egypt—to Istanbul. Equally, the frontiersmen of the Ottomans tightened the grip of the empire in North Africa with the capture of Tunis. On the negative side, two-thirds of the imperial fleet was destroyed, a major blow to the power of a Muslim ruler whose reputation rested on his success in the holy war.

Ottoman sources give no indication that this defeat constituted a turning point in imperial self-confidence; rather, in the sultan's correspondence with other Muslims about the impact of Lepanto on the empire, Selim II displayed a sober resolve to continue in the face of adversity. Citing the Koran (Sūra 2:216), "But it may happen that ye hate a thing which is good for ye," the Ottoman leader promised to revenge the defeat at Lepanto with the conquest of Christian forts in the west.[61]

In order to fulfill his pledge, Selim II set about rebuilding the shattered Ottoman navy. With extraordinary speed, the Ottoman administration, under the able leadership of the grand vizier Mehmet Sokollu, ordered the construction of more than two hundred vessels. The rapidity with which the Ottomans actually accomplished the building program set by their imperial leaders can indeed be taken as a demonstration of internal strength. Much less believable was Mehmet Sokollu's famous hyperbole that building and maintaining a fleet of 200 galleys would not strain the financial capabilities of the state.[62] As the grand vizier Sinan Paşa pointed out in the early years of Murad III's reign, just maintaining a galley in operation cost 5,000 gold pieces a year, to say nothing of the expenses of repair. If Inalcık's estimate of 6,000 gold pieces per year for each galley is more accurate, employing a 200-vessel fleet would demand 1,200,000 gold pieces a year from the treasury. This very rough figure amounted to more than one-quarter of the revenues the central administration received in the 1581–82 budget. At a time when the salaries of the military corps were taking a greater share of imperial wealth, reconstructing the 1571 armada and operating it for the next three years must have placed great pressure on Ottoman finances.[63]

One additional indication of the mounting burden of naval warfare emerges from the vast administrative effort the empire expended in finding oarsmen to man its galleys. During the early part of the century there had been extensive recruitment of paid rowers from peasant and urban sectors of the empire, but the brutal physical labor and dangerous conditions had wilted most men's enthusiasm for the sultan's wages. More and more the state turned to undesirable and unwilling elements within its population for rowers, drafting prisoners, criminals, and gypsies for service in the imperial galleys.[64] The results of such a decision could hardly have been satisfactory; for the effective use of a galley depended greatly upon the trained responses of more than a hundred groaning oarsmen.

Similarly, the prospect of military service under conditions where

horses could not be used and where land was not to be taken discouraged the Sipahis (the cavalrymen) from participating in naval
expeditions. Failure to appear at the docks for the imperial expedition then became a more common reason for depriving Sipahis of
their income.[65] The threat of punishment was not effective; and, as
in the case of the rowers, the state was compelled to call upon the
services of less well trained warriors.

If the reconstitution of the fleet met with difficulties over who
would row and who would fight, such was not the case with the
restaffing of the naval command. Here the sultan turned to his
western Mediterranean frontier for the seamen to man the imperial
fleet. Fortunately for the Ottomans, the naval losses at Lepanto in
1571 did not include the galley units from North Africa. Under the
command of Uluç Ali Paşa, the Maghribian sailors not only escaped
destruction in the sea battle but also performed well in that combat.
This untarnished command of the North African galleys earned
Kılıç Ali Paşa (his name was changed from Uluç to Kılıç) the post of
admiral on 29 October 1571. The new commander promptly issued
orders transferring sailors and ships from North Africa to Istanbul,
where they formed the nucleus for a new armada.[66]

Between the battle of Lepanto and the end of the year 1573, the
Christian coalition dissolved and the Ottoman fleet under new
leadership recovered its strength. During 1572, the members of the
Holy League disagreed over whether North Africa or the Levant
ought to be the site of the next action against the Ottomans. Unable
to agree on a common course of action, the Christian allies gave the
Muslims additional time to prepare their fleet. Then the pope died.
Meanwhile, the merchants of Venice watched the costs of their
struggle with the Ottomans mount. Corsairs flooded the sea lanes in
the Adriatic and the archipelago, and Muslim raiders pushed into
Dalmatia. Concurrently, the Ottoman client state and commercial
competitor of Venice—Ragusa—expanded her trade at the expense
of the republic. When they concluded that neither the support of
Spain nor their own efforts could reverse the course of events in the
Levant, the Venetians signed a peace treaty with the Ottomans on
7 March 1573. This agreement conceded the island of Cyprus to the
Ottomans and settled upon an annual indemnity of 100,000 ducats
as a payment to the sultan for the error of challenging the Turko-
Muslim empire.

When the Venetians acted to preserve their commercial position
in the Levant, the Spanish became free to move against the Ottomans

in the sphere of special interest for them: North Africa. In October 1573, Don Juan left Sicily with an armada of more than 100 galleys and some 20,000 troops, bound for Tunis. Duly warned by the sultan's agents of this new onslaught, the Ottoman garrison withdrew from the city in the face of the overwhelming military superiority of the Spanish army. Don Juan, following established policy, attempted to resurrect the Ḥafṣid dynasty and to fortify the harbor of Tunis. Immediately an argument began between Philip II and his general over the degree of protection to be provided for the North African outpost. Feeling the financial stresses of conducting military operations in the Mediterranean and the Low Countries at the same time, Philip wished to minimize the costs for the forts in North Africa, already above 200,000 ducats in wages alone during 1566.[67] Don Juan, representing the Mediterranean factions within the Habsburg government, called for the emplacement of a large garrison. Hardly in a position to countermand the hero of Lepanto, Philip II let his general build a new fortress at La Goletta and garrison it with 8,000 men.

For the Ottomans this same period saw a burst of activity at many levels. Dispatching messengers to North Africa, the sultan called upon the corsairs to attack Spanish shipping wherever it was encountered. At the same time, Ottoman envoys summoned the Muslim community of North Africa to arm themselves for the holy war against the Christians. Sometime late in the same year, after hearing the news of the Habsburg invasion of Tunis in 1573, the viziers made the decision to recapture the direction of political affairs in the Mediterranean with an attack on Tunis.

Everywhere the Ottomans cultivated the enemies of Spain. Under no circumstances were the French to be bothered. To placate the Christian ally, Ahmet Paşa, the governor of Algeria, sent some compensation to the Christian king for shipping losses and gave the French the right to fish for coral off the coast of the central Maghrib.[68] Again the Ottomans in Algeria were ordered to ease the flight of Andalusians from Spain.[69] Awakening the guard for both internal and external duty occurred none too soon; for in June 1573 the sultan received intelligence through the French that the Spanish intended to attack the Maghrib in the summer of that year with the aid of North African tribesmen.[70] On cue, the Banū ʿAbbās of the Lesser Kabylia revolted during August 1573; but a Christian army did not materialize.

Also sensitive to Mediterranean events, the Ottoman-Saʿdian

border conflict reflected the same reversal of fortunes as did the
frontier in Tunisia. Before Lepanto—June 1571—the sultan felt
confident enough to order the Ottoman admiral to bring down the
rule of the Moroccan emir, ʿAbdallāh al-<u>Gh</u>ālib.[71] Lepanto destroyed
that ambition. During February 1572 the viziers received the news
that agents of the Moroccan ruler had assassinated ʿAbd al-Muʾmin,
one of the Ottoman candidates for the Saʿdian throne.[72] In the same
period, the brother of the dead man, ʿAbd al-Malik, arrived in
Istanbul to claim his brother's salary and to demand assistance from
the Ottomans in establishing his right to rule in Morocco. If it would
be suitable, ordered the sultan, ʿAbd al-Malik should have his rights
in Morocco restored to him. Otherwise, he was to receive the revenues
that had previously gone to his brother.[73] On the eve of the Spanish
reconquest of Tunis, in June 1573, rumors flew of a Moroccan plan
to advance on Tlemsen. In September 1573 the sultan wrote a
conciliatory letter to the emir of Fez, the Saʿdian sultan, calling upon
him to stand with all Muslims against the infidel.[74]

However Ottoman activities between 1571 and 1574 might appear
in western histories, the Turks were determined to recover their
imperial prestige. Ottoman leaders, like their Habsburg counterparts,
knew the dangers attached to distant naval campaigns. To direct the
movement of a large galley fleet so soon after the loss at Lepanto
over a great distance into an area close to the land strongholds of the
Habsburg empire was one of the century's great gambles. No one
commanded the sea spaces, and, as one maritime disaster after
another proved, heavily loaded galleys floundered easily in sudden
Mediterranean storms.

Not only did the sultan risk vast quantities of men, arms, and
money for the conquest of Tunis, he also mobilized international
politics to assist western expansion. Informed of European affairs
through intelligence from the frontier and through the commercial
connections of the Marrano community in Istanbul, whose leader,
Don Joseph Nassi, advised Selim II, the sultan dispatched imperial
orders designed to create an anti-Spanish coalition between Protestant rebels in the Low Countries and the remnants of the Morisco
community in Spain. How much the attempt of the Ottoman agents
affected the defensive plans of the Spanish during the summer of
1574 is not yet known. But Philip II, whose frontier problems were
extraordinarily complicated, appreciated the grave danger such a
wide alliance between Mediterranean and European opponents
could hold for his state.[75]

In March 1574 the sultan promised the Ottoman governor of Tunisia that a fleet of 300 ships would attack the Spanish forts at Tunis.[76] On 13 July the Ottoman armada appeared before Tunis with a force of between 250 and 300 ships, carrying as many as 70,000 troops. These men, under the command of Sinan Paşa, joined the contingents of Ottoman troops led overland by the governors of Algeria, Tripoli, and Tunis. Backed by an armada larger than that used by either side at the battle of Lepanto, the Ottoman general directed a siege force perhaps as large as 100,000 men. On 24 August Sinan Paşa took the Christian position at La Goletta. The remaining Christian soldiers in the new fortress in front of Tunis surrendered on 13 September. Because Tunis was too far from the imperial center, the Ottoman commander partially destroyed the Spanish fortifications before returning to Istanbul in November, well after the close of the naval season.[77] Although the Ottomans had won their gamble with the weather, they were operating beyond the limits of Mediterranean galley warfare.

For the imperial position of the Ottomans in the Islamic world, the victory at Tunis had the desired consequences. A new sultan, Murad III, girded on the sword of the Ottomans with the knowedge that the empire had regained whatever prestige it had lost at Lepanto. In addition, the Turko-Muslim administration now organized all of North Africa except the far western regions. For the viziers, however, the luster of the North African achievement was dulled by the huge costs of what was probably the most expensive Ottoman campaign during the sixteenth century.

If the victory at Tunis alerted the Ottomans that they had exceeded their ability to expand in North Africa, the Spanish defeat told Philip II that he could not afford warfare on two frontiers. Between 1571 and 1576 the repression of the Dutch revolt demanded 10 million escudos from Castile's treasury. In the same period the cost of maintaining a Mediterranean navy absorbed 8.6 million escudos. Spending wildly, at times during this five-year period Philip II had exceeded his revenues by as much as 200 percent. Something had to give. On 1 September 1575, Philip II broke with his creditors, and money for an expensive Mediterranean navy became scarce.[78]

Only one frontier conflict blocked a clear drift toward the disengagement of the two empires. Morocco lay within neither the Ottoman or the Hispanic sphere of influence. Conveniently, ʿAbdallāh, the Saʿdian sultan, died during the year of Sinan Paşa's victory at Tunis (1574) and was succeeded by his son Muḥammad.

In the meantime, ʿAbd al-Malik, the Ottoman candidate for the Moroccan sultanate, renewed his appeal for aid, this time strengthening his cause through service at the siege of La Goletta. Sometime in 1575, Murad III gave his Algerian governor, Ramazan Paşa, an order to invade Morocco and establish ʿAbd al-Malik as the ruler of the western Maghrib.[79] Early in 1576, at Ar-Rukn near Fez, the Ottoman army, supplemented by a contingent of 2,000 troops under ʿAbd al-Malik, met the Saʿdian forces. Again the political combination between Hispano-Muslim exiles and the Ottomans proved effective as the Andalusian contingent deserted the Saʿdian army before the battle began.[80] ʿAbd al-Malik occupied the city of Fez in 1576 and assumed rule over Morocco as a client of the Ottomans.[81]

When he learned of the successful outcome of the Moroccan expedition, Murad III expressed pleasure that the subjects of the far west had accepted ʿAbd al-Malik, but he was distressed to learn of the defeated sultan's escape.[82] Like others before him, Muḥammad, the former ruler of Morocco, fled to the Christian side of the Ibero-African border. In Portugal he met with an interested reception from the Portuguese monarch, Don Sebastian, whose education, temperament, and political support were more appropriate for the age of the Portuguese reconquest than the era of the seaborne empires.[83] Within a short time thereafter, Murad III learned that the Portuguese might use the Saʿdian candidate to restore some of the ground they had lost in Morocco since the fall of Agadir in 1541. Murad III reassured ʿAbd al-Malik that the Ottomans would support him if an attack came.[84] At the same time, however, the Moroccan sultan, sensing that he ruled a buffer state, moved to establish peaceful relations with Spain so as to be able to balance the Habsburg and Ottoman empires.[85] But the major new political element in the give and take of the frontier struggle was the arrival in Istanbul during the spring of 1577 of Martin Diego de Acuña, an ambassador from Spain who was sent to arrange the terms of a peace with the Grand Turk.[86]

When the Ottomans reached Morocco, the Portuguese had another reason to strike back at the state that had become their main Muslim opponent in the East. There in Morocco the Portuguese could hardly ignore this new threat to the naval lines of communication that linked the Asian trade and the burgeoning African slave and Brazilian sugar commerce to Lisbon.[87] Guzmán de Silva, the Spanish ambassador in Venice, explained all this to Philip II on 23 May 1576: the Venetians would be delighted with an Ottoman conquest of

Morocco, since this would give Muslim shipping a base from which it could attack Iberia's Atlantic commerce and thereby restore Venice—and the eastern Mediterranean trade route—to its grand position.[88] Finally, a new feeling of militancy toward Islam, undoubtedly stimulated by the Catholic Reformation, merged with other strategic considerations to influence a Portuguese decision to invade Morocco.

At the time the king of Portugal elected to continue the war against Islam, Philip II adopted the opposite policy toward the Ottomans. After the state bankruptcy of 1575, Philip II made a dramatic new effort to resolve his strategic dilemma. Habsburg agents redoubled their efforts to secure a treaty with the Ottomans. In this same interval a succession crisis broke out among the heirs to the Ṣafavid state. Yet as civil war in Persia assisted the Spanish by making expansion in the east look more attractive, the Portuguese king requested military aid from Spain in order to attack the Moroccan protégé of the Ottomans, ʿAbd al-Malik.[89] Philip II then found himself in the difficult position of conducting secret negotiations with the enemy of the faith while being petitioned to carry on his role as a defender of Christendom in Africa.

In February 1578, Don Sebastian learned of the diplomatic contacts between the Ottomans and the agents of Philip II in Istanbul. Immediately he demanded to be included in the negotiations so as to ensure that no aid from the eastern empire would reach his Moroccan opponent. Philip II rebuffed his Iberian neighbor, reassuring Don Sebastian of his control over the Istanbul negotiations. The king of Portugal nonetheless obliged Philip II to provision him with men and ships. Meanwhile, in February 1578 Ottoman scribes recorded the movement in and out of Istanbul of the Spanish ambassadors who were involved in peace negotiations. In this same winter, the sultan's officials received intelligence from North Africa concerning the invasion plans of the Portuguese. Murad III warned the governor of Algeria and waited for the outcome of the impending frontier clash before settling with Philip II's representatives.

An extraordinary battle took place in Morocco on 4 August 1578. As though a complete destruction of old relations in northwest Africa was somehow necessary, the encounter between the Moroccan and Portuguese armies at Alcazar left all three contenders for the ruling position in Morocco dead on the battlefield: the sultan of Morocco, ʿAbd al-Malik, his opponent, the deposed Muḥammad, and the king of Portugal, Don Sebastian. The result of the military action, however, was much less equitable. At the close of combat on

4 August, Muslim troops had completely defeated the Portuguese army, having killed or captured a substantial portion of the Portuguese aristocracy.[90] In contrast to the difficult political history that would afflict Portugal after the death of their king at Alcazar, this definite Muslim victory, in which Hispano-Muslim arquebusiers gained a measure of revenge against their Christian enemies, quickly resulted in the triumphant accession of Aḥmad al-Manṣūr, the brother of the dead ʿAbd al-Malik, as the reigning Saʿdian sultan.

This border event in Morocco contributed indirectly to the defeat of the political faction that had ruled the Ottoman empire since the last years of Süleyman the Lawgiver's reign. Whereas the reconquest of Tunis had strengthened the hold of the grand vizier Mehmet Sokollu upon the government of the empire, the sudden death of Selim II in the winter of 1574 brought to the throne a sultan, Murad III (1574–95), who was surrounded by men determined to break the power of the grand vizier. Led by Kara Üveys Paşa, this court group fought to oust the partisans of the grand vizier from their places in the Ottoman administration and to determine the foreign policy of the empire. Their issue was that the defense of the tumultuous Persian frontier required the suppression of heterodox Islam, the Shiʿism of eastern Anatolia. Thus a Muslim victory in North Africa and political anarchy within Ṣafavid Persia changed the psychological climate at court in a manner that favored the opponents of Mehmet Sokollu. Old warriors like Sinan Paşa and Lala Mustafa Paşa now sensed an opportunity to expand their power through land warfare and joined the enemies of the grand vizier.

In the battle for his political existence, Mehmet Sokollu opposed the Persian expedition, pointing out that the Ottomans had reached the limits of their ability to expand in the east. Not only would war against the Ṣafavid lands be too difficult and expensive, but the population of the conquered regions would never accept Ottoman rule.[91] In Iberia, on the other hand, there were Muslims waiting to be liberated. How the grand vizier would have carried on warfare in the western basin of the Mediterranean, where the same arguments applied, is not known. In any case, the Ottoman court decided against the advice of this Bosnian slave. On 10 April 1576, Feridun Bey, head of the Ottoman chancery and former secretary of Mehmet Sokollu, was dismissed.[92] Sometime in 1577 Murad III approved the decision to open the eastern frontier.[93] On 5 April 1578, Lala Mustafa Paşa left Istanbul to command the Ottoman expedition in the east while Spanish ambassadors negotiated with the sultan. The next year, on 12 October 1579, a Bosnian dervish assassinated the

Ottoman grand vizier, and the empire, like its Iberian opponent, turned away from the Mediterranean.[94]

Only minor issues now stood in the way of an agreement to end large-scale conflict between Latin Christian and Turko-Muslim empires. Spain, in opposition to her reaction during the Muslim military movements in 1568–70, did not intervene in Morocco upon the news of the Portuguese defeat but continued to negotiate with the Turks. Meanwhile the Ottomans, having learned about the Portuguese disaster and the weak and scattered state of the Muslim community in Spain from their frontier commander in Algeria, reversed their direction of expansion, dispatching troops and supplies toward the Persian frontier in the summer of 1578. During this same period the sultan of Morocco signaled his desire to maintain a degree of independence between the two empires by simultaneously welcoming both Ottoman and Spanish ambassadors. Finally, in August 1580, the viziers' scribes copied into their notebooks the substance of a truce between Ottoman and Habsburg empires.

Written in the imperial language of the Ottoman court, the letter from Murad III to Philip II aimed at establishing temporary peace between the two empires. Noting that the Spanish had proposed the truce, the sultan indicated his desire to arrange a peace that would insure the integrity of imperial territories. The only condition the Ottomans attached to their proposal was that Christian corsairs be prevented from attacking the ships and territories of the sultan's subjects. If the Spanish would respect the general conditions of the truce, then the sultan guaranteed that his naval captains, corsairs, and land troops would not harm the subjects of his old opponent.[95]

From the perspective of diplomatic history, the year 1580 is clearly the best date for the beginning of a new era in imperial relations along the Ibero-African frontier. Spain, turning north and west to engage the English and Dutch with all her resources, seized Portugal in that same fateful year. Concluding that further expansion in the west would be unproductive, in 1577 the viziers of Murad III had already allied the Ottoman state with Poland against Russia in preparation for the Persian campaign of 1578. With the pacification of the western frontier assured by peace agreements, by the reality of Ottoman political and moral authority within Muslim North Africa, and by the preoccupations of Habsburg Spain in a divided Europe, there was little enthusiasm in imperial councils for a rekindling of large-scale warfare in the Mediterranean. The great empires had disengaged not at the port of Lepanto but at the Strait of Gibraltar.[96]

Six: NORTH AFRICA IN REVOLT

After this [the reconquest of Tunis, 1574] *the fleet was not sent out to make war until the Crete campaign* [1645].

Kâtib Çelebi[2]

The Turkish arsenal is only building big ships to carry heavy artillery for forts and the army; the Turks are waging war against the Persians in the Spanish manner, fortifying the strategic spots which were conquered.

Cristóbal de Salazar to Philip II

After 1580 the internal logic of the frontier's development changed sharply. The Habsburg bureaucracy intensified the authority of the central government along its Ibero-African periphery so as to entrench the claims of an early modern European society. All but the most limited expeditions against Muslim territories were ruled out. On the Islamic side of the border the internal divisiveness of the North African community reasserted itself. Ottoman and Saᶜdian sultans had in reality been able to overcome the particularistic tendencies of Maghribian society only so long as the community believed there was a major external threat to its central values. Once the military challenge waned, the prestige of the rulers slipped and local society revolted. Yet, as political authority was diffused throughout the Maghribian community, the symbols of legitimacy for the great Islamic tradition retained their vigor: no revolution succeeded in overturning the institutions that Ottoman and Saᶜdian elites had imposed upon local society. Thus the pattern of frontier history that emerged after the Hispano-Ottoman truce featured a politics of small scale based upon the heritage of the sixteenth century. Even the entry of a powerful new military technology, the Atlantic sailing ship, failed to reverse this trend; cheap iron cannons and three-masted vessels mainly benefited the corsairs, who more and more came to symbolize the life of the frontier and the times.[1]

Don Sebastian's death at Alcazar left the Portuguese state in a desperate situation. An aged Cardinal Henry inherited the burden of ruling a small seagoing empire whose economy was in trouble and whose political prestige in North Africa had been demolished. Social turmoil certainly lurked beneath the apparent stability of the cardinal's first year of rule. Yet the real danger to the independence of Portugal came not from the lower classes but from Spain. Strategic considerations associated with Atlantic commerce and a strong dynastic claim emboldened Philip II to begin maneuvers aimed at unifying the Iberian Peninsula under one monarch. When Cardinal Henry died in 1580, only Don Antonio, an illegitimate offspring of the royal family, tried to rally the Portuguese around his standard. His effort came far too late. Between June and August of 1580 a Spanish army under the Duke of Alba overcame a hastily mounted resistance and forced Don Antonio to seek refuge among the European enemies of Spain.[2]

Although the conquest of Portugal can be taken as proof of Spain's Atlantic intentions, Ottoman viziers were not quite so sure that the Christians had deserted North Africa. Murad III warned the governor of Algeria to be prepared to assist the Ottoman fleet as soon as it reached North Africa in the summer of 1581.[3] Yet beyond providing some protection against what the Spanish might do, the sultan only wished to complete his negotiations with the Saʿdian sultan—and with good reason, for according to Philip II's spies, Aḥmad al-Manṣūr had made his peace with the Ottomans at the price of 102,000 ducats.[4] Kılıç Ali Paşa, the Ottoman admiral, used falsified documents to play upon the news of the Portuguese defeat in order to convince the imperial divan that a large fleet ought to be maintained in the Mediterranean. But power at court was in the hands of men committed to continental expansion; the peace with Spain was not broken.[5]

Murad III's advisers felt that Philip II's new conquest could not prejudice the interests of the empire. According to the imperial gossip in Istanbul, the acquisition of Portugal would either lead the Habsburgs into conflict with other European powers or would create another Flanders in Iberia, which the frontiersmen of Islam could exploit.[6] In addition, Don Antonio's flight to the Low Countries internationalized the problems Philip II encountered when he imposed his administration in Portugal. Christian states hostile to Spain would surely use this candidate for the Portuguese throne to advance their own imperial purposes.[7]

The Ottomans made a strategic political calculation of this sort after carefully examining their various frontiers. They wished to determine the one border where the advantages of imperial arms could best be exploited without threatening the defense of the empire elsewhere. By 1580 the Ottomans decided to battle with the Ṣafavids rather than the Spanish.

Lazaro Soranzo listed the eight possible courses of action the viziers analyzed before agreeing to go to war in the east.[8] Their arguments opposing the reactivation of imperial conflict in the west are particularly important for the history of the Ibero-African frontier: they exposed the major differences between the Ottoman and Habsburg empires and also brought out the political tensions that threatened the stability of the late sixteenth-century border.

Those who favored a western campaign alluded to the dangers of political decentralization on the western frontier. Although the ruler of Fez—the Saʿdian sultan—now paid tribute to the Ottoman sultan, such an arrangement ought to be only a preliminary step in the eventual displacement of the local ruling class and the establishment of an Ottoman administration directed from Istanbul. In addition, the North African provinces whose governors received their appointments from the sultan—Algeria, Tunisia, and Tripolitania—should be brought under the same degree of control as existed in the territories closer to the imperial throne. Military operations along the shores of North Africa would therefore elevate the authority of the Ottoman sultan in these border regions to its proper level. At the same time, an imperial expedition could break the secret alliance between Saʿdian Morocco and Spain while preventing the Iberian empire and the Knights of Saint John from setting the local tribes of the Maghribian coast against the Turks. Placing the horsetail standards of the Ottomans on the Atlantic shores of Morocco would also enable the holy warriors to raid the Atlantic commerce of the Christians and protect the Muslim traffic in the Mediterranean.

But two fundamental difficulties confronted the advocates of an open western frontier: first, the distance between the center of Ottoman strength and the Maghrib was too far for effective naval operations; second, the yield from the conquest of Morocco would be too little to warrant the great expense of outfitting a fleet for such an ambitious project.[9]

The viziers also assessed the reality of the Spanish decision to relinquish its leadership of the struggle with Islam. Many times since the conquest of Istanbul, the Ottomans had calculated that the divisions among Christian states would blunt the force of a crusade against the House of Islam. On this occasion, spies informed the viziers that Spain was deeply engaged in a religious war in Flanders. The English, moreover, provided the opponents of the Iberian empire with military support and at the same time raided the Spanish commerce that sailed the Atlantic routes. If the war in Flanders did not occupy Spain, the old hostility between France and Spain could again be fired up to give the Ottomans a means of dividing their opposition. In Iberia itself the still unassimilated Hispano-Muslims, the Moriscos, could be encouraged to rebel. Portuguese dissatisfaction with Spanish rule offered the Muslims another means of disorganizing Spain. Confronted with this range of European dangers, Philip II could be counted on not to compound his problems with an attack on Ottoman territories. The solid fortifications at Algiers alone were strong enough to make it expensive to attempt to take those regions of the House of Islam. Even if the Spanish were severely provoked by corsairs, the Ottoman viziers calculated that they would prudently refrain from sending their expensive, slow-moving fleets into Levantine waters to confront the imperial flotilla of the Turks.[10]

Philip II's advisers likewise concluded that the Turks would not break the imperial peace. From the Spanish point of view, the Ottoman frontier had plenty of political divisions that could be exploited. To block further large-scale conflict on the frontier, Philip II's agents in Africa had long since formed the leaders of various tribes and the Saᶜdian sultan into a potential anti-Ottoman force. But the basic reason they thought the Ottomans would not resume conflict west of Tunis was the belief in Madrid that the Turks could not manage a lengthy campaign in Persia and a Mediterranean war at the same time. During an age of inflation, it strained the imagination to think that the Turks would weaken their commitment to the new continental phase of expansion by raising the enormous sums necessary to assemble a great armada. Therefore the men at the center of imperial power concluded that the Hispano-Ottoman peace of 1580 would have a long life.[11]

But nearly seventy-five years of frontier warfare had created a certain momentum that did not disappear overnight, especially when both the wealth and the honor of Ottoman march warriors depended on their continued success in war. During the spring of 1585 the ambitious governor of Algeria, Hasan Paşa, raised a serious threat to peaceful relations along the frontier when he petitioned the sultan for military assistance to conquer the Spanish fort at Oran. He informed the sultan that the infidels in the Christian outpost had allied themselves with tribesmen and raided the territories surrounding the city of Tlemsen. This news could hardly have startled the Ottoman viziers. But to refuse to deal seriously with this charge upon the military and religious values of the Ottoman ruling class would surely undermine the central administration's control over the western frontier. Murad III replied just as the Spanish had predicted. Because the grand vizier, Özdemiroğlu Osman Paşa, was occupied with the Persian war, the sultan argued that it would be impossible to send the fleet. When the Safavids had been defeated, however, the imperial armada would then be ordered to sail toward the western regions.[12]

English efforts to reverse the course of Ibero-African frontier history met the same fate. One of the objectives of their first ambassador, William Harborne, was to relieve the pressure Philip II had placed on England and her allies by maneuvering the Ottomans back into a naval war.[13] Though too late to block the Hispano-Ottoman truce of 1580, after 1583 Harborne employed a wide range of arguments designed to break the Mediterranean peace. Ottomans and Protestants ought to bring down an idolatrous Latin Christendom.[14] On a less universal plane, war should begin with the Spanish because as heirs of the Portuguese place in Asia they threatened Ottoman communications with India.[15] From the economic point of view, the English ambassador noted how the Atlantic commerce, which brought Spain 30 million gold pieces a year, could easily be raided from North African bases.[16] Conflict with Spain, moreover, would be helped because both the Portuguese and the Moriscos were ready to revolt.[17] All these embroidered inducements failed to budge the Ottomans from pursuing their protracted war with the Safavids of Persia.

On 21 March 1590 the Safavids and the Ottomans decided upon peace. Immediately the anti-Spanish coalition urged the Turks to resume the Mediterranean conflict with Spain. Old reasons for such a decision were trotted out: the advantages of a Morisco revolt were dangled in front of the Ottoman viziers.[18] Bowing, perhaps, to the persistence of the new English ambassador Edward Barton, the sultan decided upon a naval campaign for the spring of 1591.[19] Subjects, however, resisted the special tax levied for the outfitting of the fleet.[20] In addition, the imperial navy showed a calamitous lack of efficiency, mainly because it had not been used for nearly two decades. The admiral, Cağalzâde Sinan Paşa, wisely limited the operation of the fleet to the eastern Mediterranean.[21] During the following year, 1592, Hasan Paşa, the governor of Bosnia, began the raids along the Austrian border that served as the opening event in a long Balkan war.[22] This second decision to favor continental objectives left no doubt that naval affairs had low priority in the highest Ottoman councils.

It was logical that the navy would be one of the first institutions to reflect the weakening of those dynamic impulses that had brought about Ottoman expansion, not because the Ottomans possessed a congenital dislike for the sea, but because the strength of the empire was essentially based upon the ruling class's control of an agricultural surplus. When a variety of limiting conditions began to stall growth in every direction, those at the center of the empire who had previously sought rewards from the frontier naturally came to believe that a more efficient exploitation of the internal regions would maintain the ruling class in its accustomed manner. Such a sudden change from external expansion to a determined internal exploitation was bound to stimulate widespread violence. Almost all observers of late-sixteenth-century Ottoman history note how the tumultuous rite of passage from conquest to bureaucratic regime turned the Ottomans away from the sea and into an era of internal disorder.[23]

Inappropriate though it may be, historians often begin their explanation of this decline by citing the proverb "The fish stinks from the head." While the evidence is overwhelming that sultans were less able to control events after the death of Süleyman the Lawgiver, it is not necessarily true that their failure to live up to the military accomplishments of glorious predecessors was due in a great measure to their personal shortcomings. Unproductive campaigns on distant borders prevented the sultan from using war to maintain the cohesion of the ruling class. Correspondingly, the military found the risks of their profession increasing while rewards decreased. Men in high position turned to political intrigue, and the common soldier met his unsatisfactory condition head-on with what became a standard form of late-sixteenth-century protest: the pay riot.

High officials of the empire soon displaced service to the sultan in their various efforts to manipulate military discontent. Yet each victor in the internal struggle for power faced the severe dilemma of trying to administer a military empire whose motor was out of fuel and whose chief symbol of authority was the warrior sultan. Since not much could be done about changing the unsatisfactory yield of warfare, the competition to control the sultan increased and became unstable. In this manner, the sultanate was transformed from an institution calling for aggressive leadership to an office whose occupant merely carried out symbolic duties at the behest of one faction or another of the ruling class. Between the reign of Selim II (1566–74) and that of Osman II, who was killed by the Janissaries in 1622, the history of the sultanate provided a clear example of the structural changes at the very top of the Ottoman social pyramid.[24]

As the psychological unity of the holy warrior state disintegrated from the top, elements of Ottoman society that had been bypassed or excluded from office rebelled once more against the centralized political system whose heart was in Istanbul. These revolts against the "foreign" administrators, the Calâlî uprisings, convulsed Anatolia between 1596 and 1609.[25] Eventually absorbed by the central bureaucracy, the rural protest went hand-in-hand with the replacement of soldier-conquerors by tax farmers and salaried troops garrisoned in cities and towns.[26]

Not only did the rural organization of the empire go through an upheaval of unparalleled proportions, but the central bureaucracy itself showed signs of disintegration. Bribery, profiteering, misappropriation, and incompetence undermined the integrity of a scribal class caught in the turmoil of an age of fundamental change.[27]

With Ottoman history gone awry, the *ulema* exerted themselves to uphold the stability and the security of Muslim society by retreating from situations of uncertainty. Physically, the flight from the unknown was symbolized by the destruction in 1580 of Takiyyüddin's observatory in Galata in order to assuage God's anger, expressed in the form of the plague, for the human penetration of divine mysteries.[28] Intellectually, the plea of Katib Çelebi on the need for rational sciences showed that by the first half of the seventeenth century the dominant attitude toward nature was controlled by religious intuition and the sacred sciences.[29]

Students of Ottoman decline have known for some time that the waves of internal protest that shook the Turko-Muslim empire at the end of the sixteenth century were also bound up in a series of Mediterraneanwide events. One of these transcultural changes was a sharp increase in prices. Between the conquest of Egypt in 1517 and the year 1584 the empire experienced little instability in its monetary structure—a primary yardstick of price stability. For example, the relation between gold and silver during this sixty-seven-year period, which corresponded to the age of expansion, remained relatively fixed at 55 to 60 aspers (akçe) per Ottoman gold piece. During the quarter-century that followed, however, the Turkish empire was subjected to the force of an international revolution in prices whose impact corresponded roughly to the reentry into the Mediterranean of northern merchants, the arrival in Seville of large quantities of American silver, and the Ottoman government's own debasement of its silver coinage. Inflation subsequently raised the silver value of the Ottoman gold coin to almost 400 aspers by 1624, and in combination with other factors this set the price of foodstuffs on a steep climb.[30]

It would be convenient to explain pay riots, rural rebellions, and peasant discontent by simply linking sixteenth-century inflation with the cessation of Ottoman expansion. Alas, there were also other Mediterraneanwide changes at work that fed the discontent of the times. An analysis of Ottoman population statistics for the period of change offers evidence that increasing pressure was being placed on the productive capacities of Ottoman agriculture. There also appears to have been a change for the worse in the climate of the Mediterranean at the end of the sixteenth century. Too many people and too little food then set in motion that fatal connection between undernourishment and disease. Taken together, these uncontrollable events tended to create a millenarian climate in Muslim lands that excited the ignorant into believing that the Muslim year 1000 (A.D. 1591–92) would bring the end of the world.

These imperfectly documented Mediterraneanwide pressures upon man accompanied the transition of the entire region from the expansionist age of the sixteenth century to the stable age of the seventeenth century. For the history of the Ibero-African frontier they form an indispensable background for understanding the tumultuous political events that took place after the end of the conquests.

Three years before the first step in the Hispano-Ottoman disengagement, there were ample symptoms of a fundamental age of change on the North African frontier. Thus the imperial criticism that Murad III leveled at the governor of Algeria in 1577 represented a striking departure from the past: Do not give out imperial domains in the form of tax grants or *timars* (an administrative procedure that would not yield cash for the treasury) to military people; pay salaries; prevent the military from collecting unauthorized taxes; stop unearned pay increases; give justice to the subject class on tax matters; and discipline the Janissaries by cutting off their pay.[31]

Clearly, a local struggle for the control of Algeria's tax resources had broken out at a time when the territorial growth of the empire had drawn to a close. That the cessation of expansion combined with other economic trends to create a time of troubles on the Ottoman frontier was apparent from the behavior of the border governors.

An accomplished seaman and a Venetian renegade, Hasan Paşa took command of Algeria in 1577–80 and again in 1583–85. This Ottoman won his reputation not as a corsair but as a rapacious tax collector. He forced Maghribian corsairs to pay an increased share of their booty to the provincial treasury, compelled merchants to sell food to his agents at low prices, extracted greater tribute from the tribesmen, subjected the trade of the province to new taxes, and obtained more money from the provincial elite. Sometime before the end of his second administration, 1583–85, and slightly before the great devaluation at the center of the empire, Hasan began to buy and sell in the Mediterranean gold and silver market. He collected silver in North Africa, where it was cheap in relation to gold, and shipped it to Istanbul, where it purchased more gold than it would in the Maghrib.[32] Hasan Paşa's career shows that some Ottomans could contend with the economic forces of the time. By 1588 his wealth won him the post of *kapudan*, admiral of the Ottoman fleet.

If the governor of Algeria squeezed the community with uncommon vigor in order to achieve Ottoman success, the central bureaucracy also was eager to collect more taxes from the economy of the western provinces. In the year of the Hispano-Ottoman truce, the sultan signaled this determination when he ordered a major financial reorganization of the western frontier. Previously a single unit for the imperial tax collector, now all of North Africa was divided into three regions. Separate *defterdars*, provincial treasurers, were assigned to the provinces of Algeria, Tunisia, and Tripolitania and admonished to improve the efficiency of the postconquest system: the distribution of revenues to the ruling class as salaries rather than as revocable grants of taxes based on the performance of some state service.[33]

Meanwhile, a conflict arose between the center of the empire and the periphery that underlined the importance of border warfare in the economy of the frontier. When the English obtained commercial concessions from the Ottomans in 1583, they were granted the sultan's patent of protection.[34] What Murad III gave in Istanbul, the North African corsairs took away on the empire's naval frontier. Embarrassed by the privateer's seizure of English vessels, the sultan sent Mehmet Çavuş to Algiers in 1585 to return the captured ships and men to the Christian merchants, along with suitable indemnities.[35] His mission was a spectacular failure. Back in Istanbul by 1586, Mehmet Çavuş confessed to the sultan that the governor of Algiers had no intention of returning the captured men and ships. As if to confirm the envoy's report, Algerian corsairs captured another English ship, enslaved its crew, and sold the ship and its goods at the Spanish port of Oran.[36] A dangerous event, this transcultural sale raised the possibility that North African corsairs would at some point raid Muslim shipping for the benefit of the Christians.

How to check the growing disobedience of its naval frontiersmen became a vexing problem for the Istanbul government as the number of corsairs increased during the last decade of the sixteenth century. Paper protests brought no change. By 1588 the general situation had deteriorated to the point that the governor of Tunisia was given the job of patrolling the coast of North Africa so that protected shipping would be able to pass by the Maghribian shores without suffering loss.[37] In such a way had the corsairs ceased to serve as an auxiliary unit of the Ottoman navy and instead become a hazard to maritime commerce between the heart of the empire and the outside.

During the classical age of expansion elite foot units, not corsairs, set the standard of military discipline that was at the core of the extraordinary performance of the Ottoman government. This was why imperial commands addressed to the head of the Janissary corps in Algeria showed that by 1593 the centralized administration of the conquest period was a shambles. In a detailed order to the military leader, the sultan commanded his servant to prevent the provincial military units from demanding unwarranted increases in pay. Additions to the wages of the troops, *terraki*, were to be given only for valorous behavior in the holy war, not as a general rule. The reason for such an order was that the wages and salaries of the sultan's slaves in Algeria had gone up at such a rate that the revenues of the province could not cover expenses.[38] Three years before Spain's next debt repudiation, the provincial treasury in Algeria had gone bankrupt.

To overcome the financial difficulties of the border province, the governor of Algeria, Şaban Paşa, proposed a major change in the politics of frontier life. In 1593 he wrote the sultan to request that the Janissaries be allowed to participate in privateering ventures. At the same time, corsairs were to contribute a greater share of their booty to the provincial treasury. Despite the desire in Istanbul to control the corsairs, Murad III put his seal on an imperial command exhorting the Janissaries and the corsairs to act in harmony while engaged in the holy war.[39] By this desperate act, the central bureaucracy not only sanctioned the destruction of one political means by which the center controlled the naval border, but also encouraged frontiersmen to engage in a private enterprise that pulled the periphery away from the center.

Collapse came in 1595. An order from Murad III to the beys of all the *sanjaks*—major administrative subdivisions of Algeria—to the corsairs, and to the Janissaries commanded them to obey their governor and to help collect the taxes.[40]

A year later an event with even more ominous overtones for the central administration took place. The sons of Ottomans rebelled. Against the thrust of both tradition and religion, the Ottoman system denied high position to the children of the sultan's slaves. Since three-quarters of a century under the Turks had naturally increased the size of this group as well as the number of marriage connections between important Algerian families and Ottomans, the offspring of the ruling class could claim powerful local support.[41] If this was not enough, in 1598 the Berber sultan of Kūko began serious negotiations with the Spanish to acquire arms and other military support. His rebellion, the final internal attack upon the old order, came at the turn of the seventeenth century.[42]

In Tunisia a similar pattern of internal protests accompanied the breakdown of the centralized administration. During the summer of 1580 Ottoman scribes recorded an order to the governor of Tunis directing him to send the 25,000 gold florins that the western provinces normally contributed to the imperial treasury but that they had failed to dispatch that year.[43] This communication preceded other imperial correspondence detailing the illegal and violent acts of the provincial militia. Demanding and receiving pay increases for a variety of trumped-up reasons, the Janissaries exhausted the provincial treasury. In rural regions, unnamed individuals—probably local notables with some knowledge of administrative matters—took direct control of lands from which the provincial treasurer had taken taxes. The governor himself began to engage in illegal activities that were sure signs of inflationary conditions. Taxes were taken in kind by force, at prices below the market value; food and essential raw materials were sold at inflated prices by agents of military leaders; silver coinage was adulterated and forced into circulation at the old rates; property belonging to wealthy villagers was seized while the owners were held in jail on false charges. Rising salary demands, falling revenues, and official corruption quickly drove bureaucrats and tax farmers to increase taxes ruthlessly, compelling many peasants to abandon their lands.[44]

By 1585 the confusion within the Tunisian administration had become so serious that the sultan's chief officials in the province requested a statement from the center of the empire explaining the principles of government. This plea for imperial attention only evoked an order from Murad III commanding his slaves to administer the province as in the past.[45]

A time of Mediterraneanwide famine and economic disorder, the period between 1587 and 1591 marked the high point of disorder in Tunisia. Repeatedly the sultan demanded that the Janissaries not usurp the authority of the governor and the judges of the province, but military assaults on the power of the sultan's representatives only worsened. In 1587 the Janissaries appropriated the right to appoint military officials to provincial posts; they seized the personal property of the governor; and finally they began to impose their own taxes.[46] The end came in 1590 when a Janissary revolt resulted in the death of some members of the *divan*, the main governing body of the province.

Violence at the peak of the social pyramid did not destroy the Ottoman imperial idea in Tunisia; but it drastically modified its meaning in practice. Ottoman and Tunisian families with a stake in the local urban order the empire had produced came together in political agreement; the structure of Ottoman society was to be maintained, but political and administrative authority would shift from Istanbul to Tunisia. In 1591 this was accomplished when a member of the Janissary corps was elected to sit on the provincial *divan*.[47] Since this rebellious unit was the most powerful military force in the province, its representative soon became the de facto ruler of Tunisia.[48] Given the intense kinship environment of North Africa, it was appropriate that the new commander of this decentralized Ottoman province, Ibrahim Dey, took the title dey—"uncle" rather than "father"—in a manner that did not challenge the prestigious kinship role the sultan played for the empire as a whole.

By the beginning of the seventeenth century the politics of the Ottoman frontier in North Africa started to settle into this mold which the Tunisian ruling class shaped in 1591. Institutionalized local rule spread to Tripoli in 1603 and reached Algeria in 1671 after a tortuous internal history. Neither the Ottoman central government nor the Habsburg empire attempted to halt or profit from this political transformation of the Turko-Muslim frontier.

European historians have often treated this loss of direct control over the Maghribian provinces as a movement toward local independence. To a certain extent this was true. Yet each of the provinces maintained Ottoman institutions and a respect for the culture of the empire: this web of cultural and institutional ties gave substance to imperial unity in the age of decentralization. Here the history of Morocco and Tripolitania during the era of change describes the political limits of an empire composed of loosely bound regional units, each governed by men whose base of authority was Ottoman, Islamic, and local.

Tripolitania's importance seemed to depend almost entirely upon its contribution to the success of the naval war with Latin Christendom. After the Gerba campaign of 1560, however, little action took place along its shores. Internally, the coastal region from Cyrenaica to Sfax, Tripolitania's boundaries in 1576, probably yielded very little in the way of taxes. Except for a thin coastal strip of vegetation near Tripoli, there were few settled areas of any size, and the geography did not make it easy for the Ottomans to control the local population. Extensive steppe and desert regions meant that the nomad occupied a more important position in the society of this province than he did elsewhere.

Between 1574 and 1587 the military corps in Tripolitania dismantled the administrative structure of the conquest era. Hint of the impending disorder came after the reconquest of Tunis in 1574, when Murad III commanded the Maghrib treasurer to survey the financial resources of the province and correct the maladministration of the salary system.[49] By 1587, however, the tax collecting activities of Tripolitania's garrisons made it obvious that the sultan's commands had been flouted. The same dreary history of military abuses based upon the salaried corps' attempts to bring their pay into line with the inflationary conditions of the time now surfaced in the correspondence between the sultan and his servants in Tripolitania. Military units dunned the governor and the peasants for more money; unknown men seized control of property belonging to the imperial treasury; and finally, in November 1587, the Janissaries themselves took control of the provincial treasury.[50] Informed of this wrongdoing by the governor and judges of Tripoli, the central government did nothing but send one imperial command after another calling upon the servants of the sultan to obey.

During the fall of 1588, at the time of tribal movement on the steppe, a rebellion in Tripolitania gave birth to the most thorough-going internal challenge to the presence of the Ottomans in North Africa. Near Tajūra, just east of Tripoli, Yaḥyā ibn Yaḥyā al-Suwaidi proclaimed himself a Mahdi, a man anointed by God to bring about an era of righteousness.[51] He led his troops against the Ottomans, killing a thousand slaves of the sultan. After his initial success, Yaḥyā designated a lieutenant to collect taxes and to organize his army while he left for the island of Gerba, where he hoped to obtain support from the Christians.[52]

This messianic movement goaded the central government into action. When a messenger from Tripoli arrived in Istanbul late in 1588 with an appeal for help, Murad III, in an unusual break with Ottoman conventions, asked his admiral to send galleys even though the sailing season was over.[53] Hasan Paşa, the admiral, rejected the request. During the spring of 1589, however, fifty galleys loaded with troops drawn from the naval districts of the eastern Mediter-ranean arrived in Tripoli. Meanwhile, the sultan's letters to the governors of Algeria and Tunisia called for their assistance in putting down a rebellion that, in the words of the imperial document, was sure to spread. Despite the strains between Istanbul and the garrison in the eastern Maghrib, the Tunisians sent a detachment to Tripolitania. Confronted by this coordinated opposition from the center and the periphery of the Ottoman empire, the tribesmen did what they usually did: they retreated into the desert.

Hasan Paşa followed this reconquest of the Tripolitanian coast with a campaign against the causes of the uprising. He reversed the previous policy of inaction against the provincial military class and sought to punish those who had driven the subject population to reject the legitimacy of the Ottoman sultan. High provincial officials were imprisoned, fined, and compelled to return some of the wealth they had taken from subjects. Far more interesting, however, was the punishment meted out to the Janissary corps. In a real departure from the past, the old garrison was removed from Tripoli and scattered among the other provinces of the empire. Three hundred Janissaries and cannoneers, 100 bombardiers and caulkers, 200 infantrymen, and 450 men from other military organizations re-placed the discredited units.[54]

As soon as the fleet left for its winter quarters, the tribesmen returned from the desert to encircle the coastal bases of the Ottomans. When it became known in Istanbul that the revolt had not been extinguished, Murad III issued new instructions to the governors of Tunis and Tripolitania not to let this social and political disorder grow. At the same time, the sultan ordered the governor of Egypt to participate in the campaign against the Mahdi. Like the military men in Tunis, the Ottomans in Egypt dispatched troops even though military pay riots had undermined the authority of the Istanbul administration between 1586 and 1589.

Only in February 1592 could Mehmet Paşa write the sultan that his soldiers had ended the revolt of the false messiah. Betrayed, perhaps, by his own supporters when famine and the technological superiority of the Ottoman army began to tell, the leader of the Tripolitanian revolution, like the twelfth imam of the Shiʿites, disappeared in the year of Mehmet's report.[55]

After four years of fighting, the central and peripheral cadres of the empire in North Africa had underlined the unity with which Ottomans would resist attempts to destroy Turko-Muslim rule. Decentralization might occur; but the substitution of a regime based upon a new legitimacy and local society would not be permitted. This failure of the once-powerful combination of religious reformism and confederated tribesmen to create a new state within Ottoman boundaries gave notice that times had changed since the era of Ibn Khaldun. Bureaucracies, standing armies, and firearms had destroyed the theocentric means of forming an empire on the tribal fringe.

In contrast to Tripolitania, the Ottomans had not subjected Saʿdian Morocco to the direct rule of the Istanbul bureaucracy. There the political regime differed widely from the provincial system in Ottoman North Africa. No ruling class had emerged in the western Maghrib that separated itself from the kinship world to the degree that the Ottomans had. The Saʿdian army did not display the organizational sophistication or the technological prowess of their Ottoman counterparts.[56] There was little evidence of a navy. On the political plane, the legitimacy of the Moroccan sultanate did not have the sharpness of the Ottoman claim. Inside Morocco, the power of the Saʿdian family rested upon an inherited charismatic religious prestige it shared with the marabouts. Beyond the boundaries of Morocco, the Sharīf deferred, through tribute payments, to the power and wider appeal among Muslims of the Ottoman sultan. At the same time, the Moroccan ruler belied his image as a holy warrior when he consummated secret arrangements with Christians in order to defend the independence of his own dynasty from the Ottomans.

Despite the apparent weakness of the Saᶜdian sultanate in relation to the Ottoman empire, favorable conditions surrounding the end of great warfare in North Africa blessed the buffer-state independence of the Moroccan regime. A resounding victory over the Christians in 1578 put the Saᶜdian sultanate back on its holy war pedestal and yielded a handsome economic return in ransoms paid for the captured Christian aristocracy. Lucky in war, the Saᶜdians were also fortunate in peace; for the death of ᶜAbd al-Malik on the battlefield of Alcazar brought to power a capable successor, Aḥmad al-Manṣūr. His accession was contested neither by the Ottomans nor by the Spanish. Even the politics of the Atlantic world assisted the Moroccans. As additional insurance against Spanish designs upon his realm, Aḥmad al-Manṣūr struck up an alliance with England. Soon he discovered that he had access to one of the most important sources of early modern military and naval technology; that he could trade Moroccan potash, an ingredient of gunpowder, to the English for arms and naval stores.[57]

Nonetheless, a troublesome economic and political environment at the end of the sixteenth century could have stimulated the same kind of military disorder that wracked Ottoman territories. Like the Ottoman governors of Maghribian provinces, Aḥmad al-Manṣūr found himself in possession of a powerful but unemployed army. Yet the Saᶜdian ruler managed to avoid the loss of cohesion that afflicted the Ottoman administration during the last two decades of the sixteenth century. How he was able to prevent the internal division of his sultanate was woven into the history of the Saharan gold trade.

Before the mid-fifteenth century, the extreme aridity of the Sahara, the distance between the Maghrib and the Niger River basin, and the absence of an Atlantic route south of Morocco kept one of the Mediterranean world's major sources of precious metal out of the hands of North African states.[58] What effect the creation of an alternate naval route, the Atlantic, had upon the gold trade across the Sahara is not known. Perhaps encouraged by the news of the Portuguese trade at La Mina or, more likely, simply aware from the commerce in their cities of the sub-Saharan source of the ore, Maghribian commanders probed the northern portion of the routes leading to the Sudan. In Algeria the Ottoman advance toward the

Sudan reached Ouargla in 1552 and Figuig in 1584. After the reconquest of Tunis, an Ottoman, Mahmud Bey, led his men south of Gafsa on the route toward the kingdom of Bornu.[59] Somewhat earlier, during 1557, the Saʿdians sent a column to take possession of the salt (an essential element in the Saharan trade) at Taghazza.[60] Until 1590, however, the geographical defenses of the Saharan trading system and the pressure of war along the Ibero-African frontier blocked the Maghribian rulers' efforts to obtain a greater share of the commerce in gold.

In 1581 the Saʿdians renewed their interest in the Saharan oases along the main caravan route to the Sudan. Some years later Aḥmad al-Manṣūr sent ambassadors to the Songhai court, where in 1588 he demanded that the sub-Saharan state pay a *mithkāl* of gold (about 1/8 ounce) for each camelload of salt extracted from the Central Saharan mines. When the messenger from Askiya Isḥāk II (1588–91), the Songhai ruler, returned with small javelins and a sword, the Moroccan leader had the war for which he was well prepared.[61]

Few at the Saʿdian court believed an army could survive the brutal physical challenge of the Sahara. Al-Manṣūr, in a speech recorded by the eighteenth-century historian al-Ifrānī, soundly criticized the fainthearted. Noting that merchants regularly crossed the desert, the sultan refuted the argument that an army could not traverse the wastes south of the Anti Atlas. The Sudan, he said, was richer than the Maghrib; it therefore would be more profitable to conquer the territories of the blacks than to try to drive out the Turks. Room for expansion in the north was blocked by the more powerful Ottoman and Habsburg empires. Only the southern route lay open. Moreover, the Saʿdian army enjoyed a technological advantage over the Songhai. Like the Ottomans, the Saʿdian sultan looked forward to exploiting the power that cannons and muskets conferred on those who faced only swords and spears.[62]

On 16 October 1590, a long Saʿdian column left southern Morocco under the command of the Spanish slave Jūdar Paṣa. This distinctly new Saharan army, whose 4,000 riflemen used Spanish as their common language, assembled at Lektaoua near the Wadi Draʿa, south and east of Marrakesh. More than 9,000 camels provided supplies for the Moroccan column. It took approximately 135 days for the army to cross 1,500 miles of some of the world's most dangerous terrain. What the brutal march cost the Moroccans in human and animal lives is not known. Some guess that approximately

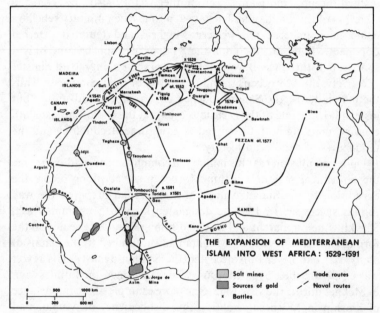

Fig. 4. The expansion of Mediterranean Islam into West Africa, 1529–91

half of the troops perished before the army reached the Niger River basin. Lulled into a sense of security by the small size of the Saʿdian unit, the Songhai slowly assembled a large force. Sometime before March 1591, the Moroccan contingent, true to al-Manṣūr's prediction, vanquished these numerous troops of Askiya Isḥāḳ II at Tondibi with the aid of their firearms.[63]

Everything comes later to Morocco; this act of expansion ten years after its time was no exception. For North Africa, the victory in the Sudan confirmed the already entrenched shape of the Mediterranean frontier. It was the only course of action that would not disturb the imperial giants. Yet another victory also preserved the cohesion of this Saʿdian buffer state at a time when military rebellion could have infected the western Maghrib and tempted external opponents. Even in the Sudan the Saʿdian invasion became only a short-run disturbance. Beyond the limits of their ability to administer effectively, the Moroccans soon lost control of their conquests. Thus the march across the Sahara touched off no imperial adventure but instead became one of those curious events at the end of the sixteenth century, marking both the spread of gunpowder technology and the uniqueness of Moroccan history.[64]

Under no illusion that his military accomplishments had overcome the centrifugal pressures within Moroccan society, long before the expedition to the Sudan Aḥmad al-Manṣūr had prepared the way for his successor. In 1581 he designated his son Muḥammad ash-Shaykh II heir apparent and installed him in Fez. Once seated in the former capital of Morocco, Muḥammad succumbed to the claims of a city that had never fully accepted the Saʿdian dynasty. His revolt was easily quashed by al-Manṣūr, who imprisoned the faithless son in Meknes during the year 1602. One more example of the importance of kinship in Moroccan politics, this disobedience of Muḥammad hinted broadly at an internal struggle to come.[65]

Upon the death of al-Manṣūr in 1603, three of his sons launched campaigns to occupy the position of the former ruler. The tri-cornered warfare that then broke out shattered the fragile political cohesion of the Saʿdian state. Without a human focus, neither Sharīfian prestige nor the memory of victories prevented tribal sheiks, religious leaders, and rulers of many factions from unleashing the spirit of division that the institutions of the Saʿdian state had made such an attempt to overcome. More power now flowed into the hands of men whose spheres of activity were institutionalized on local levels: city, town, village, guild, religious lodge, tribe.

Discredited by their internal wars, the Saᶜdians confronted a series
of internal rebellions. In 1610 a religious scholar from Sijilmassa
in eastern Morocco led a short-lived revolt against the Saᶜdians.
But the tribes of southern Morocco did not accept the messianic
claims of Abū Maḥallī, and his attempt to repeat the Moroccan
political drama failed in 1617.[66] On the Atlantic coast of Morocco,
the Saᶜdian governor of Azemmour, Muḥammad al-ᶜAyyashī, broke
with the Moroccan ruling family. Conducting his own holy war, he
formed an alliance between the Arab tribes of Morocco's Atlantic
plains and the Hispano-Muslim exiles in Salé. A merger of Morocco's
social extremes, this combination of Muslims could neither uproot
the remaining Iberian garrisons nor bridge the differences between
the tribesmen and the Andalusian exiles.[67] Even in the birthplace of
the Saᶜdians, the Sus, Abū Ḥassūn revolted during the second
decade of the seventeenth century.[68]

The death agonies of the Saᶜdian sultanate, which expired officially
in 1659, showed a wider process of decentralization than occurred in
the Ottoman provinces, where the institutions of the empire remained
intact, though under local direction. A political tradition was very
much alive in Morocco; but no one would assemble the pieces until
the end of the seventeenth century.

Such a widespread reversal of the flow of politics did not go unnoticed in Madrid. Long involvement with Islamic society had given
Spain an excellent espionage system. Reports of Ottoman and
Saᶜdian internal conflict after 1580 flooded Spain's war councils,
stimulating proposals that ran the gamut from raids on corsair bases
to plans for the conquest of North Africa.[69]

Emotion and imagination, rather than the practical interests of the
state, underpinned these thinly veiled efforts at resurrecting the
crusades. So Spain toyed with its chances of exploiting the political
and social disorder within North Africa. In almost all cases this
meant seeking out the opponents of urban Islam: the tribesmen. In
1581, when the tribes of southern Tunisia gathered near Gafsa to
unseat the Turks, the Knights of Saint John, Christian frontiersmen,
sent arms, ammunition, and a member of the Ḥafṣid family, Mulay
Aḥmad.[70] The Mahdi of Tripolitania received firearms and a few
experts in their use during the course of his rebellion.[71] Closer to
Spain, the uprising of the Kabylia Berbers between 1601 and 1604
encouraged the Spanish to send a small amount of arms, 4,000 ducats,
and twenty soldiers.[72] None of these military slivers did much more
than slightly inflame the uprisings: by themselves, tribes could not

defeat the Turks.[73] The Ottoman garrisons retained their cohesion; the population of North Africa remained resolutely anti-Christian; and the Habsburg empire did not apply even a moderate amount of its military power against the Ottoman frontier.

On the Saᶜdian border, the story was only slightly different. Between 1578 and 1583, the agents of Philip II conducted a not-too-intense negotiation with Aḥmad al-Manṣūr for the possession of Larache, a port on the Atlantic coast some fifty miles south of Tangier.[74] Close to the Andalusian termini of the Atlantic sailing routes, the Moroccan town also sat astride the main avenue of advance used by armies invading Morocco from the east. Here Habsburg generals found Larache and the Loukkas River valley a natural staging ground for a counterattack against another Ottoman invasion of Morocco; but nothing came of these negotiations, as the truce with the Ottomans held. By 1609, international conditions changed enough that a proposal to occupy Larache again interested the Habsburg court. Corsairs using Atlantic sailing ships had established bases on the west coast of Morocco, from which they raided Spanish commerce. Since the Saᶜdian state had dissolved into a welter of regional and factional conflicts, the Spanish found it simple to obtain possession of Larache in 1610 through negotiation rather than conquest. Four years later Spain added another fort to its coastal holdings in Morocco with the construction of San Miguel de Ultramar (Mehdiya) at the mouth of the River Sebou. The emplacement of these new Christian outposts was related to the effectiveness of Muslim corsairs,[75] not to any crusade into Africa.

Between the occupation of Larache and the construction of the fort at Mehdiya, the Habsburg empire stirred up frontier life in a much more thoroughgoing manner when it drove the last remnants of Hispano-Muslim society from Iberia (1609–14). One financial disaster after another as a result of the war in the Low Countries brought on an era of military mutinies (1598–1604) that ground down the energies of Habsburg Spain.[76] The swift collection and expulsion of Hispano-Muslims from Spain after Philip III's truce with the Dutch in the spring of 1609 was no coincidence. If exiling Muslims to North Africa—the eventual destination of most of the Moriscos— served the cause of Spanish unity by diverting attention from the poor outcome of war in the Low Countries, the injection of a new group of Hispano-Muslims into the society of North Africa threatened to touch off an explosion of Muslim wrath. But this last wave of Morisco exiles entered Africa at a time when the Ottoman empire

had broken up into regional units and the Sa'dian sultanate was en-
gulfed by factionalism.

The way the Moriscos settled along the Muslim edge of the frontier
reflected this localization of Maghribian life at the turn of the
seventeenth century. In the eastern Maghrib, where the process of
decentralization had all but destroyed the administration of the
Sa'dians, the exiles established independent city-states like that at
Salé, entered Andalusian communities such as Tetuan, or submerged themselves in old Moroccan cities, Fez being the most
popular.[77] A more organized reaction to the plight of the Moriscos
took place in Tunis, where Osman Dey presided over their resettlement in agricultural regions.[78] For other regions of the Maghrib,
especially those areas where the tribes prevailed, the Moriscos were
often unpleasantly received. In Istanbul the policy of the central
bureaucracy was to assist the Hispano-Muslims to settle in whatever
regions of the empire they happened to reach, making a special
provision in Syria for the distribution of agricultural lands to the
Andalusians.[79]

Thus the last wave of Muslim exiles from Iberia provided no
grist for imperial mills. Neither the Ottomans nor the Sa'dians
grouped the immigrants into organizations determined to roll back
the frontier of Latin Christendom. No doubt the corsairs of the
Maghrib found their ranks swelled by numerous Morisco recruits.
These new exiles added to the mixture of human motivations the
bitter ingredient that earned early seventeenth-century privateering
such a bad reputation. Yet Muslim freebooters, armed with the
technology of the sailing ship and raiding as far north as England,
Ireland, and Iceland, did not provide the cutting edge for Turko-
Muslim armadas.[80] Where the Hispano-Muslims were absorbed in
North Africa as individuals or as self-conscious units, they mostly
added to the strength of local Islamic society. Correspondingly, their
absence from the Spanish side of the border made a desert in some
regions and everywhere hastened the process by which Iberians
separated themselves from Islam and Africa.

Had the Ottoman sultan risen to the level of his early sixteenth-
century performance, the Hispano-Muslims might have had a less
severe experience. One reason why this did not take place was that
the empire responded most conservatively to a structural crisis
involving naval technology. As the naval history of the last half of the
sixteenth century demonstrated, the fleet could not be effectively
employed beyond Tunis. Either a new type of vessel with a greater

range of operation had to be designed, or the navy had to develop Mediterranean bases far enough away from Istanbul to store supplies for the armada. After 1580 Ottoman leaders did not explore either of these alternatives.

Meanwhile the continental inclination of Ottoman policy let viziers march off to Persia with funds that might have gone toward building new ships. Then the opponents of the Ottomans licensed corsairs who, although causing great damage, posed no territorial threat to the empire. Since these Christian privateers spread the burden of defense, the empire placed the work of coastal protection in the hands of provincial officials.[81] Naturally the viziers reduced the flow of resources to an unemployed imperial fleet and relegated its few serviceable units to lesser tasks such as supplying eastern armies and protecting the annual convoy from Egypt.[82]

While the Ottomans reduced the size of their navy, English and Dutch ships entered the Mediterranean with the naval technology they had developed on their ocean voyages. Ottomans, who had an opportunity to observe the new technology close at hand in Istanbul during 1593, noted the range and especially the heavy armament of the English sailing ship.[83] Moreover, the purveyors of this new maritime equipment entered the Mediterranean as friends, not as enemies. Yet the Ottomans still did not adopt the sailing ship. Even when Christian corsairs began to use the Atlantic technology, the imperial officials clung to the galley. It was true that for a long time the contest between the galley and the sailing ship was not necessarily an unequal one. The maneuverability of oared vessels in light winds, their ability to beach, and the short range of sixteenth-century cannons often gave them the advantage over the heavier sailing ships.[84]

Furthermore, the most serious naval challenge to central regions of the empire at the turn of the seventeenth century came not from the sailing ship but from the small riverboats, the *shaykas*, of the Cossacks. In that essentially Black Sea conflict the galley was far more suitable than the sailing ship for the task of destroying the river bases from which the large numbers of dugouts were launched.[85]

If the nature of warfare at the turn of the seventeenth century offered no reason why the technology of the oared vessel ought to have been overturned, the reduction in the size of the imperial fleet also acted to preserve old ways. When northern sailors entered the Mediterranean to engage in privateering, many of them used North African bases. There they taught the sailors of the Ottoman frontier the arts of the Atlantic sailing ship. Had the naval success formula been operating as it had in the age of expansion, the center would have drawn these men and their technological experience to the heart of the empire. But after 1580 the decentralization of the empire and the economic pull of the robust Atlantic economy acted as a centrifugal force. At this same time the empire narrowed the opportunities for sailors. In 1581 the sultan appointed Cafer Paşa, an administrator who had not risen through the ranks of the corsairs, governor of Algeria.[86] Ten years later, upon the death of the admiral, Hasan Paşa, the highest naval offices in the empire began to fall into the hands of Ottomans who had not acquired their experience as corsairs.[87] This reshuffling of the criteria for advancement paralleled not only the disappearance of naval expeditions west of the archipelago but also the decline of the Ottoman military spirit. Then, as the central administration's interest in the abilities of the corsairs waned, so also did the march warriors lose respect for the authority of an inactive sultan whose prestige rested upon his descent from a long line of holy warriors.

The question why Ottomans failed to accomplish the transfer of Atlantic naval technology from their western Mediterranean periphery to the center of their empire when they had earlier moved with such alacrity to acquire powder technology must be understood within a much larger cultural framework than can be dealt with here. Yet, as with so many other problems concerning Ottoman history, not even the beginning of an ideological framework is present.

For whatever impetus it might give to such an investigation, it seems that the conservative policies of the Ottoman government were most to blame for the widening gap between Europe and the empire in the ability to exploit the naval fringe. Viziers applied no major resources to acquiring a cannon and sailing technology that had gone far beyond the experience of Ottoman artisans, because such a decision meant modifying the structure of the navy and of society itself. On the seas the Europeans took the initiative in organizing commercial advantages for the benefit of the state, whereas the Ottomans devised no imperial policy resembling the emergent mercantilism of the European states. Equally, there were no attempts to create a Muslim form of state capitalism to exploit maritime commerce. And, curiously for a civilization with a long record of international commerce, there was little evidence of the merchants collectively pressing the Ottoman government to either defend or expand their rights.[88] This suggests that the commercial

community valued the economic and political stability the Ottomans
brought and therefore deferred to rather than challenged the Muslim
ruling class. Ottomans in turn treated the merchants like the great
tribes: they were to be taxed, kept in their place, and discouraged
from forming confederations. The result on the frontier was that the
new technology benefited corsairs, who operated not as robber
merchants on the edge of an expanding commercial economy but as
parasites whose hosts were the declining trade of the Mediterranean
and the booming economy of the Atlantic.

By the first quarter of the seventeenth century, complaints from
every coastal region of the Mediterranean bore witness that the
unusual severity of corsair violence was related to a Mediterraneanwide event. During the following two centuries, when the guerrilla
warfare of the freebooters was regularly practiced in the Mediterranean, the Barbary corsairs—the Scourge of Christendom—won
the reputation for being the most violent of these lawless seamen.
Yet modern research has shown that many of the most successful and
peripatetic corsairs based in North Africa were Atlantic seamen.[89]
Also neglected in older descriptions of privateering was the degree
to which Latin Christendom participated in this form of warfare.[90]

In 1601 the Council of State in Madrid deliberated whether it
would be profitable to license corsairs to operate against the Turks.
Two years earlier the Venetian ambassador in Spain had filed a
complaint against the viceroy of Sicily's wife, the Duchess of
Maqueda, who had armed several corsairs that the Venetians felt
would surely raid Christian as well as Turkish shipping. Ignoring the
general threat to commerce that any stimulation of the little war
represented, Philip III's advisers listed the reasons why the crown
ought to continue to send corsairs against the Turks. The Council of
State first noted that the precedent for using the corsairs was
established by Charles V. Proceeding to the objections of the
Venetians, the council took into consideration the Republic of Saint
Mark's position in the eastern Mediterranean: her proximity to the
Turks and her trade with Muslim territories exposed Venice to the
anger of the Ottoman sultan. On the other hand, the success of
Christian privateers hurt the enemy, gained respect for Spain, and
gave hope to the Christian captives held in Muslim territories. By the
same token, the corsairs acted as a standing navy, augmenting the
power of the imperial fleet just as the Turkish flotilla profited from
the effectiveness of the North African galleys. Certainly the time was
ripe for deploying the privateer against the Turk; for the campaigns

in Hungary exhausted both the Ottoman army and the sultan's treasury at the same time as civil war raged in Anatolia.

On 28 March 1602 the Council of State agreed upon the need to license the corsairs. Reciting the familiar arguments for justifying war against Islam, the Habsburg officials concluded that the corsairs would do damage to the Turks and Moors. This form of warfare had the additional advantage that it did not involve the dignity of the state. Because the Turkish and Moorish privateers against whom the crown wished to direct its naval effort were not public enemies, they could be attacked privately. Moreover, the enemy counterattack from such a low level form of combat would not result in great damage to the state. In addition, the crown would have a naval force in arms paid for out of the yield of frontier conflict, not from imperial revenues—an important point for a government whose record for combining military activity with financial disaster was well known. On the basis of these arguments the crown approved the licensing of the corsairs who, it was hoped, would avoid attacking friendly ships.[91]

Universally condemned by the Mediterranean states of the seventeenth century, the corsairs accomplished what both Habsburg and Ottoman empires required of their frontiersmen in a period of disengagement. Despite a vigorous commerce in prisoners and captured goods, the privateers turned Mediterranean coastal waters into a no-man's-land that, although full of passageways, nevertheless kept the populations of each civilization within the boundaries of their lands. The dangers of travel and the difficulty of dealing with many officials restricted the unbelievers who made the perilous journey between one face of the frontier and the other to a small number of specific categories—merchants, prisoners, ambassadors, and religious leaders. Missionaries no longer left for Africa with much hope of capturing new souls; the New World was infinitely more promising. In addition, the trade in slaves—so much a part of frontier economics among both Christian and Muslim privateers—limited men of religion to serving those who were unfortunate enough to be caught in the corsairs' nets.[92] No better example of the freebooters' role in intensifying the differences between the Mediterranean civilizations can be found than the history of Venice's difficulties with privateering. As Spain's Council of State observed, the glory of the Republic of Saint Mark depended upon its trade with the Muslim Levant. When corsairs from North Africa and other areas of the Mediterranean raised the costs of protection along Mediterranean shores at the same time as European companies carved out profitable oceanic routes for the Asian commerce, the yield from the trade through the Mediterranean declined.[93] Linked with the structural changes that displaced the Mediterranean world from the centers of commercial innovation, the appearance of the ubiquitous corsairs did not imply that the societies of the two civilizations shared a common internal history. Quite the contrary; for the war of the corsairs also screened those remaining acts by which the political representatives of the two religions forming the Ibero-African frontier accentuated the differences between the societies of the two Mediterranean civilizations.

Seven: ISLAM EXPELLED

Above all it was because the Morisco had remained inassimilable.
Spain's actions were not inspired by racial hatred ... but by religious
and cultural enmity. And the exposition of this hatred, the expulsion,
was a confession of impotence, proof that the Morisco after one, two or
even three centuries, remained still the Moor of old. ... He had refused
to accept western civilization and this was his fundamental crime.

Fernand Braudel, *The Mediterranean*

With the fall of Granada in 1492, Catholic Spain placed its political,
but not its cultural, boundary on the southeastern edge of the Iberian
Peninsula. Swiftly the victors cast out the vanquished military elite
and came to grips with the complexities of an alien society.[1] Unlike
previous Christian rulers of Muslim Valencia, the monarchs of
Catholic Spain did not accept a mixture of civilizations. The forced
conversion of Muslims, the mass expulsion of border populations,
and the destruction of Islamic institutions soon testified to their
aggressive consolidation of a unitary state and society, struck off
in harsh opposition to Islamic civilization. All this was accomplished
in Spain at a time when the intensification of warfare between the
Habsburg and Ottoman empires caught the Hispano-Muslim border
population in a struggle between states whose bureaucracies starkly
defined the social differences between two congealing versions of
Mediterranean civilization. Attracted by the resurgence of Islam
under the imperial administration of the Ottomans in North Africa
and rejected by a Spanish society increasingly hostile to any form of
cultural ambiguity, the Hispano-Muslims could do little to avoid the
complex pressures that would draw them into conflict and sweep
them out of their homeland.

127

In 1492, however, the cultural gap between Spain's two civilizations was not yet of great consequence. How to govern the newly conquered populations absorbed the attention of the royal bureaucracy. For the crown, the end of the Reconquista complicated the task of ruling the peninsula's Muslim minority. An irregular passage of Islamic territories into the hands of Christian rulers since the eleventh century had given birth not to one large Mudéjar society but to a mosaic of separate groups. This spasmodic progress of the reconquest had also formed a varying set of relationships between the subjected populations and the aristocracy the crown had established as the local rulers of its new Muslim subjects. In Valencia, for example, the attachment between the Muslims and the Christian nobility had begun in 1238 and had evolved into a stable form.[2] In contrast, the ties between the bulk of the Muslim population in Granada and their Christian overlords started only during the last years of the fifteenth century. Equally, the attitudes of the Old Christian population toward the Muslims differed substantially between the two realms. In Castile a fierce adherence to the values of the Reconquista sustained a more militant approach toward Mudéjar society than in more cosmopolitan and Mediterranean Aragon.[3] Taken all together, the Islamic community in Spain on the eve of the sixteenth century could be divided into four groups: the Mudéjares of Aragon and Catalonia; Castile; Valencia; and Granada. Among these regional divisions of the Muslim community those of Valencia and Granada stood out for both their size and their cohesion.[4]

Last to be conquered, the former Naṣrid kingdom of Granada became the first to experience radical change. Causes for the turbulent nature of Granada's social history after the fall of the Alhambra are not hard to find. A long history of survival as a Muslim state left behind a tradition of independence that the Valencian community had lost. Since the bulk of the Muslim population in the new province lay along a mountainous coastline not far from Muslim Africa, Christians believed—with plenty of reason—that Granada could easily become the focus of anti-Christian activity in Spain. Castilian crusading traditions then merged with a clear need for security to produce a firm conquest policy that at once deterred rebellion and perpetuated religious hostility within Granadan society. Conflict between Muslims and Christians was therefore more likely to arise in the lands of the former Naṣrid sultanate than in other realms of the Catholic kings where the polyreligious settlement of a much earlier conquest had become a fundamental part of social life.

Already the troubles of Spanish Jewry indicated that the old communal life built around autonomous religious groups was about to collapse. Beginning with the massacres of 1391, the intolerance of Spanish Christians for the Jewish community and for those of Jewish parentage who had converted to Christianity soared. Old Christians brooded over the high position many of the Conversos had maintained in Spanish society. By the middle of the fifteenth century, when the atmosphere within the peninsula had become charged with religious fervor and when the pressures associated with the formation of a modern state had increased, the hostility between the Old Christians, the Jews, and the Conversos boiled over into anti-Semitic legislation in Valencia (1412) and popular demands in Toledo for the exclusion of Conversos from public office (1449). Old Christians then applied the first of the decrees on *limpieza de sangre*— purity of blood—after the Toledo riots of 1449 as a means of marking the social distance between those who were truly Christian and those who were not.[5] This formal means of describing loyalty through the examination of lineage made the process of assimilation more difficult.

Social movements stimulated by the reconquest intensified this imbroglio. As it had before, expansion attracted to the edge of Muslim territories an aggressive and upwardly mobile element from Christian society. Everywhere there were those who wished to take the possessions of the defeated and acquire the prestige that would legitimize their newfound wealth and power in the presence of the older Spanish nobility. In fifteenth-century Castile the distinguishing traits of these ambitious frontiersmen were a warriorlike attitude toward non-Christians and a pride in the purity of their own Christian ancestry. When, like the Jews, men from the Muslim upper classes converted and somehow managed to retain their social standing and wealth, they limited the opportunities of Old Christians who wished to acquire new status and wealth and thus forced the New Christians to become ardent champions of the Christian regime. Conversely, the desertion of former Muslim leaders in an hour of need angered the members of the community they had left, producing a deadly situation in which the loyalties of both the convert and the faithful to their respective groups increased the difficulties of moving between the religious societies.[6]

By the last quarter of the fifteenth century the Catholic kings began to exploit the dynamics of Spain's internal social frontier for the benefit of the state. From July 1477 to October 1478, Queen Isabella

listened in Seville to the sermons of Alonso de Mojeda. Enemy of the
Conversos, the militant priest called upon the state to counteract the
danger represented by the lax acceptance of Christianity among
the Jews. Soon after leaving the Andalusian city, the queen joined
her husband in a petition to bring the Inquisition to Spain. On the
first of November 1478, Pope Sixtus IV granted a bill authorizing the
Catholic kings to establish such an organization in Spain. By 1483
the scale of the state's involvement in matters of religious loyalty
became evident when the Inquisition acquired its bureaucratic form.
The Consejo Supremo de la Inquisición, the new organization for
religious investigators, acquired three ecclesiastical members and an
inquisitor general, all selected, unlike the medieval tribunal, by the
crown. This new arm of royal power was eventually applied to the
entire realm in such a way that it became the only institution whose
authority extended over all of Spain at the time Granada fell.[7]

On 31 March 1492, the Catholic kings ordered the expulsion of
the Jews—an entire religious community. Though both a victory for
religious uniformity and a statement of social radicalism, the royal
command left the problem of the Conversos unresolved. To decide
upon their social admissibility, now that the obviously Jewish
element had been excised, the crown possessed a bureaucracy whose
principal charge was maintaining Christian orthodoxy, especially in
those territories where Old Christians did not predominate. Spectacular in operation, the Inquisition would earn a reputation for the use
of terror in the service of Latin Christendom. Yet the novelty of its
establishment was not its tortures or the ceremonies of the auto de
fé but the way the Catholic kings exploited the religious and social
tensions of the conflict between civilizations to extend the power of
central government by imposing cultural uniformity. The Jewish
community was merely the first element of the old polyreligious order
to migrate in response to the actions of a state whose bureaucratic
organization showed that it was more willing than ever to tinker
with the shape of society.

Although the removal of the Jewish community from Spain did
not touch Muslims—the Mudéjares—nevertheless Castile was well
on its way toward defining them out of Christian society. From the
laws enacted before 1492 concerning their position in Castile, two
basic themes can be extracted to show how the crown's administrators perceived the Muslim subjects. For them, Islamic society was
tolerated only because it had both formidable external allies and a
royal grant of protection. This defense of a foreign element was

couched in the language of feudalism: the crown personally guaranteed the safety of Muslim communities, and each king renewed that grant as a legal duty owed to loyal vassals, But because the Mudéjares belonged to another dangerous civilization, they were to be administered in a way that would not contaminate Christians.[8]

With great power on its side, Castile circumscribed the life of its Mudéjares—17,000 to 20,000 persons in the reign of Isabella—within increasingly well defined social boundaries. As with the Jews, it was a long-established practice to prohibit Muslims from inhabiting the same quarters as Christians. In 1480 Isabella strengthened the walls of Muslim enclaves—the *morerías*—when she revived the legislation requiring that Muslims maintain separate quarters and wear distinctive clothing. Although unevenly enforced, other legislation prohibited Mudéjares from taking Christian names, from eating with or visiting Christians, and from sending medicines and special foods to Christians. Over time, this social exclusion of Muslims from the mainstream of life in Castile confined the Mudéjares to peripheral jobs in urban areas. A cultural defensiveness born of defeat, a preference for endogamy—first-cousin marriage—and a declining economic position then cemented the minority character of the Mudéjar quarters.[9]

In all the legislation bearing upon the Muslim communities, the spirit of the struggle between civilizations lay beneath the surface. Separateness was to be maintained so error did not creep into the ways of Christian society. On the other hand, the rules of behavior for the Mudéjares also rested upon another strong consideration: the hope of conversion. Obtaining a victory for Christianity involved not only presenting the Christian message to the Muslims but also creating conditions favoring a change of religion. Conversion to Islam was prohibited, and Muslims' migration from the clearly unpleasant conditions of their life in Castile was checked. Isolated and immobilized in the middle of a solidly Christian population, it was believed the Muslims would soon come to the faith through the good works and suitable preaching of the church. Yet this path narrowed suddenly when religious emotions were stirred by Converso riots and by the half-modern, half-medieval campaign for the conquest of Granada.[10]

On the surface the crown's social policy toward Islam seemed unchanged after Granada was conquered. Administrative plans for the new subjects were based upon the idea that the Muslims who remained would be loyal vassals like the Mudéjares of Castile. Yet the defeat of the last Muslim state in the peninsula occurred in circumstances different from the earlier movements of the Hispano-Muslim frontier. Since the removal of the Naṣrid regime completed the reconquest, the event naturally heightened the popularity of both the crusade against Islam and the social struggle to eradicate the influence of non-Christian civilization in Spain. On the other hand, the realities of administering a large block of solidly Muslim peoples located in a strategic spot close to Africa compelled the crown's officials to permit freedoms for the practice of Islam that had not been seen in Castile for some time. Thus the conditions of the conquest placed conflicting claims on the energies of the crown's officials while raising the expectations of Hispano-Muslims that life would go on somewhat as it had in the past.

From 1484 to 1489 the outline of the Castilian conquest state in Granada emerged in the texts of the capitulations that were signed with the Muslims after each major advance. In every case the primary objective of the concords under which the defeated surrendered was to establish Spain's sovereignty. First the new subjects recognized the Catholic kings as their rulers. In turn, the Mudéjares received the protection of the crown on the condition that Christian captives be released. All important military facilities quickly passed under the control of the new government. In general, the Muslim population of cities also had to divest themselves of their weapons, especially firearms. But if the new Mudéjares lived in open areas where security depended upon defense by the male members of a household, then some personal weapons could be retained. In no circumstances were Muslims to bear arms in frontier areas or to establish any contact with their coreligionists on the non-Christian side of the military border.[11]

During this same period the social content of the various agreements with the conquered maintained an official respect for the laws and customs of Islam. Local administration remained in the hands of Muslims. The leaders of the non-Christian society were to be consulted in matters involving contacts between the two communities. Legal problems that crossed religious lines, social difficulties attached to the migration of Christian and Muslim peoples, and tax matters all were to come before the local notables of Muslim society. Understandably, a dual administration emerged to carry out the orders of Granada's Christian rulers. However, a hierarchy already existed between these two institutional orders. Despite the thin veneer of Christian rule, all realized that behind the crown's administrator stood the power of a victorious Christian army.[12]

Near the end of Granada's life under Islam, the Catholic kings signed capitulations that embodied wholesale concessions to the operation of Islamic social institutions. While the political and military pillars of the earlier compacts maintained themselves in the new agreements, the sections covering the preservation of Islamic customs and religion were amplified. Wishing to keep the Muslims on the land and at work in the cities, the Christian rulers pledged to maintain irrigation networks and markets. Muslim religious buildings and the economic institutions supporting them were not to be disturbed. Even the call to prayer could be made in Granada. Islamic law was to be applied in cases involving the faithful. Taxes were lightened. Scrupulous respect was to be shown for personal rights. The inviolability of the home, the maintenance of private property, and the conservation of local administration all guaranteed that the daily life of Muslims would remain relatively unchanged. Christians were not to enter mosques without permission. The high point of official support for Islamic culture was reached when the crown guaranteed not to force renegade women to return to the Christian faith and to insure the sincerity and freedom of choice of any Muslim women who became Christian "for love."[13]

If the thrust of Castilian administration in Granada at the time of the reconquest seemed to maintain Islam in Spain, its support of the emigration and the conversion of Muslim elites had an altogether different objective. In earlier agreements, the Catholic kings offered these Muslims the opportunity to move either to Africa, to reconquered lands away from the frontier, or to Castile. Of the three alternatives Africa clearly held first place. As the last Islamic outposts in Granada fell, the crown made emigration to North Africa easy, offering free passage and, in the end, monetary inducements to those who wished to leave Spain. For the elite who remained, the crown provided rewards that, if not sufficient to encourage conversion, at least discouraged rebellion. In some cases, as with the Venegas family, the new administration succeeded in attracting to its side important members of the Muslim political class. The object of this conservative conquest policy, then, was to deprive the community of its elite either by encouraging their flight to Africa over a "bridge of silver" or by appealing to their cupidity.[14]

A year after the conquest of Granada, unknown persons spread the frightening news that the Catholic kings intended to drive the Muslims from their homes. Ferdinand and Isabella quickly recognized the disruptive impact such an idea might have upon the administration of their new territories. Unwilling to add the expenses of another campaign in Granada to the heavy charges upon state finance, the crown instructed its officials on 3 December 1493 to inform the Moors of their right to a place in the society of Catholic Spain. No one was to make statements that might result in any offense, injury, or maltreatment of the Muslims who resided in Granada.[15]

Three men—Hernando de Zafra, López de Mendoza, and Hernando de Talavera—dominated this new Christian administration of Granada and at the same time represented the major components of Castile's conquering society. Hernando de Zafra had risen from the lettered class to a place of influence at court through his loyal work in the bureaucracy. Given the responsibility of running the province, the royal secretary favored a greater effort to rid Spain of the Muslim elite, to populate Granada with Old Christians, and to continue the crusade in Africa.[16] The Count of Tendilla, member of the aristocratic Mendoza family, whose power the crown had reason to watch, assumed the military duty of defending Granada. At the same time, he acquired large estates worked by Muslim peasants.[17] The third appointee of the crown, Hernando de Talavera, was the first archbishop of Granada. A Converso himself, the priest had some sense of the cultural gap dividing a Muslim community that he was pledged to evangelize.[18]

For eight years Ferdinand and Isabella maintained through these men the agreements under which the Muslims of Granada retained their religion. To force the conquered to be baptized was neither a just nor a pious act; and, realistically, an aggressive evangelization of the Moors would only provoke another expensive war, which would then impede the process of assimilation.[19]

Nonetheless, Hernando de Talavera began the work of conversion. An advocate of persuasion rather than compulsion, he attempted to publicize his Christian message through religious debate. Under his direction, Christians who knew Arabic and could deal with the cultural medium of Islam began to obtain some converts from the other society. But the success of the archbishop's program rested on the assumption that the clash between civilizations had not reached a level that excluded individual persuasion.

One major reason why the campaign of evangelization had such a short life was the crown's encouragement of immigration. Between 1485 and 1498, 35,000 to 40,000 new inhabitants from the north were settled on lands taken from the Naṣrids.[20] This visible evidence of Christian society's demographic momentum heightened the internal

tensions within Granadan Islam. Other signs that the policy of
toleration masked a strong desire at court to reduce Islamic society
rapidly through an unvarnished use of state power appeared when
Ferdinand issued a decree on 31 October 1499, requiring that all
Moorish slaves who had been baptized since the surrender of
Granada be freed and their owners compensated. In the same
breath, the crown sweetened the process of conversion by decreeing
that recently converted Christians were to receive both their legal
share of any inheritance under Muslim law and the portion that
would normally go to the crown.[21]

Until the turn of the sixteenth century, the Muslim community
behaved, despite the crown's repeated violation of the capitulations,
as though coexistence with the Christians were possible.[22] In
October 1499, however, the climate of relations between the two
cultures changed dramatically when Jiménez de Cisneros preached
to former Christians—renegades—converted the mosque in the
Albaicín quarter of Granada into the church of San Salvador, and
engaged in other symbolic acts whose anti-Muslim character was all
too clear. Religious emotions reached a flash point when, according
to the Spanish historian Mármol, the renegade daughter of a converted Muslim cried out publicly that the Christians were forcing her to
accept their faith.[23] No doubt the story was a good piece of propaganda for a cultural world with a high order of sexual jealousy;
nevertheless, Mármol's suggestive language did expose the social,
as well as the sexual, intentions of the Christian invaders.[24]

The surface events that attended the first revolt of the Alpujarras
(1499–1500) obscure many of the reasons for the Muslim violence.
Paradoxically, the removal of the Granadan political elite through
conversion, emigration, or imprisonment did not undermine the
cohesion of Islamic society. Far from stripping the community of its
leadership, the destruction of the Naṣrid ruling class had placed
public responsibility for the operation of society in the hands of
Muslim religious men and elders. This assumption of a political
role by a local religious and social elite gave over the direction of
affairs within the community to men whose world view and duties
made them more sensitive to the social and religious boundaries of
society than were their predecessors. These new rulers of Granadan
Islam did not look upon Cisneros's conversion campaign as just
another political skirmish. In the cultural milieu of late-fifteenth-
century Granada, it was perceived by the Muslim elders as an intolerable attack upon religion and society.[25]

Alarmed by the fury of the 1499 rebellion, the crown demanded an explanation from Cisneros. The militant priest, according to Spanish sources, refused to be cowed by violence. Condemning the rebellion, the archbishop argued that the revolt should be regarded as a breach of the capitulations, and that this act of disobedience should permit the state to offer Muslims the harsh alternative of baptism or exile.

It was the crown rather than Cisneros that then made another radical decision on social policy. In February 1502, the Catholic monarchs called for the conversion or expulsion of all Moors in the kingdom of Castile by the end of April 1502. Given the numbers of Muslims living on Spain's southeastern periphery, the state's action must have been thought out in far more detail than previous historical accounts imply.

Whether the decision was planned or not, the crown offered all but a handful of the Muslim community only one choice. Those who wished to leave Spain were to surrender their sons under fourteen years of age and daughters under twelve. Only the wealthy could avoid this cruel requirement. Even if Granadan Muslims could preserve their families, life in North Africa, the goal of most immigrants, would be hard. Consequently most Muslims accepted Christianity. It was not difficult. The speed with which the priests flung the holy water over the converts left the newly baptized with the feeling that the sacramental act of the Christians had little meaning.[26]

Shorn of their old protection, subjected individually to the laws of a different society, and confronted with Old Christian immigrants, the newly converted Muslims—the Moriscos—dissembled their religion and held fast to Muslim social customs as a means of sustaining their identity.[27] This superficial acceptance of Christianity caused no end of trouble for the party of religious orthodoxy. Unwilling to charge large numbers of the New Christians with apostasy, to launch a massive campaign of evangelization in an area that was officially Christian, or to attack the frontier aristocracy who often defended the Moriscos against the centralizing institutions of the state, the advocates of rapid assimilation intensified their campaign against what they could identify as wrong: Islamic social practices.[28]

Once more the Muslims of Granada sought aid from the east, from the emerging champion of Sunnī Islam—the Ottoman empire. In an Arabic poem, the Hispano-Muslims explained to the sultan, Bayezit II (1481–1512), how the Christians had compelled the faithful to dissimulate in order to preserve true belief. Stressing their intention to remain among the believers, the Moriscos called upon the Turko-Muslim state to intervene on their behalf. While the Spanish Muslims waited for their deliverance, they accepted sorrowfully the injustice of a world that let Christians act against Muslims in a manner so much in contrast with the mild treatment the infidels received while living under Islam.[29]

Here and there in the poetical appeal to the Ottomans the Hispano-Muslims drew a vivid picture of the Christian war against Muslim society. Aside from the symbolic defilement of Islamic territories—church bells in the place of the oral call to prayer—the most revealing evidence of the depth of the frontier conflict comes from the verses that condemn the Christians for tampering with the Muslim family.

Islamic society in fifteenth-century Spain did not have a family structure resembling the "European" model with its delayed marriages, sizable amounts of celibacy, and small conjugal families; rather, it possessed a strong sense of social solidarity that rested upon the patriarchal extended family and larger kinship units—the *linajes* (bloodline relationships).[30] Two distinctive features characterized the extraordinary stability of these structures in Muslim Spain, as elsewhere in the Islamic world: the maintenance of social identity by a line of descent running from parents to children on the male side, and the advancement of the extended family's interests through carefully planned marriage alliances.[31] When, therefore, passages in the Muslim ode to the Ottoman sultan commented upon the dropping of the veil, the arranging of forced marriages not sanctioned by Islamic law, and the exchange of Muslim for Christian names, the poet signaled real social distress. It may have been true that the Granadan bard only wished to rally holy warriors around the standards of Islam; yet the regularity with which other Muslims and Christians repeated the same message tended to support the truthfulness of his charge.

Sometime before his death in 1543, the Ottoman admiral Hayreddin Barbarossa dictated his memoirs. This lengthy account of wars against the infidels in the western basin of the Mediterranean, the *Gazavatname*, despite its polemical nature, is a major source for the sixteenth-century history of the Hispano-Muslims.[32] Early in his manuscript the famous Turkish corsair gives his listeners a brief account of how Christians took advantage of Muslim weakness in Iberia to defeat the true believers and destroy their society. Once in control of the Islamic community, the Christian conquerors changed mosques into churches and forced Muslims to practice their religion secretly. Only in hidden places could the faithful pray and teach their children to read the Koran.[33]

Hayreddin takes note of Catholic Spain's effort to impose cultural uniformity. As the *Gazavatname* describes it, the Spanish monarch called his priests to a meeting and asked them whether it was good to have Muslims living among Christians. The priests replied no to this reference to the old policy of coexistence. Pressure ought to be put upon the Muslims, they argued, because they threatened the security of the state by aiding the Turks and by undermining respect for Christianity with their Islamic practices.[34]

The Ottoman corsair pursues his Islamic version of Granada's history with a description of the crown's attack on the Muslim extended family. Christians, Hayreddin alleges, separated the children of Hispano-Muslims from their families and trained them in Christian ways. More alarming was the effort to block Muslim women from marrying within their communities in order to keep the Islamic population from increasing.[35]

In Spain this program to obliterate the memory of Granada's Islamic past by destroying social institutions gathered steam in 1505. The practice of the public bath, the celebration of circumcisions and weddings, the hidden observance of Muslim dietary laws, the use of clothing not worn by Old Christians, and other customs of the pre-Christian era were prohibited by royal decree.[36] One of the leaders in this social crusade was the Duke of Alba. During 1514 he subjected his Moriscos to a vigorous program designed to break the means by which Muslims reaffirmed personal ties. They were to marry like Christians, use Christian names, avoid heating baths on Friday, open the doors of their houses on selected days, shave their beards and cut their hair in the Christian manner, discourage the use of the veil, and finally cease celebrating holidays and wedding engagements in the Muslim manner.[37]

What checked the implementation of these draconian measures in the first half of the sixteenth century was the difficulty of their enforcement and the fear that economic dislocation would result. In Granada, for example, the poverty and isolation of many Muslims prevented the wholesale adoption of Old Christian clothing. The other major reason why social homogenization was not accomplished overnight was that Muslims provided cheap and skillful labor for irrigated estates owned, especially in Valencia, by aristocrats.[38]

Aragonese Muslims, however, could not escape the forces molding the early modern society of Spain. In 1519 the plague broke out in Valencia, setting off a revolt by urban groups—weavers, spinners, artisans—against the city officials and aristocrats who had fled the outbreak of sickness. Paralleling the uprising, the rebellion of the Comuneros in Castile created a widespread climate of violence that soon expanded from a protest against the influence of Flanders in Spain and the irresponsibility of the Valencian aristocracy into a social revolution. Radical leaders in Valencia, like Vicenç Peris, organized angry urban groups into Germanías, or brotherhoods, and directed them against the nobility. During the civil conflict that followed, the Muslims, faithful to the bonds of their polyreligious society, supported the aristocracy in its military actions against the brotherhoods. At an earlier time, when Valencian Muslims occupied a less well defined, second-class position in society, such an alignment of forces might not have turned this classic riot against the upper classes into a religious pogrom. But in 1521 the internal war within Valencia ripped the cloth of Christian-Muslim compromises apart at the seams.[39]

On 4 July of that year a Franciscan monk preached the crusade against Islam. Quick to see the advantages such a claim had upon the emotions of the Christian population, the leaders of the Germanías launched a campaign for the baptism of the Muslims. The revolutionaries profited doubly from this adroit exploitation of the religious issue: their movement was legitimized in terms of the crusade; and the Christianization of the Muslims deprived the aristocrats of their feudal rights over the non-Christian communities.

The result of this confrontation between the heirs of the thirteenth-century conquest and the newer society of the Old Christian cities was bloody. After the victory of the Germanías at Gandía on 25 July 1521, rebel bands raced through the countryside of Valencia forcing Muslims to submit to baptism under conditions that made the conversions in Granada seem tame. Although some Christians showed compassion for the victims of this social explosion, the level of respect for the other culture—or more often the indifference toward Islam—disappeared during the course of the Germanía. Mosques were turned into churches with the most perfunctory motions, and newly converted Muslims were compelled, as though it was possible to change their civilization overnight, to attend Christian services in their former places of worship.[40]

Like the first revolt of the Alpujarras, the Germanía ushered in a
new era of social history for the Valencian frontier. It demonstrated clearly that the pressure for the exclusion of Islamic culture
had much wider social support, especially in urban areas, than that
provided by the ambitions of prominent ecclesiastical and bureaucratic figures. In addition, the rebellion exposed the weakness of
the union between the frontier aristocracy and the Hispano-Muslims
when circumstances accentuated the cultural differences between
Muslim and Christian communities. The crown would not fail to
profit from such a situation.

When the Valencian revolt was suppressed in 1522, Charles V
found himself in a delicate political position. The rebels had baptized
thousands of Valencian Muslims who, since their conversion to
Christianity was not freely chosen, should have reverted back to
Islam. Yet the state itself had just brought the Muslims of Granada
and Castile into the Christian fold under somewhat similar conditions.
To perpetuate religious inconsistency within the realm would surely
exercise the purists and strain the resources of Charles V's own
authority. On 13 September 1525, the emperor issued an imperial
order excluding from Spain all Muslims except slaves and instructing
the nobles to cooperate in the rapid conversion of the remaining
Muslims. On 25 November of that same year Charles V signed a
decree for the expulsion of all Moors from Valencia by 31 December
and from Aragon and Catalonia by 31 January 1526. With no real
alternative before them, Spain's remaining Muslim population
became Christian. Again the result of imperial action did not so
much remove Islamic culture from the peninsula as extend the
authority of the imperial bureaucracy and create conditions under
which the rapid assimilation of the New Christians would proceed—
or so it seemed.[41]

With the official expulsion of Jews and Muslims between 1480 and
1526, Spain ended a long history of mutual toleration—convivencia—
between religions and between portions of its society. This double
divorce was not solely related to the victory of religious emotion over
reason or to the closing of Spain's internal frontier; for the pressure
to achieve religious unity had mounted hand-in-hand with population
increases within Castile and the arrival of a period of strong economic
growth.[42] These powerful developments could have produced
additional changes in the complexion of border society; but after
1526 Charles V's ability to rule Spain increased, while the opening of
other imperial frontiers relieved some of the pressure on the south-

eastern border. The assimilation of the New Christians quickly descended on the list of state priorities; Charles V, with vast imperial projects in mind, had little interest in disturbing the seignorial order in Granada and Aragon.

The hold of tradition on the border peoples led to a prompt redefinition of old social and political alignments and a continuation, in new clothing, of the social war between the two civilizations. Aristocrats with substantial landholdings along the frontier became the defenders of the newly converted Moriscos, who under a veneer of Christian customs preserved the substance of Islamic ways. Few Old Christians believed in the sincerity of the average Muslim's conversion. Those who were not members of the nobility could not refrain from sympathizing with efforts to alter the Moriscos' social customs, the grounds upon which the Old Christians could both challenge the continuing influence of Islam and contest the privileged position of the nobility.[43]

Economic motives also inspired campaigns against the Moriscos. Though the details have not yet been studied, the economic history of relations between the Moriscos and the bulk of the Old Christian population on the frontier featured a relentless shift in wealth from the New Christians to the immigrants from the north. To a certain extent the border nobility checked this polarization of society where their properties and income might be threatened. Yet the stiff judgments levied against Morisco property in Christian courts and the parallel complaints of New Christians on the quality of local justice indicated the drift of events.[44]

Deserted by the lords who emigrated or converted, the Granadan Moriscos saw all too clearly how little they could directly influence the course of events. With political leadership in the hands of Christians who controlled the main sources of Granada's wealth, the former Muslims resigned themselves to positions in the lower ranks of society. They became artisans, city laborers, small farmers, peasants, and other middling and poorly rewarded workers.[45] Their social and economic rank, moreover, was fixed, unless they wished to become truly a part of the Spanish community and move up the social scale by either marrying into Old Christian families or joining the church.

Their world could also be dangerous. Once converted to Christianity the former Muslim faced other terrors, for establishing Christian credentials was difficult, and the punishment for a suspected apostate was extreme. Seeking allies, the Moriscos found the frontier aristocracy, led by the Mendozas in Granada, ready to offer some protection against the charges that the more militant representatives of the church and the bureaucracy leveled against their social order. Thus arose the strange combination between the victors and the vanquished along the social frontier.

With the church, however, an opposite process took place. The hierarchy of the Hispanic priesthood reacted to the shallow conversion of the New Christians with a call for a more vigorous attack upon their separateness, which, given their conversion, could be phased only in social terms. Armed with powerful institutional weapons such as the Inquisition and the civil law supporting the church, priests marched against the vestiges of Islamic society. With the aid of the aristocracy, the Moriscos were often able to buy off or temper the measures that the militant elements within the church wished to have enforced during the reign of Charles V. Frustrated by the refusal of the Moriscos to assimilate, the Christians held meeting after meeting—Granada (1526), Toledo (1539), Guadix (1554), and Madrid (1566)—at which they defined and redefined the differences between the Moriscos and the Old Christians so that the enemy might be known.[46]

Bureaucrats entered the struggle for the right to shape the conditions of the frontier later than either the church or the aristocracy. When Hernando de Zafra began his administrative work for the crown in Granada during 1492, there were two laws to be applied— Muslim and Castilian—and therefore two administrations to be operated. The quick conversion of the Muslims to Christianity officially removed the presence of Islamic law but implicitly denied the Moriscos a position in the new Granadan administration. Old Christians then flooded the newly established bureaucracy with requests for assistance in one form or another. Since the crown had an interest in repopulating Granada with loyal subjects, government favored their requests. This partiality that the clerks displayed toward the Old Christians and the feelings of illegitimacy the Moriscos harbored toward an alien law inevitably forged a bad relationship between the lettered classes and the New Christians.[47]

As the century progressed, these divisions between the members of this frontier society did not blur but became more intense. Moriscos were increasingly viewed by Old Christians as covert Muslims. Not only did they border on being apostates, but according to their critics they also employed witchcraft, divination, and other sinful forms of worship. Always ready to return to their former religion, the New Christians conspired with the foreign enemies of the crown, the corsairs of North Africa, the Ottomans, and later on the Protestants to threaten Spain internally and externally. Old Christians, moreover, saw the customs of the New Christians not as a purely Spanish phenomenon, but as part of a uniform Islamic civilization. The persistence of these social practices therefore represented an intrusion into Christendom of a powerful alien civilization, an issue on which no quarter could be given at a time when the armies of Süleyman the Lawgiver threatened Europe. Similarly, as the temperature of religious dispute soared during the second half of the sixteenth century, this distrust that the New Christians evoked seemed to threaten the physical and moral ordering of Spain.[48]

By mid-century Old Christians had identified the crucial cultural differences that separated the New Christian from Spanish society. Leading the list of social errors were the clothing and language of the Moriscos. Even though men in the cities had adopted the dress of Old Christians, women and the rural Morisco population continued to wear clothes of the Muslim pattern. Especially repugnant to state and religious officials was the use of the veil by Morisco women. New Christians also maintained an intolerable linguistic difference between themselves and the Old Christians even when they lost the ability to speak Arabic. Mispronouncing Castilian and writing their new language with crude capital letters, the Moriscos set themselves apart by failing to adopt two of the most visible traits of an emerging national culture.[49]

If clothes and language were the obvious means of discerning who was socially acceptable and who was not, there were other less pronounced Morisco customs to be destroyed if the New Christians were to be brought into the mainstream of Spanish life. Former Muslims, holding to the dietary laws of Islam, avoided eating pork, drinking wine, or buying meat from which the blood had not been drained. By extension, carrots, radishes, and turnips did not find their way into Morisco markets because they were regarded as food for pigs, whose flesh is denied to Muslims. Hygienic customs of the Moriscos, in particular the use of the public baths, which, in the words of the synod of Guadix in 1554, "were nothing more than the houses of the devil," scandalized the ecclesiastics. Church officials attacked those and other Islamic customs through a system of fines.[50]

In the face of such an assault on their traditions, the Moriscos carried out a silent revolt. Turning inward to oppose attempts to break their kinship relations, they created a dual system of names, Muslim to indicate their place and lineage in their own society and Christian to satisfy the social policies of their masters. What preserved the cohesion of Morisco society at lower levels was the control that elders exerted over the extended family. To maintain bloodlines and religious loyalties, family heads made marriages keeping in mind the traditional Islamic virtues of kinship solidarity. In the home, where repressed emotions could be expressed, Morisco children picked up their parents' hatred for the Old Christians and thus provided a generational continuity to the cultural division. With the gap between the two communities already large, the heads of households found it easy to maintain separateness: they stiffened their control over Morisco women; they avoided Christian institutions where possible; and they nurtured a silent anger against traitors that exploded in the revolt of 1568.[51] Finally, a millenarian expectation that help would come from the outside provided hope for this beleaguered society.[52]

But whatever the strength of this reaction to the events, the Muslim community also displayed evidence of internal disintegration. The emigration of its elite stripped Granadan Muslims of their high culture and exposed them to a powerful alien civilization with little means of fighting back. Moreover, the absence of a generally recognized cadre of leaders at the upper levels of Morisco society encouraged the spirit of division in the particularistic Muslim community and abetted the political objectives of the Christians.[53] Forced to the edge of society by pressures well beyond their control or understanding, weaker elements among the New Christians showed signs of distress. Since drinking wine was a Spanish custom and a positive sign of conversion, the conquerors approved its sale to the conquered. For the cities of Granada in 1500 and Guadix in 1505 and for the province as a whole in 1515, the state soon discovered the necessity of acting against the public drunkenness of New Christians.[54] Another response of the Moriscos to a world that was not theirs was banditry. Here the robbers of the Sierras—the *monfíes*— increased their activities to such an extent that they became a serious problem on the eve of the 1568 rebellion.[55]

Until 1556 the tolerant policy of the emperor, Charles V, and the strength of the conquest aristocracy maintained the old frontier order. But all this changed when Philip II began his reign. Between his accession in 1556 and the concluding sessions of the Council of Trent in 1563, the dogmatic spirit of the Counter Reformation entered

Spain. This age of the statutes of *limpieza de sangre* and the persecution of allegedly Protestant groups in Seville and Valladolid brought to power men who were determined to impose religious uniformity.

In the same span of time, Ottoman Turks reinforced the wave of religious militancy when they advanced dramatically in North Africa and the western Mediterranean. Whether it was true or not, Old Christians believed that the Moriscos aided the Ottomans.[56]

After 1552 a conjunction of militant religion, political fear, and local economic problems attached to the declining Granadan silk trade prepared the ground for another social explosion in southern Spain. A primary industry of the city of Granada and a principal economic activity in the Alpujarras, by the mid-sixteenth century the silk industry had suffered permanent damage. Its export trade was prohibited in 1552; its raw material declined in quality; and its economic health was undermined by a massive increase in taxes between 1561 and 1564.[57]

Under these conditions, the President of the Audencia of Granada, Pedro de Deza, announced the publication of a *pragmatica* on 1 January 1567, designed to remove once and for all the cultural differences between Old and New Christians. Within three years the speaking, writing, and reading of Arabic was to cease. All contracts in Arabic were to be voided, and books in that language would be examined to see that their contents supported right belief. Moriscos were to dress in Castilian clothing, and their women were to be unveiled. Celebrations in the Muslim manner could not be conducted, even secretly. Friday was not to be regarded as a holiday. Moorish names and surnames were forbidden. In short, the fabric of crypto-Islamic society was to be destroyed.[58]

A year passed before the Moriscos reacted to what they now believed would be a serious campaign to enforce cultural conformity. On Christmas eve, 1568, a band of mountaineers scaled the walls of the Alhambra, while another group entered the city through one of its gates. Proclaiming a new era of righteousness in the name of God and his prophet, Muḥammad, the rebels called upon their coreligionists in the Albaicín quarter of Granada to rise up against the Christians. There was a disappointingly small response. Nonetheless, the news of the incident spread rapidly to the Alpujarras, where the tougher mountain people rallied to the cause of the rebels.

Treated in great detail by Spanish historians, the short-lived rebellion of the Moriscos—24 December 1568 to the autumn of 1570—was remarkable not for its military character, for it was a short and dirty little war, but for its political and social consequences. Politically, the war in Granada undermined the power of the Mendoza family and elevated the importance of the alliance between the bureaucracy, the church, and Old Christian society while removing the Morisco community as a force in the life of the province.[59]

Though the Morisco revolt was nothing more than a flash in the pan on the military level, the extraordinary expression of violence that accompanied the uprising underlined the deepening cultural division between the two civilizations. Only the sudden and uncontrolled release of long-repressed anger mixed with a rising fear and hatred of an alien social order can explain the vicious behavior that accompanied this collapse of a polyreligious society.

At every opportunity the rebels attacked the cultural representatives and symbols of the other society. Moriscos executed Christian priests, being especially hard on those members of the church who came from Morisco families. Just as the rebels eliminated the missionaries of the other society, so also did they destroy the visual symbols of the Christian religion—the churches. Intoxicated with their sudden freedom, the Moriscos systematically profaned the Roman Catholic religion. Iconoclastic assaults on the interiors of churches were accompanied by burlesque performances of the mass designed to parody the rites and beliefs of Latin Christendom. Wherever Old Christians were unlucky in their resistance, the hint of their social cohesion often drove the victors to extremes. Despite local friendships, Morisco rebels sporadically killed their prisoners, sold them into slavery, or exacted a supreme form of revenge—executing men in front of their wives and children.[60]

Old Christians behaved no less violently. Whipped up by the demagoguery of lower clergy and state officials, they executed Morisco hostages and seized the property of New Christians. The brutality of the Old Christians was matched by the undisciplined behavior of the Spanish soldiers, who repeatedly turned their military campaign into raids against Morisco lives and property. Even the state did not regard the repression of the rebellion as a war to pacify populations whose labors would be taxed as soon as the army restored security. On 19 October 1569 Philip II gave the Spanish army the unlimited right to take booty from the Moriscos in a war of blood and fire. On 1 November 1570 he ordered the expulsion of the Morisco survivors from Granada.[61] If the state could not destroy the influence of Islam in peacetime, it would do it through war and the relocation of populations.

A radical act by any standards, the expulsion of the Moriscos in 1569–70 drastically reduced Granada's crypto-Muslim community. Favored by Deza, the campaign to root out the Moriscos from the province, to expropriate their property, and to scatter them among the larger population of Old Christians in other regions of Spain began under the command of Don Juan.[62] The process was not without its bloody incidents, and 70,000 to 80,000 Moriscos reluctantly left their homeland.[63] Only a few loyal New Christians of high social standing were allowed to remain—Pedro Venegas, Gonçalvo Zegri, Geronimo de Palaçios. Even for them the criteria for residence in Granada had a cultural edge: service in the war against the Moriscos, high personal sacrifices for the crown, marriage into Old Christian families, and prominent public behavior in the manner of an Old Christian.[64]

Philip II gave the bureaucracy the formidable tasks of expelling the Moriscos, preventing their return, and repopulating the province with Old Christians. Royal administrators paid more attention to the first two requirements than to the last. Frequent cadastral surveys and numerous documents of all varieties demonstrate the care with which the crown maintained both a control over the property of the expelled Moriscos and a blockade against the resurgence of Islam in Granada.[65] In Galicia, Asturias, and the environs of Leon and Burgos, the agents of the repopulation council extolled the virtues of life in the south, promising immigrants the cattle and agricultural implements necessary to begin farming. Soon the new settlers from the well-watered northern regions of Spain found themselves in strange territories that required elaborate irrigational techniques. For a while the crown lightened the tax burden of the new cultivator.[66] But soon the relentless need for money drove taxes up above the level the Moriscos had paid. Northern colonists also discovered how quickly choice Morisco lands passed into the hands of the original Old Christian population rather than being made available for the new settlers. Discouraged by the rough demands of life in the Alpujarras or other mountain regions, many of the cultivators left.[67] Gradually, however, the population of the province increased either through natural growth or through the covert return of an undetermined number of exiles.[68]

These drastic changes in the composition of Granada's population opened a new chapter in the social history of Spain's Muslim border. Expulsion did remove a dangerous element from a region now threatened by the expansion of Ottoman power into North

Africa. After 1570 no disloyal population stood ready in Granada to welcome the Turks from North Africa; and the mountain ranges of southeastern Spain no longer sheltered rebel bands whose actions could tie down royal armies.[69] But the cost of unifying the cultural and political frontiers in southeastern Spain was high. Although Granada had not quite become a desert, the revolt and the uprooting of populations depressed even further the economy of a once-prosperous region.[70] This deliberate disruption of society along the border also had its price in terms of forgone solutions to one of Spain's major internal problems: the expulsion of the Moriscos from Granada had established a precedent for other regions heavily populated with Moriscos.

Whatever the long-run implications of the Granadan upheaval, the exile of the New Christians raised two new questions: Should the Morisco community in Aragon be allowed to remain on the southeastern border in light of the Turkish advance in North Africa, and could the exiled Moriscos of Granada be assimilated by submersion among the Old Christians of Castile?

Against the expectations of many, the Moriscos of Aragon did not rise up against the crown during the war in Granada. What seems to have prevented an explosion in Valencia, where a substantial number of New Christians resided, was the strength of Aragonese traditions, the special history of its Morisco community, and the organizational failure of the rebel elite. When the cities and towns rose up against the nobility during the Germanía, the aristocracy defeated their opponents and thereby tightened an old bond between the lower rung—now crypto-Muslim—of society and the seignorial regime. Another major difference between the Valencian social order and that of pre-1568 Granada was the absence of an important Muslim—or Morisco—population in the cities. The slow ruralization of the Valencian community after the thirteenth century not only isolated the Muslims somewhat from the economic tensions of urban life in the second half of the sixteenth century, but also gave them a degree of cultural invisibility not present in Granada. Aragon, moreover, preserved a healthy concern for its independence throughout its long history before the Union of the Crowns in 1469. Thus the institutions of the central government—the royal bureaucracy and the Inquisition—appeared not only as threats to the privileged classes but also as a foreign encroachment upon Aragonese society.

Nonetheless, the objection to the lingering influence of Islamic society made its weight felt in Valencia as it did elsewhere. The aristocracy, however, protected its seignorial privileges after the baptisms of 1526 by obtaining from the crown a grace period of forty years during which the New Christians were to be instructed. With some care the Inquisition acted to propagate both the faith and the power of central government. Characteristically, it was the acquisition of Morisco lands by the Inquisition that caused the nobility to rain protests upon the crown in the Cortes of 1533, 1537, and 1542. A political compromise between the center and the Aragonese periphery of Spain, however, stipulated in October 1571 that the Inquisition would refrain from seizing the property of Moriscos being tried for heresy if an annual payment of 2,500 ducats was tendered to the tribunal. In the same document, a system of fines, with a limit of 10 ducats, was established to punish the inattention of Moriscos to their religious duties as Christians. This financial rather than social solution to the religious and political strains created by the times proved satisfactory—for a while.[71]

During the long period between 1526 and the end of the Morisco rebellion in Granada, the attempt to evangelize the New Christians in Aragon floundered because of both political and social opposition. In 1534 the inquisitor general, Manrique, launched a program to educate Morisco children and to provide schools where they would learn Christian doctrine. By 1564, just before the end of the forty-year grace period, the Cortes of Monzón alarmed the crown with a report that every plan for the instruction of the converts had failed. Archbishop Matín de Ayala responded to this news with a moderate program, proposing to publish the catechism in Arabic and again to set up schools for the instruction of Moriscos. Philip II also joined in the effort to find a peaceful path through the religious and political thickets created by the failure of the assimilation campaign. In contrast to his actions in Granada, he called upon the Inquisition to lessen the severity of its approach to heterodoxy in Aragon; still, Muslim ministers, teachers, and midwives were not to be tolerated. Meanwhile the archbishop of Valencia, Juan de Ribera, strove in 1568 to make religious service among the Moriscos attractive.[72]

An increased toughness toward the Valencian Moriscos did emerge during the 1570s. New methods of using informants and new proposals to close off the Moriscos from coastal regions and to disarm them were symptomatic of an increasing tension. Yet when internal violence came in Aragon between 1584 and 1588 it pitted the mountaineers against the Moriscos and had no more than local consequences. Both the strength of the Aragonese aristocracy and the fragmentation of the New Christians apparently inhibited rebellion during the last years of Philip II's reign.[73]

If inquisitors watched the Moriscos of Valencia with greater care after 1570, the church also redoubled its efforts to lift the exiled Moriscos of Granada to the level of good Christians. The archbishop of Cordoba was one of those so inspired. On 15 January 1573 he sent Philip II a detailed program of the measures he had ordered to assimilate the Morisco within his diocese. No better example can be found of what lay at the base of the Iberian reconquest; for the archbishop's program called for an institutionalized annihilation of Morisco society.[74]

Moriscos were first of all to be taught pure Christian doctrine, on Sundays and at Christian festivals. This not only subjected the New Christians to a different religious calendar but also prevented them from interpreting the Christian message in terms of Islamic beliefs. No less important was the need to envelop the new convert in the symbolic and sacramental order of the Catholic church. Parish priests were to be notified of all births so they could baptize the infants promptly, with more ceremony than usual. Attendance at mass was required of all New Christians, and they were to behave in church like Old Christians.

Far more was required of the Moriscos than participation in the ceremonies of the church. Plunging ever deeper into the cherished privacy of Muslim family life, the archbishop admonished his vicars to be extremely discreet so that women would confess sexual relations. In general, priests must be firm with Moriscos, calling for true, not superficial confessions. Though adults might mask their real beliefs, the young could be properly indoctrinated; therefore Morisco children of four years and older would be placed with Old Christians in order that they might be properly schooled. Sacristans were to see that Moriscos did not hide their offspring in the fields to avoid Christian instruction. On that same point, the father would bear the responsibility for training his children in the faith. Contrary to the practice in Islamic society, where formal religious ceremonies were dominated by males, the family was to attend mass together.

The bishop of Cordoba did not restrict his proposals to religious matters, but also entered fully into the social arena. New Christians were to be dispersed among Old Christians so that the extended family linkages characterizing Islamic society could not be renewed. Marriages were not to be arranged among relatives, and wedding ceremonies must be celebrated according to Old Christian practices.

This point was to be watched carefully, since the engagement ceremony and its celebration was an important part of Islamic culture. Moriscos were to dress like Old Christians and to butcher their animals in the Christian manner, without draining the blood from the carcass. No one was to speak or write Arabic. Moriscos should not celebrate Muslim holidays. In particular, their form of dancing and singing should be prohibited, for they often used words with double meanings and gestures by which they mocked the Christian religion. They should not be compelled to make offerings on Sundays and at festivals; rather, they should be treated with Christian charity and not be called dogs or *Moros*—Moors. A fine should be provided for such acts. Finally, the Moriscos should be checked every six months or, better, every three months, to see whether they were assimilating the ways of the Old Christians.

Reports from both Andalucia and Valencia soon demonstrated that a Morisco society maintained by informal traditions was still impervious to the bureaucratic acts of the state.[75] In Aragon, as elsewhere in Spain, this failure of the Moriscos to adopt Old Christian ways worked dialectically to increase the difficulty of their entry into Christian society. Even after the Hispano-Ottoman truce of 1580, the Morisco was still regarded as a potential source of major violence. His industry became not a sign of his useful place in society but of his avariciousness. His frugal mode of existence marked him not as a person forced by circumstances to live on the periphery of society, but as a miser. Finally, the fertility of Morisco women was both a sign of the animallike sexuality of the other civilization and a warning that the New Christians were a population threat that could make the Old Christians a minority in their own land. In the presence of such a powerful negative stereotype, there was little incentive for the Old Christian to provide the Morisco with a marriage partner who would carry the former Muslim over the threshold of Latin Christian civilization.[76]

Aware of their increasingly isolated position among Old Christians, the Moriscos attempted what the archbishop of Cordoba had feared: a reinterpretation of Christianity that would preserve both their place in Spain and their attachment to Islam. It began with the discovery in Granada during 1588 of leaden books written in a curious Arabiclike script, the *Libros Plúmbeos*. The translation and publication of these tracts touched off an angry religious controversy between 1595 and 1597. Propounding an Islamic version of the Trinity—"There is no God but God and Jesus, the spirit of God"—the unknown

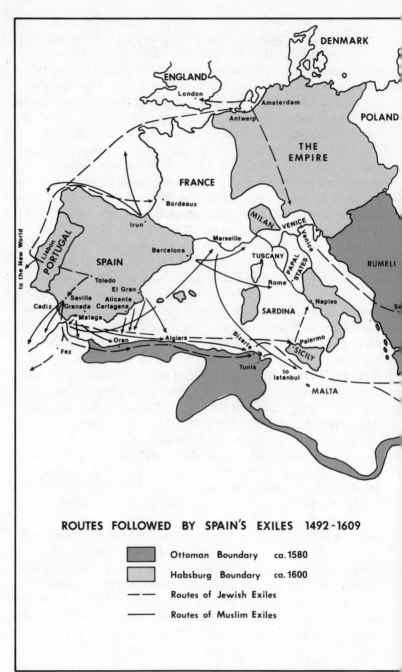

ROUTES FOLLOWED BY SPAIN'S EXILES 1492-1609

Ottoman Boundary   ca. 1580

Habsburg Boundary   ca. 1600

- - - Routes of Jewish Exiles

——— Routes of Muslim Exiles

Fig. 5. Routes followed by Spain's exiles, 1492–1609

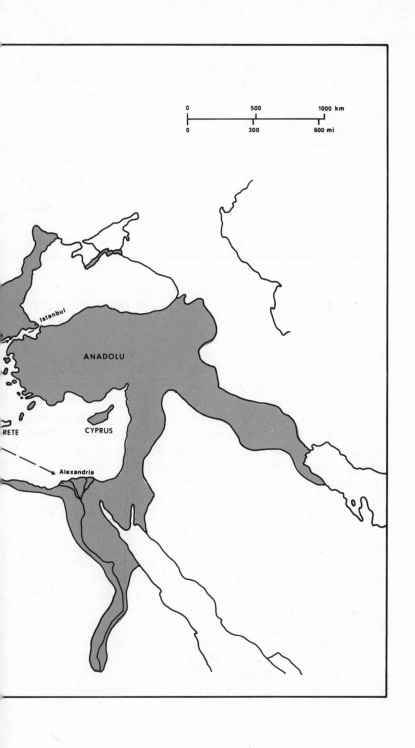

authors of the Lead Books tried to cast Christian dogma in terms of a strict monotheistic theology acceptable to Muslims. Thus the scriptural forgeries advanced the liturgical argument that the chalice used in the mass contained not wine, which was prohibited to Muslims, but water that the priest used to wash his mouth, face, and hands just as Muslims performed their ritual ablutions. To legitimize the presence of the Arabs in Spain within the framework of Christian religion, the writers of these religious documents depicted the invaders as God's chosen people and the bearers of the Christian message to Spain! Yet such a fanciful distortion of the past could hardly check the powerful movement toward the cultural unification of early modern Spain.[77]

Long before the Lead Books were unearthed, bureaucrats had planned the definitive resolution of Spain's internal war. As early as 1582, Philip II considered a proposal to eject all Muslims from the peninsula.[78] Although The Prudent King refused this advice, such a policy continued to be discussed at the highest levels of government as Ottoman power receded and as Spain plunged even deeper into the war in the Low Countries. By 2 January 1602, an outline for the removal of the Moriscos had been prepared. Economic and political difficulties during the early years of the seventeenth century then converged to provide a background for imperial deliberations on their expulsion. The debt repudiations of 1596 and 1607, and the disastrous course of the war in the Low Countries, sharpened internal conflicts between the aristocracy and the urban classes in Spain, intensifying the search for a visible scapegoat.[79] On the same day the twelve-year truce with the Dutch was signed—9 April 1609—Philip III ordered the expulsion of the Moriscos, while unknown persons floated the rumor that they were conspiring with their coreligionists in North Africa to launch another rebellion. Agents of the crown then supervised the emigration from Spain of some 275,000 New Christians, out of a population of perhaps 300,000.[80]

Preceded over a century before by the other casualties of early modern state formation, the bulk of the Morisco emigrants crossed the Ibero-African frontier at the beginning of an era of economic contraction to pick up the threads of their life in the cities of North Africa, where Muslim governments had rejuvenated Islamic civilization. This major human movement, organized and carried out by the Habsburg bureaucracy, completed the social changes that Spain had initiated on the Iberian side of the military border between Spain and Africa since the conquest of Granada in 1492. Victims of the rapid differentiation of Mediterranean civilizations and the religious wars of the sixteenth century, the Hispano-Muslims were soon absorbed by their North African coreligionists. The Spanish, whose own origin owed much to the confrontation with Islam, then resolutely turned their backs upon Africa and upon Muslim civilization, pausing only for a moment in the literary creations of the Golden Age to indulge in an amusing nostalgia about their oriental past.[81]

Eight: ONCE AGAIN THE EAST

Order to the governors of Tripolitania, Tunisia, and Algeria: the treasurer of the North African provinces, Mustafa, sent an administrative report to my Threshold of Felicity. All of the above mentioned provinces are Imperial Domains—havass-ı hümayun—and all their revenues are to be collected by the state treasury.

MD 39 215:436

Throughout the era of expansion, both Ottoman and Saᶜdian sultanates refreshed the great Islamic tradition in the Maghrib. This richly textured civilization of the eastern Mediterranean achieved its supreme social expression in the growth and embellishment of the frontier's capital cities. As urban worlds under the authority of a military elite with imperial ambitions, the sixteenth-century Maghribian cities became the arena where the values of a well-developed religious code of conduct mixed with the local population's fierce loyalty to its indigenous culture. Such a combination dictated social policies for the Muslim political elite that bore no resemblance to the Spanish movement toward a unitary state and a mobile society: Ottoman and Saᶜdian ruling classes preserved and even strengthened an underlying social particularism. Neither society nor the ruling classes approved efforts to impose universal loyalty to religious doctrine or to change the basic structure of society by homogenizing speech, controlling education, imposing uniform clothing, supervising marriages, or dictating the contents of ceremonies. Yet like their Iberian neighbor, Ottomans and Saᶜdians were responsible for a social formalization of frontier life: they played their part in sharpening the cultural division between an increasingly "Old Christian" Spain and an increasingly Islamic North Africa.

156

When Hayreddin Barbarossa placed the Ottoman sultan's name in the Friday prayer and on the coinage that circulated in Algiers, the territories taken by the corsairs became part of the Ottoman empire. Süleyman the Lawgiver acknowledged the extension of the "protected domains" as far west as the Central Maghrib by conferring the title governor of western Algeria—Cezayir-i Garp—upon the corsair. For the North African community, this seaborne arrival of the Turks was a revolutionary political event, comparable only to the Arab conquests of the seventh century.[1] Rather than coming from the steppe or the mountains, the Ottomans came from the east—from the heartland of Islamic civilization—at a relatively late stage in their history, to install an alien military class in place of local dynasties. Yet though this disembarkation of the Turks in North Africa was indeed unique, the conquest system they imposed upon society represented much less of a departure from the past.

For the development of newly conquered communities, Ottomans were guided by ancient Near Eastern precepts that emphasized the prosperous management of the state rather than the creation of a highly integrated society. The first of these ancient canons called for the paternalistic direction of society. Sovereigns—here Ottoman sultans—were to use their absolute power to remove conflict, to bring justice to the subjects, and to embellish the provinces, providing caravanserais, bridges, irrigation ditches, and other public works necessary for the relief of the poor and the support of religion. In the language of the Ottoman chronicler, the sultan was the shepherd of his passive charges, who were regarded protectively as the flock—the *reaya*.[2] This structural separation of government from the underlying population could and often did lead sultans and their slaves—the ruling class—to be contemptuous of the subjects. Yet both the moral demands of Islamic law and the experience of imperial rulers checked abuse of the *reaya*—or at least that was the hope of those who advocated good government. All this ancient wisdom was schematized for future rulers in a list of aphorisms that normally were written in a circular fashion to show the interconnected nature of good relations among the various units of society:

1. There can be no royal authority without the military.
2. There can be no military without wealth.
3. The subjects—*reaya*—produce the wealth.
4. The sultan protects the subjects by making justice reign.
5. Justice requires harmony in society.
6. Society is a garden and its walls are the state.

7. The foundation of the state is the Holy Law.

8. There is no support for the Holy Law without royal authority.[3]

Like the Spanish, the Ottomans first attempted to impose their political authority within the newly acquired lands. In all cases where the creation of a buffer state was not sought, as in Morocco, this meant the elimination of native rule. Before the late fifteenth century, the Ottomans had often integrated the military aristocracy of Christian lands, as well as the political elite of Muslim territories, into their ruling class. But with the passage of time the leaders of the conquered peoples tended to be excluded from the ranks of the Turko-Muslims, especially if they were Christians. A mature recruiting and training system for the slave corps of the army and a heightened sense of both imperial and Muslim identities after the conquest of Egypt in 1517 were two of the more important manifestations of this increasingly exclusive character of the Ottoman ruling class.[4] Since North Africa was conquered late in the history of Ottoman expansion, the Maghrib's political institutions—with the exception of Morocco—were subjected to the full force of a developed Ottoman government.

By the second half of the sixteenth century, provincial rule in North Africa meant, at the political level, government by men who had risen to power through success in border warfare or through the Turko-Muslim slave system.[5] Though conquered at first by naval vagabonds, whose attachment to the sultan was ill defined, Algeria quickly came under the control of Ottomans who had been trained in some prescribed manner, in schools, barracks, and courts, to be servants of the sultan. In the terminology of the empire these men were *kullar*: slaves who represented the sultan and who, in his absence, were rulers.[6]

This installation of a new political elite was the Maghrib's most visible sixteenth-century social revolution. These new men, the Ottomans, did not identify themselves with society at large, except as defenders of *Sunnī* Islam. To emphasize their independence of local kinship attachments, they set themselves off from the subject class through language, training, clothing, and their relation to the sultan, which was sustained on the basis of service, not on hereditary privilege. In addition, their offspring were excluded, except in unusual circumstances, from all but minor government positions.[7] Thus, a nonhereditary, single-generation class of warriors and administrators was superimposed over a North African population that differed from their overlords in language and social organization.[8] During the sixteenth century, these Ottomans tolerated no challenge to the paramountcy of this political and social organization of the peak of society. Power was exercised autocratically by the alien elite, with what appeared to be few concessions to local interests until the time of troubles at the end of the sixteenth century.[9]

If superimposing an imperial ruling class that was neither local nor aristocratic upon a large part of the North African community partook of violence, the introduction of the other hallmark of the Ottoman conquest system—its bureaucratic organization of imperial revenues—was somewhat less radical. As soon as the Ottomans controlled settled areas, military leaders dispatched clerks to extend the web of the Ottoman tax system beyond the walls of the coastal cities. Without fail, old families and tribes ferociously resisted this second rank of invaders because they threatened their economic status; they attacked the independence of a society based upon kinship or other local alliances; and they surely preceded other changes. In North Africa they were right. Yet nowhere in Ottoman administrative plans was there any idea that the empire would benefit by destroying a portion of the communal order, even when tribes continued to be disloyal and other communal units, the Jews, remained non-Muslim.[10]

Ottoman bureaucrats probably began their administrative organization of North Africa's fragmented society sometime before Hayreddin Barbarossa left Algiers on his voyage to Istanbul in the summer of 1534. In the manner of most conquerors, the Ottomans started off with a policy of leniency, *istimâlet*, after occupying a centrally located city within the new lands.[11] The object was to encourage tranquility and the resumption of economic activity by lessening the subjects' tax burdens. At about the same time, scribes were commissioned to supervise the registration of the population, of the sources of revenue, and of the customary laws relating to taxes and to the possession of land. This survey—the *tahrír* in Ottoman Turkish—whose results were entered in a detailed register, was usually undertaken by scribes who studied old records, traveled through the country, and examined local notables. When the requisite information had been compiled, the administrative personnel calculated the income the state could expect from new possessions, given past production and the reduced rate of the conquest taxation. This figure was then recorded in the register along with any special conditions pertaining to the administration of the province. The complete survey was then sent to the center of the empire, where provincial traditions were adjusted to conform to a more general Ottoman pattern. Once it was approved in Istanbul, the central bureaucracy returned a copy of the detailed register to the province, where it supplemented the holy law as a means of governing the territories of the empire.[12]

On the whole, this conquest fiscal system had a conservative impact. It is true that the Ottomans revolutionized the control of land: ownership of productive regions passed from the hands of numerous tribal sheiks to the Ottoman sultan. Yet peasants and tribesmen retained hereditary rights to the usufruct of their lands. Meanwhile, at this early stage of conflict Ottoman bureaucrats rewarded conquering warriors with revocable grants of taxes collected at the source, the *timar*. When these men went to the countryside to apply this system of military fiefs, they limited the ability of the existing social regime to change, because their military power prevented local upheavals and because their pay was based upon the assumption that the old society would remain in place. No massive, long-standing resettlement of the North African countryside paralleled this imposition of a veneer of conquest officialdom. Ottomans were known to have relocated tribes and repopulated cities; but the goal of resettlement in the Maghrib was culturally neutral: tribes were moved about to make the rural population more manageable. Economically, the Ottoman administration profited from rural stability when the removal of internal violence led to an increase of population and productivity of the existing social units— just what the imperial bureaucracy wanted in agricultural regions, where the main problem was the scarcity not of land but of labor.[13]

By no stretch of the imagination could the Ottoman fiscal organization of the central Maghrib be compared to the seignorial regime in Spain. Only the sultan theoretically "owned" the land in the Ottoman empire.[14] In practice, sultans permitted some private property to exist in North Africa,[15] and they also allowed the revenues of lands and other income-producing agencies to be dedicated in perpetuity to the support of pious activity.[16] During the age of expansion the sultan's slave could, in theory, pass on only a portion of his tax grant or his salary to his heirs; on the other hand, he could lose his income if he was delinquent in his duties.[17] Since no tribal or landed aristocracy capable of challenging the Ottomans existed after mid-century, and the bureaucracy was able to redistribute regularly the province's taxes, bonds of vassalage between the ruling class and the subjects did not develop. What did happen was that the bureaucracy applied a more fiscally sophisticated system that was related to the strength of the urban sector of provincial society.[18]

Beginning, perhaps, with the early Balkan campaigns of Süleyman the Lawgiver, the Ottomans adopted measures at the heart of their empire that everywhere made the bureaucracy more important. The relatively simple grant of tax rights at the source—*timar*—worked well for the age in which Ottoman generals relied on horsemen and the central bureaucracy had not fully matured. In the sixteenth century, however, the advancement of powder technology and the mushrooming of the empire obliged the Ottomans to expand the ranks of their urban-based professional soldiery, to acquire ever more expensive weapons, and to place greater emphasis on centralizing financial resources. Under these conditions the sultan wished to reduce the number of *timars* because they neither yielded the necessary revenues for the treasury nor supported what became the most powerful unit in the army, the Janissary corps. To accommodate the demand for money, which became voracious after the price revolution of the late sixteenth century reached Ottoman territories, the imperial bureaucracy laid great stress on producing revenue for the central government. All over the empire this meant a reduction in the number of *timars* and an increased use of the more elaborate fiscal device, the tax farm.[19]

With greater administrative efficiency in mind, the sultan dispatched his clerks to North Africa shortly after the reconquest of Tunis in 1574 to impose the fiscal demands of the late classical period upon the western frontier. In each province new tax surveys were conducted; three distinct units were designated for financial purposes (Tripolitania, Tunisia, and Algeria); and the administrative goal was clearly enunciated. All sources of wealth in the province belonged to the sultan, and the products of his imperial possessions were to be applied to the wages of the ruling class.[20] The Maghribian provinces had become, like Egypt, *salyane*—salaried—provinces.[21] Behind this administrative revolution lay the desire of the central bureaucracy both to extend its most advanced fiscal techniques to the rim of the empire and to increase the flow of money into the imperial and provincial treasuries.

From the Fezzan in Tripolitania to the oasis of Figuig on the edge of Morocco, tax farming during the second half of the century became part of a decisive shift of social relations between city and countryside within Ottoman North Africa.[22] Both Ottoman and modern scholars have commented upon the connection between the widespread application of this fiscal method and the waning power of the rural militia. Tax farmers and salaried troops—Janissaries— now collected imperial revenues under conditions that implied the solid predominance of the cities over the countryside. It was truly the beginning of a new era for Ottoman North Africa. Even the collapse of Istanbul's direct influence on the frontier after 1580 did not alter this internal social balance. The ascendency at the provincial level of urban society and its bureaucratic devices continued into the seventeenth century.[23] Sedentary culture had finally taken firm root in North Africa.

Just as the history of the Turko-Muslim fiscal system testified to the rising influence of the city, so also did the experience of the tribes under the Ottomans confirm both the power of urban society and the conservative character of Ottoman social policy. Once a military encounter with the Turks taught the kinsmen something about the deadly superiority of firearms, the tribesmen usually avoided combat, withdrawing to the highlands or to the desert where Turks found the pursuit unrewarding.[24] Victories by foreigners, however, compelled the kinsmen to delegate greater authority to their chiefs. Yet the rising power of the tribal leaders assisted the Ottomans. Far from excluding them from the political system, the Turks gave the tribal rulers the option of moving between loyalty and opposition to the Ottoman regime. The fragmented system of tribal politics, where each tribe had its opponent, then allowed the Ottomans to pit the chieftains of large tribal gatherings such as the Banu ʿAbbās and the Kūko Berbers against each other. At a less spectacular level, Ottoman *kaids* worked at a smaller version of the same structure, preserving their power as well as the authority of the sheiks by formalizing the divisions of tribal society for the benefit of an urban-centered regime.

Other ways of controlling the tribes were always available. The ancient tactic of turning the inner barbarian against the outer often lay beneath the surface of an Ottoman summons to the holy war. Most Maghribian states employed allied tribes to check other less loyal inhabitants of the mountains and the steppe. Ottomans continued this practice. They enlisted members of the Zwāwa Berber confederation as auxiliaries and granted tax concessions to allied tribesmen in order to create a buffer zone of friendly tribes around the cities and the agricultural sectors of the provinces.[25]

On another plane, the Ottomans employed the economic dependency of the rural communities upon the cities and towns to perpetuate their rule. In noncritical areas powerful tribes were often left alone. What the Ottomans did not do, however, was to relinquish control over the communications routes. These either came under the protection of allied tribesmen or were garrisoned at strategic points by detachments from one of the military corps. *Kaids*, meanwhile, organized the rural markets of the province so that they could exclude the rebellious not only from the place of exchange but also from the wider cultural world of Islam to which the Berbers and Arabs belonged. When the tribes of dissident regions—the Kabylia mountains or the southern steppe—revolted, an Ottoman economic blockade of the tribesmen through the domination of the routes and markets usually prevented tribal strong men from collecting the wealth necessary to maintain their authority. The high population density of the Kabylia region and the low agricultural productivity of the mountain slopes aided the Ottomans just as the barrenness of the steppe drove the Bedouins to compromise with settled peoples in order to exchange animal products, gold dust, slaves, and dates for the manufactured goods of the cities.[26]

One often misunderstood expression of the Ottoman willingness to live with tribal society was the *mahalla*, the annual campaign among the tribes to collect taxes. Janissaries, assisted by tribal allies, conducted the expedition. This Ottoman column not only reminded the tribesmen of urban power, it also offered rural leaders an opportunity to renew the honor of their tribe and the prestige of their own position by mounting a fruitless revolt and then playing a role in subsequent negotiations with the Ottomans.[27] The cost of putting down these gestures of manliness may have exceeded the revenues from the *mahalla*; yet this never drove the Turks to the extreme of eliminating the tribes. Doubtless, the real alternative to Ottoman rule in tribal regions would have been a free-for-all until some new leader with a religious message replaced the old order or until some unstable balance of power emerged between the elements of tribal society. As was indicated by the failure of the Mahdi in Tripolitania during the last decade of the sixteenth century and the Kūko rebellion of 1603-8, the tribes in the end preferred the Ottoman tax collector to the uncertainties of a revivalist movement or an alliance with Spain designed to excise the Turk.

What the Ottomans had done was to plaster a thin layer of imperial authority over a dynamic and yet stable rural society. The object was not to drag the kinsmen into a new era for which there were no guides, but to manipulate the balance of power in a highly fragmented society so as to produce in those regions the degree of tranquility necessary for the growth of urban life. But by becoming the supreme arbitrators of tribal affairs, Ottoman governors guaranteed the existence of the tribes; and, in a society where tribalism was endemic, such a limitation of change accentuated the divisions between the kinsmen, producing a crazy-quilt distribution of the tribes throughout the hinterland. This predominant social, but not political, role that tribalism played in North Africa was one of the traits that distinguished this Ottoman frontier from the center of the empire.

What happened to North Africa's cities under the Ottomans was as much a manifestation of the revival of urban Islam as was the pacification of the tribes. During the first quarter of the sixteenth century, Leo the African's picture of life in North Africa showed that the Muslim city had fallen on hard times. Ottoman governors and Saʿdian sultans reversed this decline of the social arena where Islamic civilization found its most comfortable expression.

Its location on the edge of the Mediterranean conferred upon Algiers, a previously undistinguished Maghribian city, the cosmopolitan advantages of most seaports. This coastal position put the inhabitants of the port in touch with the commercial and political events that drew the sailors of the Mediterranean basin along the coastline and out into the Atlantic Ocean. Yet unlike Cadiz or Seville, the maritime culture of Algiers remained predominantly Mediterranean. Until the late sixteenth century, when the arrival of northern sailors brought the naval practice of the Atlantic to Algiers, the dominance of Mediterranean ways stood out in the complexion of the port's population, in the commercial life of its merchants, and most characteristically in its lingua franca—the frontier language, made up of words and phrases of various Mediterranean tongues, that was spoken in the city.[28]

Algiers entered a time of rapid growth under the aegis of the Ottomans soon after the Barbarossa brothers penetrated the central Maghrib and killed the local ruler of Algiers, Sālim at-Tūmī. More than an isolated example of frontier violence, the execution of the Algerian leader signaled an alteration in both the politics and the social history of the city. Not only did this urban center pass out from under the protection of the Thaʿāliba tribe of the Mitija region, but the city became a major political center for the Ottoman empire in North Africa.

Under the rule of the Turks, Algiers entered a period of rapid expansion. At the beginning of the sixteenth century, Leo the African listed the population of the city as a respectable 4,000 hearths— 20,000 persons if we assume a multiplier of five.[29] After Hayreddin's followers defeated both the tribesmen and the Spanish, the economy of Algiers began to grow. Concurrently the pacification of the interior prevented the biological strength of the rural population from being dissipated in internal warfare. Since the high death rate of Maghribian cities ruled out any dramatic increase from within the walls of Algiers, the rural population reservoir now provided ample material for the growth of Algiers. Shortly after 1580, the Spanish priest and historian Diego de Haëdo recorded the population of the provincial capital as 12,000 houses, or 61,000 persons. Comparing this figure with the number reported by Leo, the population of the city had tripled in slightly more than half a century of Ottoman rule.[30] That this growth rate also corresponded to an increase in the wealth of Algiers is attested to by the Moroccan ambassador at-Tamgrūtī, who passed through the Ottoman port on the way to Istanbul at the end of the century and described the city as the richest in the Maghrib.[31]

Algiers impressed everyone with its military facade. Whereas the major city on the Spanish border, Seville, submerged its old fortifications with new buildings related in one way or another to commercial growth, Algiers bristled with structures dedicated to warfare.[32] At the beginning of the sixteenth century, Oruç Barbarossa initiated the construction of a new casbah on the high ground at the rear of the walled enclosure and above the former Berber fort. The wall itself—some one and a half miles in length—was continually strengthened throughout the period of warfare between the Ottomans and the Habsburgs. This sharp military rather than commercial image of Algiers was accentuated when governors repeatedly cleared away the houses and gardens near all fortifications.[33] With a good sense of how the Turks had impressed their military ethos upon Algiers, Haëdo compared the outline of this Ottoman border city to a crossbow.[34]

If the enclosed shape of Algiers pointed out its frontier role, its labyrinthine configuration of homes, markets, and mosques unmistakably placed it among the broad spectrum of Islamic cities belonging to the Turko-Muslim era. Overseen by a grim-looking casbah that symbolized architecturally the division between rulers and subjects, the inhabitants of Algiers lived in homes that descended from the high ground to the heart of the city near the waterfront.

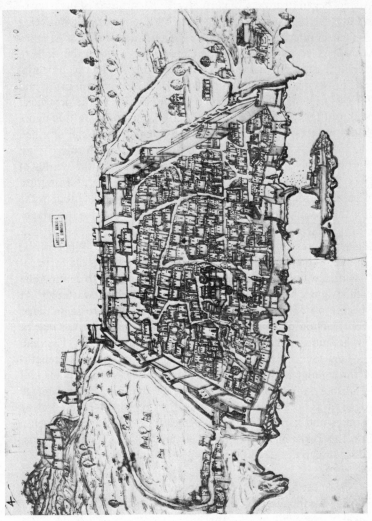

Fig. 6. The city of Algiers, ca. 1560. The irregular pattern of the streets is clear

Row upon row of closely packed, low-level white houses set into the land on terraces undulated down toward the sea, following curved streets suitable for camels and donkeys rather than for the carriages the successful classes in Cadiz and Seville used to mark their status. At the base of the city all passageways converged on the main market just above the congregational mosque to the west of the governor's residence. Like the pattern of other Islamic cities, the haphazard route of the thoroughfares did not reflect the rectilinear geometry of wide plazas and paved streets that the urban planners of Renaissance Europe demanded. Rather, the social concerns of a subject population relatively free to group itself into semiautonomous quarters on the basis of religion, origin, profession, and all other significant elements of social identity made up what only appeared to be an anarchical arrangement.[35] Finally, the congregational mosque of the Ottomans bore witness to the cultural influence of the eastern Turkish dynasty in religious matters. Its rounded white dome, circular minaret, and crosslike ground plan mingled the spirit of Anatolia and the Balkan frontier with the rectilinear minarets of North Africa's green-tiled mosques.[36]

In keeping with Near Eastern and Islamic traditions, the Ottomans attempted to make the city prosper through public and private works. Members of the ruling class commissioned the construction of major mosques and the attached buildings that together formed an architectural complex, the *imâret*, where both religious and social goals were pursued: Koranic schools, fountains, baths, and facilities for the poor were clustered about the main religious centers. Each of these focal points of formal religious practice (a Spanish map drawn during the last quarter of the sixteenth century indicates nine major mosques) supported men of religion who received salaries for duties ranging from teaching the Koran to officiating at funerals.[37] From time to time high Ottoman officials commissioned lesser public projects, constructing fountains or beautifying the tombs of either holy men or their own families. Not always so altruistic, Ottomans like Ramazan Pasha, the governor who ruled Algeria from 1574 to 1577, built large homes with luxurious interiors and fortresslike exteriors that stood in opposition to the opulent decoration the merchants of Seville lavished upon the outer walls of their houses.[38] The frontiersmen of the Turko-Muslim state also built the monuments of their profession. Two of the most significant of these Ottoman constructions that dealt with the less humane side of frontier life were the Janissary barracks and the prisons for the Christian slaves.

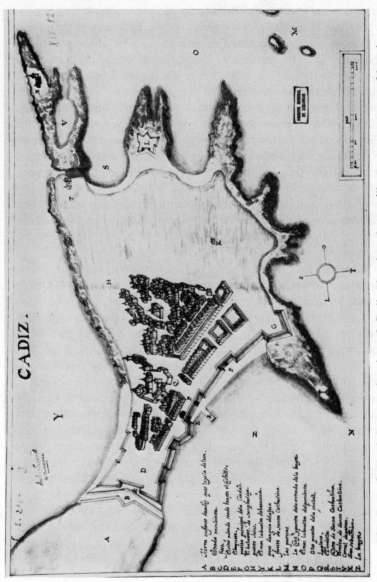

Fig. 7. A sixteenth-century drawing of Cadiz showing the rectilinear arrangement of housing

The Ottomans in Algiers conceded a small place in their scheme of administration to officially recognized posts held by town dwellers. No council with any legal standing represented the subject population. The government of the city during nearly a century of direct Ottoman control began at the threshold of the governor. With a personal staff modeled, with slight differences in terminology, on the Ottoman sultan's own palace cadre—chief deputy, doorman, treasurer, keeper of the horses, taster, secretary, chief paymaster, messenger—the governor both ruled the province and administered the city through personal contacts between the members of his staff and those who sought justice or privilege.[39] In the day-to-day operation of the city, however, the Ottomans again blended their imperial institutions with the culture of the frontier, borrowing the forms of management, as well as the terms, from the urban heritage of both the Hispano-Muslims and the North Africans. A _shaykh al-balad_, selected from Muslim elders, was responsible for the proper functioning of the city. Under his authority two subordinate officials were placed in charge of the orderly conduct of public activity: the _mizwār_, or chief policeman, and the _muḥtasib_, or custodian of public morality. In addition to these two posts, the _ağa_, or provincial commander, of the Janissary corps retained responsibility for the overall internal security of the city. When his men were not on campaign, they served as an additional police force, receiving in turn the fines levied for infractions of urban ordinances.[40]

On the judicial plane the Ottomans against struck a compromise between the frontier and the center of the empire. When laws or customs were violated, the police hauled the offender before the _kadi_, the judge, who administered justice in accordance with the holy law of Islam and the civil law, _kanun_, of the empire. In Algiers, however, the Ottomans divided the judicial arm of their bureaucracy between two Muslim officials: one judge for the Malikite rite followed by their Maghribian subjects who were Muslims and one for the Hanafite rite to which the ruling class belonged. Non-Muslims were judged by their own courts unless the legal matter involved Muslims, whereupon Islamic law prevailed.[41] If the judges decided upon punishment— European observers usually complimented the North African Muslims on the speed of their justice—then the _çavuşlar_, or attendants, executed the orders of the court.[42] Whatever the imperfections of this justice, the strength of Ottoman government and its urban orientation simply produced a much wider forum for the _Sunnī_ view of how Muslims ought to behave.[43]

Beyond the duties of these officials, the city possessed no institution that expressed any sense, historical or otherwise, of its independence. In place of the legal instruments that regulated the relations between city and territorial state in Europe, the Turko-Muslim ruling class relied upon an informal and personal system of control that was invisible to the foreign observer. All who derived some tidbit of authority from their position or had some social or religious prestige among the multitude of groups within Algiers—the notables of the city—collaborated with the Ottomans once their rule was firmly entrenched. These elders were largely committed to maintaining social discipline through a system of personal ties based upon convention rather than through the sanctions imposed on individuals by a complex judicial system as in Spain.[44] They therefore supported the limited authoritarianism of the Ottoman ruling class because the Turks both guaranteed the existence of the established order and relied heavily upon their managerial abilities.[45]

Aside from the Ottoman defense of the basic social order, urban notables had good economic reasons for an alliance with the Ottomans. Beyond the walls of the city the relative peace imposed upon the once-powerful tribesmen opened up a large interior market. In keeping with the practices of Near Eastern governments, Ottomans used this domination over the countryside to insure the supply of scarce raw materials at a fair price for a profusion of urban guilds. Within Algiers the ruling class exerted a great deal of energy to prevent economic instability through the control of prices and to avoid unemployment through public works projects.[46] These measures were all grounded upon the state's fear that rapid changes in prices would, as in the period of inflation, provoke urban disorder. Guildsmen and merchants did not fail to see how closely their affairs benefited from the policies of the Ottoman regime. Thus the actions of the provincial government and a guild structure linked to the heterogeneous nature of society prevented, except in extreme circumstances, the emergence of upheavals based upon economic classes. Moreover, this alignment of the guilds with the state coincided with the conquest of the countryside and the economic takeoff of Algiers. Taxes collected from the various arms of the provincial economy yield one measure of the capital's economic good fortune. According to Haëdo, by the 1580s the income of the provincial treasury was a respectable 400,000 to 500,000 ducats a year. This sum paid the salaries of the ruling class and, until the time of troubles, permitted the treasurer for the frontier to send an annual contribution of 25,000 florins to Istanbul.[47]

Even though the economy of the city grew during the sixteenth century, there was little indication that a thirst for wealth tended to dissolve social institutions. Similarly, the political turmoil that followed the Hispano-Muslim truce of 1580 did not overturn the corporate, rather than unitary, structure of society in Algiers.

"Turks" were the essential ingredient of the city's society. In the age of Barbarossa the Turks were adventurers; those recruited by the provincial government during the second half of the sixteenth century came to Algiers through a more formal process. Using an old procedure, representatives of the Maghribian military corps sent out recruiters to the coasts of Anatolia and Ottoman Europe, where they convinced young men of the advantages of life in the military corps in North Africa. Thereupon galleys carried those who had enlisted to Algiers. If they were to be enrolled in the Janissary corps, the recruits were issued new clothing, assigned a pay grade, and quartered in one of the Janissary barracks in Algiers. Soon they were distinguished from the rest of the city population by their professed loyalty to the sultan, their acceptance of Islam, and their Ottoman mannerisms: special clothing, an esprit de corps shown in their haughty, authoritarian demeanor, and, finally, their ability to speak some form of Turkish.[48]

Not all of the recruits to the various military organizations serving the provincial leaders were brought to Algiers under such pleasant conditions. The large numbers of renegades who flocked to the Maghribian port—the Turks-by-profession in the European sources—testified to both a general increase in population of the Mediterranean world and the success of the corsairs. Invariably from the poorer regions of the Mediterranean coastline—Calabria, Sardinia, Corsica, southern Spain—the renegades climbed a difficult social ladder when they converted to Islam: provided, of course, they were not caught by their former coreligionists. Welcomed into the Ottoman regiments with a simple ceremony, they were set off from the Janissary corps not so much by different clothing as by a standard of behavior that permitted them to retain customs—such as drinking wine—that were abhorrent to good Muslims.[49]

Sailors were the most heterogeneous of the warrior organizations. Called by a variety of names—Levanters, corsairs, and other less neutral terms—the seamen who served on the raiding galleys in the hope of obtaining booty formed the least organized of Algiers' military communities and were enrolled in no formal military organization. Converted to Islam superficially, if at all, the privateers survived on grants doled out by their captains until the raiding season began. Then their promotion depended entirely upon merit or, more accurately, upon luck. If fortunate in combat, they could move from the margin of the city's military society to become salaried members of the Ottoman naval organization in Istanbul.[50] Yet, like the military corps with whom they feuded, the corsairs became less interested in the attractions of Istanbul when the empire decentralized.[51]

Religion, not national origin, separated the subject class of Algiers into its three most distinguishable groups: Muslim, Jewish, and Christian. Of these religious communities, the Muslim was by far the most complex. At the top of the social order among the believers were the long-term inhabitants of the city. Granted tax concessions during the conquest and other privileges afterward, many of them had become prestigious merchants, religious leaders, or holders of tax farms. These men prospered under the Ottomans, founding family organizations that undoubtedly grew wealthy as the Turkish empire expanded. Yet compared with the booming business activity of Seville, the structure and scale of Muslim economic development lagged far behind: no *casa de contratación* emerged in Algiers. Long-distance merchants displayed a comparative lack of aggressiveness; they avoided the Atlantic world and retained old business practices that, if we can believe Haëdo's comment about the lack of record-keeping among the commercial men of Algiers, did not go beyond the social boundaries of the Muslim extended family. Nor did merchants challenge the Turko-Muslim slave system, which excluded urban notables from positions of high political power.[52]

Below the level of the merchant or tax farmer stood the artisans. The growth of this key element within society was fostered not only by the expansion of the city under the Ottomans but also by the migration of Hispano-Muslims to North Africa. Here, later waves of immigrants were especially important in bringing to the city carpenters, masons, gunsmiths, silk workers, tailors, and a host of other skilled workers whose home was the city and whose trades diversified and strengthened the existing guilds. Again the social contrast between this Muslim city and the commercial cities of Mediterranean Europe was strong. To the north, the aristocratic nature of society, the low status of the working classes, and the freewheeling movement of the economy had all but eliminated this old socioeconomic unit. It was the other way around in Algiers, where urban society had married ethnic, religious, and cultural variety to the division of labor among artisans. Every guild had its distinctive life-style, clothing, physical appearance, education, diet, recreation, and form of worship. A vital organ of society, guildsmen often attracted retired Janissaries to their ranks.[53]

But the alliance between the Ottomans and their prestigious Muslim subjects was not without its social problems. Gradually, marriage between Ottomans and local women expanded the number of children who had a direct connection with the ruling class—the *kuloğulları*. Excluded from positions of high rank, these offspring of the Ottomans began to challenge the two-class imperial social order in the last decades of the sixteenth century. Behind their discontent, which resembled to some degree the situation of the cadet in Spanish society, rested the question whether the stability that the alien rule represented justified the denial of those family rights Islam sought to protect. Long ago the Ottomans attempted to siphon off the anger of the *kuloğulları* by providing them with minor positions or by exporting them.[54]

Fixed outsiders, formed a second major element· of Algiers' population at the high point of its sixteenth-century development. Although physically urbanized, these tribesmen and mountaineers— peasants had less freedom to move—retained the fundamentals of their rural social organization. Crowded conditions and economic complexity did force the new entrants to modify their social institutions: tribes could hardly roam through the quarters of Algiers. Nonetheless, through intermarriage the immigrants constituted new individual-related kin groups of a size appropriate to urban life. Once established, they behaved in the cities like tribes, forming parties, splitting into factions, and seeking alliances.[55] Ottoman social and political policies merely assisted the proliferation of this human arabesque because it perpetuated the subservience ‘of a divided urban population and maintained the attachment between the city and the countryside.

One sign of the powerful hold rural social institutions exerted upon the life of this half-urban, half-rural element was the way the division of labor in the city crudely expressed the kinship relations of the countryside. Mountain men from the Kabylia region worked as gardeners or petty merchants. But some preferred the warrior role and served the Ottomans as auxiliaries, the *Zwāwa* units, or staffed the forts and watchtowers in the interior. Mzabites from the Saharan oases obtained a monopoly over positions in public baths, butcher shops, and small industries. Exploiting their long-standing knowledge of the trade across the desert, this same group managed the commerce with Black Africa. Men from the city of Biskara specialized in carrying water, refuse, and small items of commerce during the day and acted as watchmen at night.

The floating proletariat of the city was composed of poor nomads and mountaineers who had been driven out of their homelands by their own kin. Entering the city at a social level just above the slaves, these poorly dressed and hungry city dwellers performed the rougher work of hauling and cleaning. Sometimes they were able to develop roots in one of the poorer quarters of the city, but the poor and the transient were more often than not carried off by one of Algiers' recurring plagues.[56]

Like other entrants into the city, the Hispano-Muslims settled in Algiers as a unit under their own sheik. Whereas the first group of immigrants brought the upper class of Naṣrid Granada to North Africa, the later waves of Hispano-Muslims delivered men skilled in urban arts to North Africa at the same time as the Ottomans began to rebuild high Islamic society in the cities.[57] Characteristically, the migration of these exiles to Algiers did not produce a single group but populated the port with two distinct communities. The 6,000 members of the Andalusian quarters were divided into Mudéjares (and probably Moriscos from southeastern Spain), and Taragins (Hispano-Muslims from Valencia, Aragon, and Catalonia). According to Haëdo, most of these immigrants were small businessmen and artisans, the key social elements of a Muslim city. Their identification with the Islamic culture the Ottomans were bent on defending was reflected in their attitude toward the Christians of Spain, one of uncompromising hostility: "They are altogether the greatest and cruelest enemies the Christians had in Barbary."[58]

The Jewish community made up another well-defined element of Algiers' social network, and its existence also gave evidence of the Ottoman allegiance to the polyreligious organization of the Muslim city. Under the supervision of their rabbis and elders, the Jews lived in two small quarters. They paid, collectively, a capitation tax as an acknowledgment of Ottoman sovereignty and an outward recognition of the religious superiority of Islam. Otherwise the Jews were able to seek their own form of life in an atmosphere that gave them the religious freedom they were unable to obtain in Christian Spain. The Jewish community itself, being affected by the social ethos of the society in which it lived, split into three groups: those of African origin, those from the Balearic Islands, and those from Spain. Iberian Jewry, the group that had suffered most from Spanish social policies, became the upper class of the small community in Algiers. There in the Maghrib, as elsewhere in the Ottoman empire, many of the Hispano-Jewish exiles employed the talents they had gained in the more advanced culture of Iberia—knowledge of language, of commerce, of banking—to act as brokers between Europe and North Africa, handling regular items of trade as well as the exchanges generated by corsair warfare. Noted for its humane treatment of slaves and for its probity, the Jewish community served a ruling class that did not turn communal hostilities based on religion against non-Muslims but preserved religious difference in order to exploit the talents of the minorities.[59]

Christians in Algiers comprised two groups. Merchants and their assistants constituted a small number of foreigners who resided in the city on the basis of a special agreement with the Ottoman governor. They carried their own law with them and were free to return to their respective countries. A much larger group, the Christian slave population of the city, reached 25,000 during the last two decades of the sixteenth century. Sold to merchants from the east or ransomed by their families in Europe, the slaves were valuable possessions.[60] They were rented out to local businessmen or worked for their owners on some project while awaiting exchange. Rescued from complete degradation by the exemplary service of Christian religious orders who struggled to save lives and souls rather than to convert, the captives hoped for release, converted to Islam, or died under miserable conditions.[61]

By the last quarter of the sixteenth century this Ottoman society in Algiers had hardened into forms whose boundaries were clearly visible. Both the richly brocaded caftans of the provincial dignitaries and the uniforms of the Janissaries, which if worn falsely brought the death penalty, distinguished the most powerful members of the ruling class from the sultan's subjects. In fact, everyone's place in the Turko-Muslim community could be determined by clothing—from the highly honored members of the Prophet's family with their green turbans and shaved heads to the new recruits from the eastern Mediterranean with their "Turkish" clothing. The elevated social standing conferred on the *ulema*—men of religion—by their high religious affiliation, lofty family status, and age was accentuated by their flowing garments of a somber color and by their serious public demeanor. Merchants wore clothing of a lighter hue and, like the *ulema*, grew long beards to claim the respect given to elders in a patriarchal society. One's trade and origin were also known by physical symbols—from the tattoos of the Berber merchants to the rough clothing of the less prestigious Arabs from the Sahara. Ottomans, whether members of the Janissary corps or corsairs, were singled out by their luxuriant black mustaches and their haughty behavior.[62] In this rich and complex society, the Old Christian image of proper attire—doublet, hose, short hair, and closely trimmed beard—fit only a few foreign merchants.

At the base of this well-organized Islamic society lay that other pole of social loyalty, the extended family. Haëdo, the most astute of the Spanish observers, sensed here an institutional order and rhythm different from that of the Latin world when he remarked that something was wrong with the inheritance laws of this Muslim city. Unlike the aristocratic society of Spain, the holy law of Islam spelled out a complex system of passing on wealth with the hope that the Muslim extended family, not only the firstborn son, would survive. In Algiers it did; and in keeping with the high sense of privacy that surrounds the family in Islamic society, its inner history remains obscure.[63]

Nonetheless, by studying women in Algiers the Spanish priest was able to convey a sense of the Islamic mode of existence that the security of the Ottoman regime fostered in family matters. First, the scented hair, the hennaed feet and hands, the Berber tattoos, and the veil were noted as the surface differences between the Latin Christian female and the Muslim. Still more interesting was the cultural framework that determined the separated place of women in a society vastly different from that of Old Christian Spain. Muslims took exceptional care for the security of their women, for the honor of the family and the purity of the bloodline could be drastically affected by female behavior. Secluded in houses whose fortresslike exteriors revealed the great value Muslims placed upon family purity, females moved in patterns quite different from those of males. And in public the distinctly different roles of the sexes were maintained by the veil and by uniform outer clothing whose form and decoration might suggest the woman's status but would not reveal her identity. Given unusual control over family matters, the mothers of Algiers brought their children up in their own enclosed world, rearing them to serve the family into which they were born.

Among the social tasks for which the children were prepared, the most important was making a proper marriage. Again Haëdo noted Muslim practices that differed from Christian custom: polygamy, dowry payments to the bride, and marriages between parties who might never have seen each other or who might be first cousins.[64]

Far from being powerless, the women of Algiers maintained their position in urban life through their control of food, honor, sex, sons, inheritance, and the supernatural. Women from the upper levels of the subject class and wives of Ottomans regularly visited the homes of female friends from the same general level of society and attended parties where matters affecting the family—in particular, marriage— were invariably discussed. Excluded from the high religious and intellectual life of male society, females of all elements of society visited women who were reputed to have control over the spirits, hoping that an amulet would solve some pressing personal require- ment, such as guaranteeing the birth of a son. Women of leisure worked at strengthening their social ties, looked over prospective daughters-in-law, and demonstrated their status by visiting the public bath under close guard. In good weather the link between the rural world, the religious culture of North Africa, and the family was maintained when mothers took their children to visit the tombs of marabouts or of their own kin. Yet the high point of social life for Muslim women came when the negotiations over marriage had reached a conclusion and eventuated in those ceremonies that the archbishop of Cordoba so roundly condemned.[65]

A continual use of ceremony in Algiers heightened both the sense of collectivity and the common dependence upon the spiritual beliefs of Islamic society. At the family level, circumcision, marriage, and death provided this most fundamental unit of society with the public opportunity to demonstrate its obligations to the wider Muslim community. The regular call to prayer, especially the pressure to conform during the month of fasting, Ramaḍān, compelled almost all reasonable men to accept a common temporal rhythm and to acknowledge their ties to a larger cultural unit. Public recognition for the pilgrims who returned from Mecca and Medina added a cere- monial element to urban life that expressed respect for self-sacrifice, bravery, and religion. The great public feasts of Islam, the festival of the sacrifice, ʿīd al-aḍḥā, the breaking of the fast at the end of Ramaḍān, and the Prophet's birthday cut across the social differences within the Muslim community to bring the city population together in enthusiastic celebrations. Ottoman governors were well aware of the unifying effect of a public demonstration of the faith. In 1579 an unusually severe famine struck Algiers, provoking, in the North African tradition, pilgrimages to the tombs of marabouts. During this period of great tension, the governor of Algiers, Hasan Paşa, assembled the population of the city and publicly broke and burned three Christian images. The city restated its profoundly Islamic identity in this symbolic reenaction of Muḥammad's destruction of the idols in Mecca.[66]

East of the Moulouya River basin, where Ottoman sovereignty was not imposed, for a time high Islamic society experienced under the Saʿdians the same renaissance that occurred in the central Maghrib. Yet the Moroccan community was again a reluctant bride of the east. The S̲h̲arīfian lands showed all the evidence of the shaded-off eastern Mediterranean version of Islam: the powerful family dynasty with a competing legitimacy, the wide concession to rural religious practices, the incomplete conquest of the tribesmen, and the lack of a monumental religious emblem of eastern Islam. Also muted, and strikingly so, was the creative spirit of Hispano-Muslims. Bereft of its Iberian cultural pole and on the fringe of Turko-Muslim civilization, the Saʿdian sultanate found its own resources insufficient to maintain the balances demanded by high Islamic society beyond the era of expulsion. After 1603 the civilization of the city receded once again.

Why the swift rise and fall of urban society in sixteenth-century Morocco? A great part of the answer lies in the influence of tribalism. Though the Saʿdians profited from the military abilities of the kinsmen at the foundation of their dynasty, they could never quite get this sharp sword back into its scabbard.

Since the resurgence of tribalism in the centuries after the fall of the Almohads had reduced cities and towns to frightened spectators of widespread internal disorder, the beginning of a new sultanate did not originate in the cities. Instead, those who wished to rejuvenate the Moroccan community found support among the religious representatives of rural Islam. Ideally placed to lead a movement that could cut across kinship structures and local loyalties, the leaders of brotherhoods employed their connection with the larger world of Islam and their brokerage function among the tribes to summon the kinsmen to a higher task. Elevation of the Saʿdian sultans above the fragmented society of the tribes and religious lodges then required the rural religious leaders to combine the Maghribians' widespread veneration for holy men with the Islamic habit of showing respect for the family of the Prophet.

With this legitimacy the Saʿdian family began a long climb along well-known social paths toward political power in the western Maghrib. Tribesmen were assembled from the southern steppes, and taxes from the Sus valley were collected to fuel a religiopolitical movement launched from the steppe periphery toward the agricultural plains where the great cities lay. In 1525 the Sa^cdians made their ultimate social orientation clear when they settled in Marrakesh. Yet the selection of a capital city, the establishment of a rudimentary administration, and the formation of a permanent military force, the ^ɔAhl al-Sūs, from the Sus valley, was not accompanied by the destruction of the religious bonds that attached the dynasty to rural Morocco. The Sa^cdians were unable to style themselves, as did the Ottomans as leaders of the holy war or protectors of *Sunnī* Islam. Rather, their failure to achieve a wider legitimacy in the face of Ottoman competition drove them toward a unique version of Maghribian Islam. In Morocco their combination of Islamic cultures produced a pompous stress on the importance of the ruling families' tie to the house of the Prophet, Sharīfianism, an exalted celebration of the Prophet's birthday, the *Maulid*, and a lavish concern for the tombs of saintly men, among whom the Sa^cdians included themselves.[67]

Their military history also shows that the Sa^cdians were not able to escape the kinship environment to the degree that the Ottomans did. Competition in the powder era inevitably demanded technical and organizational abilities that the tribal allies of the Sharīfian state did not possess. Yet the nonkinship implications of war in the sixteenth century did not push the tribesmen to the margin of Moroccan society; nor did it compel the Sa^cdian rulers to establish formal institutions that would socialize military men so that they would both be efficient with the new technology and be loyal to the rulers.[68]

Sa^cdians, however, centralized government and pacified the tribesmen. Meager indeed is the information on their conquest of the countryside. Political expansion and the growth of an urban bureaucracy were certainly part of the inner history of the Sharīfian success. Protests against non-Koranic taxes alone offer proof that the Sa^cdians placed increasing pressure on rural society. By the reign of Aḥmad al-Manṣūr (1578–1603), the financial demands of maintaining a large army elevated the importance of the bureaucracy, leading the Moroccan sultan to adopt some Ottoman practices. But the Sharīfian dynasty made no formal break with old patterns of administering society. It was a matter of degree. No Sa^cdian ruler was able to impose the impersonal administrative devices—regular cadastral surveys—that characterized the Ottoman administration.[69]

How closely this dynasty remained enmeshed in the local culture of the western Maghrib can be observed in its delegation of authority within settled communities. Following Marinid practice, the sultan assigned the governance of major cities to members of his ruling family. Provinces, especially those with a tradition of independence, were ruled not by an alien elite but by a *khalīfa*, a deputy, from another part of the Saʿdian territories—mainly from the southeast, the Sus. For areas of lesser importance, the peripatetic court of the sultan met and accepted pledges of allegiance from local leaders, sheiks, *kaids*, and pashas, who were then charged with the administration of their regions.[70]

In an environment where tribalism was so vigorous, the strength of the Moroccan state depended, more than with the Ottomans, upon how well the *Sharīfs* could control the centrifugal tendencies implicit within such a society. Although the state had little difficulty entrenching itself in the central plains where town dwellers and peasants were relieved of the perpetual tribal conflicts, subjecting the mountains and steppe to some sort of supratribal authority was an entirely different matter. The Saʿdian rulers first attempted to influence the internal politics of the tribes, favoring candidates that would be pliable. Yet even if the chosen sheik was elected he customarily measured his strength in terms of how much he could lighten the obligations to the outside world. Thus the tribes paid taxes irregularly, if at all, and served on military campaigns only as long as the direction of warfare favored their interests.

Saʿdian sultans attempted to collect their revenues and impress their authority upon these tribes with many of the same techniques the Ottomans employed: economic blockades, political division, religious pressure, holy war, financial concessions, and finally punitive expeditions. But the difference between Saʿdian internal rule of the tribes and the Ottoman was characteristically the more formal role it gave to the place of the kinsmen, especially those drawn from the Arab *Maʿāḳil* tribes. Institutionalized in the latter part of the sixteenth century, the military tribes allied to the Saʿdians—the *gīsh*—were located within cantonments where their military responsibilities and their exemption from taxes marked them off as representatives of the *Sharīfian* state. No matter how efficient the sultans were in applying this instrument of rule, the tortuous geography of the southern steppes and the High Atlas mountains generally furnished dissident tribesmen with a refuge zone, a hazy area beyond the pale of governmental authority—the land of *ṣiba*, where the authority of the state administration, the *makhzan*, did not run.[71]

Upon the death of Aḥmad al-Manṣūr in 1603, the strength of the kinship factor in Moroccan society was a major reason for the

collapse of political cohesion. In contrast to the Ottoman provinces of
North Africa, where the slave class regrouped around a decentralized
version of the imperial social regime in Istanbul, the struggles between
the sons of al-Manṣūr decreased the influence of urban government
and increased the power of social structures whose base was rural.
At the same time, the resurgence of the kin factor in the political
turmoil that afflicted the western Maghrib was strikingly reflected
not only in the familiar basis of the internal war between the sons
of al-Manṣūr, but also in the early-seventeenth-century failures to
regenerate a centralized government. Abū Maḥallī, al-ʿAyyāshī, and
the adepts of the religious lodge of Dilāʾ all attempted to bridge kinship divisions within Moroccan society with some form of religious
appeal. But the spirit of division was in the air, and neither the religious leaders nor the warriors found a message that persuaded the
tribesmen to submerge their independence for the benefit of the cities.

This decline of Saʿdian government did not destroy Moroccan
society. Within the zones of tribal independence the competition
between clans, tribes, and leagues, the functioning of a balance of
power at many different levels of association formed a system of
relations well known to the tribesmen. Meanwhile, men of popular
religion continued to function through their brotherhoods at the
margins of the tribes, tempering in the process the feuding inclina-
tions of the kinsmen and acting as mediators between the tribesmen
and Islamic civilization. The rural way of life in Morocco constituted
an elaborate organization with its own motion, leaning, after the
turn of the seventeenth century, toward more internal fragmentation.
Tribes nevertheless preserved their attachments to a wider world even
during this time of general economic and political decline. The markets, the religious brotherhoods, and the veneration for the family
of the Prophet were institutions full of meaning for the entire
Moroccan population. With time, the building blocks for high Islamic
society would again be cemented into a new foundation by a dynasty
that emerged not on a wave of national sentiment thinly disguised by
religion, but out of this religiotribal background during the seventeenth and eighteenth centuries.[72]

The short duration of Saʿdian control over the Moroccan countryside set narrow boundaries for the recovery of high Islamic society.
Nonetheless, this Moroccan dynasty left an impressive record of
dedication to the values of Islamic civilization, to those cultural ties
that bound this frontier to the eastern Mediterranean rather than to
Europe.

Marrakesh, the Saʿdian capital, was an exception to the general movement within North Africa and Iberia toward the sea; it nestled up against the High Atlas mountains at the southern end of Morocco's Atlantic plains, well away from the coast. The tribesmen and peasants that contributed to the bulk of the city's population were local, deriving their livelihood from the surrounding plains and mountains and from the communication network leading into the interior of northwest Africa. Its favorable location had already made it the capital of previous dynasties whose birthplaces were thoroughly interior, and the Saʿdian appropriation of the large oasis was the third changeover within four and a half centuries.

Marrakesh turned a corner in its history when the Saʿdians secured control of the casbah in 1525. But war with the Portuguese, the Waṭṭāsids of Fez, and the Turks of Algiers left Muḥammad ash-Shaykh (1525–57) little in the way of time and resources to improve urban life. By 1558, however, the Saʿdians found themselves ringed by foreign states too powerful to attack. Since the Moroccan army had grown to a point where the tribes no longer were an immediate danger and neither the Ottomans nor the Spanish appeared ready to invade, ʿAbdallāh al-Ghālib (1557–74) shifted the resources of his state from war to the construction of an impressive capital.

There already existed the framework of an old city whose shape was determined as much by the nearness of water—the Wadi Tensift—of an agricultural region—the plain of Haouz—and of communication routes as it was by the structure of Moroccan society. Visually, however, the exterior forms of early-sixteenth-century Marrakesh clearly linked this city with other urban areas in the Islamic world. Walled, with gates on major routes, the city was anchored at its southern end with a royal enclosure that was both a palace area and a citadel. Separated from the home of the rulers and near the center of the city were the congregational mosques, surrounded by markets graded in relation to the religious and social status of their merchants. Centrally located residential areas also shared the densely packed core region of the city. Physically, the divisions of the living area seemed indefinite. Subunits of society were juxtaposed higgledy-piggledy, destroying linearity and open space. Yet socially the shape of the city's quarters corresponded to well-defined local, ethnic, and religious groupings. Some remaining space between the residential clusters and the wall provided room for limited agricultural activities, malodorous trades, and recent settlers. Finally, the living citizens gave way to the dead, the near dead, and the outcasts as the inhabitants laid out their cemeteries, leprosariums, and animal markets for the nomads just beyond the city walls.[73]

The renaissance of Marrakesh began in a truly Sharīfian fashion with ʿAbdallāh al-Ghālib's construction of a small burial chamber for the remains of his father, Muḥammad ash-Shaykh (d. 1557). This respect for the Moroccan religious sensibilities underlying the political power of the dynasty soon produced the beautification of Saʿdian tombs, as well as those of other religious men such as Sīdī Yūsuf ibn ʿAlī, an Almohad saint, and became a regular practice of the dynasty, culminating in the construction of the Saʿdian necropolis. Improvement of the royal residence, which may have begun under Muḥammad ash-Shaykh, also identified the political power of the Saʿdians and separated them from the entangled and complicated patterns and patronage loyalties of the townsmen. New shelters for the court, the harem, the treasury, the armory, and other state institutions were also erected to handle the diversified requirements of ruling Morocco.[74]

The improvement of Marrakesh's buildings went hand-in-hand with a renewed commitment of the Saʿdians and the religious elite of the city to a social organization based upon the polyreligious institutions of Islamic civilization. In 1562 ʿAbdallāh moved the small Jewish community of Marrakesh from a space near the center of the city where he intended to erect a large mosque. Granting the Jews a large tract of land—approximately twenty eight hectares—to allow for expansion, the sultan constructed a separate city within the city for the non-Muslims. The *al-mallāḥ*, or Jewish quarter, was surrounded by a thick wall that divided it from the rest of the city. Within this protected square was a small-scale replica of the basic urban order—except in terms of religion and its inner life. Synagogues, cemeteries, merchant clusters, residential quarters, gardens, fountains, all emerged under the authority of the sultan, who delegated responsibility for administering the non-Muslim society to a caste of rabbis and wealthy Jewish merchants.[75]

If the population now knew where non-Muslims lived and by contrast could identify itself, the erection of a grand mosque firmed up the Saʿdian tie with the Malikite ʿulamāʾ and their urban allies, the merchants, the artisans, and the city notables. According to the Moroccan historian al-Ifrānī, construction of the cathedral mosque of the Saʿdians began in 1562 and was completed about ten years later. Named after a family of *sharīfs—Mawwāsīn*—this monumental statement of cultural loyalty and political power included annexes:

library, bath, fountain, and school for the study of the Koran. If there was any doubt that ʿAbdallāh planned to shape his regime in accordance with the holy law of Islam and the advice of the orthodox, this was removed by the construction of a new *madrasa*, or religious school, in 1564–65, next to the central mosque of Ben Yūsuf. Finally, it is the duty of all Muslims to ameliorate the inequities of this world— to give alms to the poor and to care for the sick. The Saʿdians set the example for discharging this moral duty of the community by dedicating the funds from a religious trust to build a hospital and an insane asylum.[76]

During the four years between the end of ʿAbdallāh's reign and the battle of Alcazar in 1578, the architectural growth of the city languished, only to be resumed with fervor during the reign of Aḥmad al-Manṣūr (1578–1603). Bringing peace, booty, and new taxes to Marrakesh, this sultan rebuilt the casbah on a grand scale. All previous architectural tasks shrank in comparison with the plans the victorious sultan drew up for a royal palace within the city. Begun five months after the battle of Alcazar, the construction of al-Badīʿ, the incomparable, was not inspired by Moroccan invention, but took its name from one of the pavilions of the Umayyad Palace at Cordova and its design from the Alhambra in Granada. If its name and scale preserved the lost grandeur of Islam in Spain, its extravagant cost, so the historian al-Ifrānī reports, is remembered as a pound-for-pound exchange of sugar for Italian marble.[77] To glorify his family in Moroccan fashion, al-Manṣūr presided over the construction of two buildings covering the main Saʿdian necropolis. For his own symbolic attachment to formal Islam, the sultan supervised the work on the mosque of Bāb Dukkāla, which his mother had commissioned in 1557–58.

Divided into an unknown number of quarters based upon religion, origin, and other social criteria, the city experienced an increase in population during the sixteenth century, reaching, perhaps, 75,000 by al-Manṣūr's reign. Most new inhabitants came from the surrounding Berber and Arab tribes, filtering into the city through a network of personal ties that linked immigrants to kinsmen already settled in the city. Migration from a greater distance manifested itself in an increase in the size of the quarters dedicated to foreigners and non-Muslims. Leaving only the name of a street—*odabaşı*—as a trace of their ephemeral presence, the Turks reached Marrakesh as members of the Saʿdian army. The much larger contingent of Hispano-Muslim troops put a deeper mark on the city than the Turks did; for Spanish Muslims and Iberian renegades probably made up the bulk of the elite units in the Moroccan army. Also influential were the numbers of Muslims from Spain who brought to Marrakesh those crucial talents required for cannon casting and architecture. At the bottom of Muslim society, black African slaves increased in number after the Saharan campaign in 1590–91. Whatever the weight of the immigrants from the outside, the culture of the city remained intensely Muslim and North African, indicated by the emotional celebration of the Prophet's birthday, the extensive influence of maraboutism within the walls, and the general unwillingness of the merchants to travel outside the state.[78]

As elsewhere in the Islamic world, the non-Muslims of Marrakesh lived under the protection of the reigning dynasty. An old and well-established community, the Jews prospered until the first decade of the seventeenth century from growing internal and external trade. Because Marrakesh occupied an important commercial position near the edge of the Atlantic world and at the end of the African trade routes, the city attracted foreign merchants. When the victory at Alcazar elevated the prestige of al-Manṣūr, Christian traders and adventurers wandered into the Moroccan capital in increasing numbers as the Ottoman pressure upon the eastern Maghrib subsided. To accommodate the foreign merchants, the sultan reserved a small space in the city for free Christians. Christian prisoners, on the other hand, occupied two jails. Under the conditions of the time, life in Saᶜdian prisons was far from pleasant. But even here the sultan tempered the brutality of the age by constructing a hospital for the prisoners—they were, after all, valuable for their ransom—and by allowing Christian priests to establish a church. However, in deference to Muslim tastes the Christians could not ring a bell but had, like the Muslims, to call their coreligionists to prayer orally with *Ave Maria, hermanos.*[79]

The outburst of political violence that followed the death of al-Manṣūr in 1603 showed the notables of Marrakesh all too vividly how close to the surface conflict was even in the reign of a powerful sultan. Internal violence, fed by a thinly disguised factional spirit, visited Marrakesh in the form of warfare between the partisans of Fez and Marrakesh, between the armies of Mulay Zaydān and ᶜAbdallāh, and between unidentified groups who took the opportunity to settle old scores. In 1607 these combatants so brutalized the city with bloody street fighting that the urban population began to flee the Saᶜdian capital, leaving in its wake another age of urban expansion.[80]

This return of decline after only three-quarters of a century of Sharīfian administration could have labeled the entire Saᶜdian effort in Marrakesh as nothing but a recasting of old structures and symbols. Certainly the southerners were hardly innovative in molding the architectural and social forms of their capital city. They built on the urban skeleton of the eleventh-century Almoravid city; they attempted to bring back the architectural glory of Muslim Spain in North Africa long after it had disappeared in Iberia; and they brushed aside whatever urban influences the Turks and Latin Christians had carried into the western Maghrib.[81] Conservative though they may have been, the Saᶜdians strengthened the high Islamic traditions of communal existence in a land where the culture of Islam bent heavily under the weight of tribalism.

If the history of these capital cities is any measure, the influence of the Muslim east had, on the whole, increased west of Tunis during the sixteenth century. The Spanish had brutally erased the old manifestation of the western frontier's cultural autonomy. In the place of Hispano-Islam, only the Saᶜdians carried on the West's traditions of independence. Yet a strong bias toward the tribal form of life restricted the long-run development of this sultanate and gave political and cultural predominance in North Africa to the Ottoman provinces. There the lasting impact of this eastern empire was not the short imposition of Ottoman political supremacy over its western periphery but the renewal of high Islamic society under a Turko-Muslim shield; that is what survived and what intensified the difference between North Africa and Spain.

Nine: THE FORGOTTEN FRONTIER

Válgame Dios! ¿ qué es esto ? Moros hay en la costa.

Cervantes, *Los Baños de Argel*

From the influence of Arabic literature upon the poetry of Dante to the impact of the arabesque upon the European illuminator, the culture of Latin Christendom bore witness during the High Middle Ages to the creative impulses that a mixture of Islamic and Christian civilizations could provoke.[1] The Hispano-Muslim community, benefiting from its relatively autonomous position, played an important role in this exchange. Latin Christian receptivity to Islamic arts and sciences, as they were mediated through the palace culture of Muslim Spain and Sicily, showed that at certain levels the two civilizations were moving along compatible lines of development. But by the first decade of the seventeenth century the cultural history of the Hispano-Muslim frontier had experienced a revolution. Gone was the cross-cultural synthesis of southeastern Iberia. In its place an introverted North African Islam confronted Spain in the midst of her Golden Age. Xenophobia and widely different intellectual traditions joined with a lack of any meaningful economic contact to reinforce a mutual rejection of cultural pluralism. Visible and yet invisible, the frontier lost its function as a ground for intercultural invention and became a rampart against the impure.

In the final stages of this cultural division, corsair warfare erupted along the coastline of the Mediterranean. Neither the ubiquity nor the violence of the private warrior was particularly new. What made this surge of naval vagabondage unique was that it did not foreshadow the resumption of grand warfare but introduced an era of decline. Ottomans simply wrote off oceanic expansion in favor of exploiting a vast internal economy based on continental conquests. Spain down-graded the importance of her Mediterranean borders and rushed to the defense of New World and northern European possessions. Of course more was at issue in these strategic decisions than the inflated costs of naval warfare. Even contemporary observers were aware that the momentum of the economies of the two empires had diverged.

On 11 January 1611, the comendador mayor of Leon left a record of these separate economic orders of the Mediterranean world when he pointed out in the council of state that "the caravan from Alexandria [to Istanbul] is there what the convoy from the Indies is here."[2] From one point of view this statement said much about the similarities between the imperial economies of the Ottoman and Spanish states. Although both empires did develop extractive economies, they differed geographically. What concerned Spain after 1580 was the protection of an entirely new system of economic exchanges whose axis ran through the Atlantic rather than the Mediterranean. A much less understood but nevertheless crucial difference was that Spain, but not the Ottoman empire, had become a peripheral part of the emerging capitalistic economy whose center was northeastern Europe.[3] Great wealth arrived in Seville each year; yet the money passed through Spain without producing a qualitative change in the economic structure of Hispanic society. In a vain effort to control developments spawned by the revolutionizing economy of northeastern Europe, Habsburg rulers sent armies and navies northward to conquer this entirely new, and for them elusive, source of power.

If Atlantic commerce and the precapitalistic development of Europe tilted the interest of Spain away from North Africa and the Islamic world, the interior wealth of a large empire and the commerce with Asia bound the Ottomans to a Near Eastern economy. Like the Genoese, long-range merchants of the Turkish empire hastened to exploit the growth of a huge imperial market during the sixteenth century.[4] Their trade generally followed the well-known silk and spice routes that linked eastern Europe with Asia. The troubles attending the cessation of expansion merely intensified the importance of this eastern Mediterranean economic network. Ottomans sought to protect, in an era of contraction, both the agricultural centers of their empire and the naval and land routes that fed the commerce of the Levant. By the middle of the seventeenth century, it was still the flow of money over the routes from the center of the empire to Asia, rather than to Europe, that attracted the attention of the court chronicler Naima.[5] Some Ottomans dreamed of capturing a portion of Europe's commerce; and Ragusan merchants did participate in Atlantic trade. On the whole, however, the subjects of the sultan saw little reason to neglect the profits of a known economic structure for the uncertain yield of commerce far beyond the boundaries of the Islamic world.[6] In any event, the development of Europe's oceanic trade just did not generate, at the end of the sixteenth century, enough strength to shatter the cohesion of a huge and still vital Near Eastern economy.

On the frontier itself the history of the long-range merchants of Muslim North Africa and Seville offered additional evidence of the qualitative differences between the two economic blocks. In Seville, the commercial boom of the sixteenth century tended to loosen the behavior of merchants, allowing them to advance upward into the ranks of the aristocracy and encouraging them to be more innovative. The scale of the new ventures also stimulated the use of complicated business techniques that pushed mercantile organizations beyond ancient geographical and institutional boundaries. In comparison with Spain's past, the Atlantic traders in Seville displayed less attachment to traditional practices, to kinship considerations, and to the use of religious minorities for special tasks.[7] Yet the merchants of Seville did not become the vanguard of a new socioeconomic system of Spanish origin but yielded precedence in the development of Europe's nascent capitalistic economy to northern merchants.

In contrast to the entrepreneurial spirit of Seville's merchants, the Muslim traders of North Africa did not gamble with the Atlantic commerce created by the Oceanic Discoveries. Trade did evolve between the merchants of Europe and North Africa.[8] Yet the exchange of European manufactured goods for the sugar, saltpeter, coral, hides, and other raw materials of the Maghrib did not provoke a migration of Muslims to the North or to the New World, where the Spanish attempted to exclude Islam.[9] Maghribian traders, moreover, ran their long-distance commerce at a low level of organization, rarely offered trust beyond members of their extended family, and gave a prominent position in European trade to non-Muslim communities (the Jews) or to recently absorbed Hispano-Muslims. Thus the depressing impact of the corsairs on transcultural commerce, the strength of traditional Muslim trading patterns, and the European domination of the oceanic economies kept the majority of the Maghribian merchants confined to the continent of Africa and to

the southern and eastern coasts of the Mediterranean—to the
territories within the House of Islam where, as in the interior of
sub-Saharan Africa, European economic activities had only a
peripheral impact.[10]

Ottoman sultans were not unaware of the many advantages
Europe derived from its oceanic commerce. Lufti Paşa warned
Süleyman the Lawgiver that failure to control the seas would in the
end harm the empire. The sultan therefore expanded his imperial
fleet. Yet with the exception of Hadim Süleyman Paşa's relatively
unsuccessful campaign from Suez to the west coast of India in 1538,
there was no major attempt to compete with the Christian navies
outside the Mediterranean. Later on, at the end of the sixteenth
century, when the Ottomans decided to invade Persia (1578), the
choice of an Asian frontier and the persistent commitment of resources to eastern campaigns more and more came to be a judgment
against the maintenance of a large navy and therefore against seaborne expansion. This view of state politics, which rested upon the
enormous terrestrial acquisitions of the past, stressed the separation
of the political elite from the merchants, and placed agriculture at the
base of political power, inclined Ottoman sultans to reject naval
adventures in favor of continental expansion. The Spanish, who were
afflicted with the problems of managing a disjointed empire, regarded
this continental cohesiveness of the Turks as a great source of their
strength. On the other hand, the choice of a Persian battleground at
the end of the sixteenth century froze the Ottomans within a continental and Mediterranean framework at a crucial point in the
economic and technological history of the world.[11]

One consequence of this turn toward the old routes of Turko-
Mongol expansion in Eurasia was a decreasing curiosity about the
geography of the world outside the western basin of the Mediterranean. On the margin of his maps of 1513 and 1526 and in his
introductory poem to the second version of his *Book of Sea Lore*, Piri
Reis had brought high Ottoman officials up to date on the latest
voyages of European sailors. At mid-century Seydi Ali Reis, whose
fleet was wrecked off the coast of India, composed a geographical
treatise that described the Indian Ocean and devoted one chapter
to the New World. In 1559, Hacı Ahmet drew a map of the world,
and a year later he produced a manuscript that included only one
page on the Americas. During 1572 Ali Macar Reis constructed a
map of the world showing the regions reached by the European
voyagers. In the reign of Murad III, selected portions of European

geography books describing the New World were translated and presented to the Ottoman court. Yet all these attempts to broaden the western horizons of the Turko-Muslim rulers by calling attention to overseas expansion rapidly died off.[12] By the middle of the seventeenth century the Ottomans were operating with an intellectual deficit in an old Islamic science, geography, that the Ottoman scholar Kâtib Çelebi charged was responsible, in part, for the infidel conquests of the lands beyond the seas.[13]

This constriction of information about the western naval frontier joined a conservative intellectual movement at the heart of the Turkish empire that separated Habsburg and Ottoman elites just as the corsairs marked the no-man's-land between the two empires. Although the Ottomans had absorbed firearms and the political and social consequences that evolved from their use, the same ruling class did not welcome the printing press and its social and intellectual implications.[14] True to the eastern practice of using literacy as a means of separating the ruling class from the subjects, scholars and writers instead intensified the abstractness and complexity of their work. This growth of a complicated court literature stood in sharp contrast to the simple Turkish of the naval manuscripts, which had recounted the adventures of the pre-Ottoman Ümer Bey or the holy wars of Hayreddin Barbarossa.[15] Concerned with creativity within a stylistic framework that accepted the external world as given, rather than yet to be discovered, Ottoman authors looked to the elegant organization of expression as the measure of literary accomplishment.[16] At the same time, the use of foreign information as a device for exciting intellectual interest declined; not until the last half of the seventeenth century did the later writer Evliya Çelebi employ descriptions of lands outside the empire to stimulate his readers.[17]

This inward literary development, which effaced the personality of the Europeans and ignored their accomplishments, arose along with religious difficulties within the House of Islam. In response to the late-sixteenth-century challenge launched by the followers of Shiʿism and varieties of mystical Islam that surely bordered on irreligion, the Ottoman religious leaders naturally fell back upon the same position taken by other urban-based regimes at the hour of an assault from the periphery: adherence to rigid interpretations of orthodox Islam. This emergence of a religious reaction in the empire took on a public form in 1580 with the destruction of an astronomical observatory in Istanbul. If, as the Şeyh ül Islam argued, the attempt to explore the revolutions of the heavenly bodies had caused the plague of 1579–80, then other matters not in conformity with received wisdom—the very shape of the world—had dangerous implications for public order in Istanbul as in Algiers.[18] The conclusion of this line of thought, which appeared at a time when the scientific advances of Copernicus survived in the West, was the need to draw nearer to the given—to the Holy Law—and to stabilize the Turko-Muslim society that three centuries of expansion had created.[19]

In an entirely different manner from the Ottomans, Spanish authors produced a literary genre dealing with the Turks and the Muslims of Spain and North Africa. They also reflected the same tendency toward cultural separation that was implicit in the works of Ottoman authors. But the form and size of the Spanish literature on its Muslim neighbors differed greatly from its Ottoman counterpart. Three major reasons accounted for the quantity and complexity of the literature on the Turks: the printing press was used; the state and society supported a large university system; and the tastes of a growing audience permitted a rapid expansion in the publication of secular literature.[20] The upshot of these differences between the place of Spanish literature on Muslims and the parallel effort in the Turko-Muslim world is that the Iberian works mirrored shifts in the political judgments of the elite concerning the Turkish threat and also changes in the attitude of society as a whole about Islam.

From Süleyman the Lawgiver's German campaign of 1532 through the battle of Lepanto in 1571, the serious study of the Turks built upon an established tradition of scholarship concerning the Islamic world. Although Charles V had sponsored a propaganda effort against the Turks that resurrected the anti-Islamic diatribes of the crusades, the mid-sixteenth-century histories of the Turks belonged to a more objective and critical stream of knowledge that emerged during the Renaissance period.[21] Aggressive and expansive, the Turks were too dangerous a foe to be treated lightly. Thus, documents on their organization, studies of their political intentions, and long histories of their rise to power formed the body of the early literature on the Ottomans. In these works, the Spanish consistently viewed the conflict with the legacy of Islam in Spain, the battle against the corsairs, and the major wars with the Turks as part of a single cosmic struggle between Christendom and a monolithic Islam. The simplicity of this viewpoint, which grew out of Spain's assumption of the providential mission to win the world for Christianity, was complicated at mid-century by the revolutions of the Reformation.

But Spanish writers—with some reason, as it turned out—soon claimed that the Moriscos, the Turks, and the Protestants formed a single international conspiracy against Latin Christendom.[22]

Until the battle of Lepanto in 1571, histories of war, of imperial campaigns against the Turks, emerged regularly. The preparation for naval operations, the actions of valiant generals and admirals, and the explanation for victory or defeat filled one book after another.[23] If victories were celebrated with elaborate detail, defeats, such as the emperor's campaign against Algiers in 1541, were also subjected to careful analysis. There the Spanish acknowledged the martial abilities of the Turks—especially their discipline; but the reasons for Christian failure were attributed not to the strength of the enemy but to bad leadership or the positions of the planets.[24] No one argued that reasons of state should be substituted for the spirit of the crusade as the basis for making decisions about whether to war against the Turks.[25]

Between 1565 and 1571, the image the Spanish authors projected of the conflict with the Turks began to change. Improbable though it may seem, there was a connection between Philip II's decision in 1565 to emphasize the importance of his European border over his Mediterranean frontier, the unsuccessful Turkish siege of Malta, and the publication at the same time of a romantic history of the Abencerrajes, one of the last of the great Hispano-Muslim families. The victories over the Turks that Christian and Spanish soldiers earned at Malta, and especially at Lepanto, provided psychological underpinning for the elevation of Christian self-confidence in the relation with Islam and for a change in the literary portrait of the now so much less dangerous Muslim opponent. No longer a terrible threat to be carefully analyzed, the Turks could appear in works of fiction for which the history of the noble Moors, the Abencerrajes, could act as a guide.[26] Assisted by the printing press, Spanish authors swept their former opponents into works of imagination after 1580, the year of the Hispano-Ottoman truce.

Between 1580 and 1640–50 the fictional representation of the Turks came to be a mechanism by which Spanish authors exalted country and religion in the absence of large-scale warfare against Islam. Since the Ottomans had not collapsed under the weight of Christian arms, Spanish writers held out the hope that the imperfections of Turkish society would do what the sword had failed to accomplish. On this level of discussion authors devoted a great deal of attention to the enemies of urban Islam: Tamerlane, Skanderbeg, and the

194 CHAPTER NINE

"kings" of Kūko and the Banū ʿAbbās in North Africa. Meanwhile, Ottoman sultans such as Selim II and Murad III were endowed with negative virtues—drunkenness and lechery—that allowed authors to praise the Spanish ruling class by contrast. The Turk himself was charged with all those shortcomings—polygamy and divorce were most often cited—that excluded the Moriscos from Spanish society. This turn toward the fictional representation of the Turks and Islamic society at large occurred at the same time as the Catholic Reformation gathered steam in Europe. Here the Turkish possession of the Holy Lands, the corsair raids, and the Morisco refusal to assimilate were periodically employed to revive the crusading spirit. But the frontiers for religious activity had shifted greatly at the end of the sixteenth century. Missionary enthusiasm among Latin Christians was now either for the conversion of the New World or for the much more difficult war against the European heretic. Under such conditions the tendency to exaggerate the fictional character of the Turk, to emphasize the reasons for keeping a moral distance from Islam, increased as the two Mediterranean civilizations drifted apart.[27]

Meanwhile the literature produced by men who lived along, as well as within, the Ibero-African frontier also left a record of the changing relationship between the societies of Spain and North Africa. Far from abundant, and rarely examined as a unit, this vital source of information can be divided into the following subunits: the Old Christian's view of the Moriscos, the literary response in Spain to the corsairs of the Maghrib, the descriptions of North Africa by Spanish captives and traders, the literary expression of Spanish Islam in decline, the Islamic propaganda in North Africa, and the secular literary tradition in the Maghrib.

The Spanish domination of the Moriscos permitted the Hispano-Muslim to be absorbed into the world of imagination earlier than the Turks. Moreover, this passage of the once-hated enemy from the realm of historical detail to the world of nostalgic fantasy was more than an amusing literary ploy. The publication in Granada between 1592 and 1600 of Miguel de Luna's fictional history of a brilliant but decadent Hispano-Islam undoubtedly was designed to ease the path into Spanish society of former Muslims by drawing favorable comparisons between the high culture of Hispano-Islam and the chivalric society of Europe in the Middle Ages. At the same time the embellished treatment of the Moor in other literary works became a backhanded way of praising Spain's ability to overcome a powerful opposition. But the gap between the idealized picture of the noble Moor and the miserable circumstances of the Moriscos tended to confirm the belief of Old Christians that the maximum social distance, including expulsion, ought to be placed between the truly Spanish and the mass of the recent converts.[28]

If the literature of the Golden Age accepted something from Spain's Muslim past, the imaginary treatment of Islam in North Africa was a matter of total rejection. Here the fictional encounter between Spanish authors and the Muslim corsairs of North Africa gave birth to what became a standard plot: captivity, suffering, romantic adventure, longing for freedom, and eventual liberation from the slave quarters in Algiers. That this literary genre also reinforced the religious dikes separating the two societies is revealed not only by its major theme, the escape from Islam, but also by its treatment of two special subjects, love and apostasy. However complex the situation, no enduring love, or for that matter marriage, was possible between members of the two religions. In the end, romantic adventures either collapsed or concluded in a totally Christian ending with the conversion of the Muslim partner. Firm on the question of apostasy, the great crime of this age, Spanish authors were compelled to offer reasons for the substantial defection of Christian males to Islam in the coastal cities of North Africa. This aberration was explained away by attacking the firmness of the renegades' attachment to Islam: the converts were insincere, the conversion was motivated by self-interest and low birth, and the new Muslims secretly remained Christian despite wealth and honor.[29]

Just as these products of imagination captured public attention after 1580, the efforts of the Spanish historians of the North African frontier failed to attract support. The cause was not a decline in the quality of their histories. Among the most important of the authors who were outflanked by events was Luis del Mármol Carvajal. In 1535 he departed from the peninsula to fight with Charles V at Tunis and to serve in the African regiments of Spain until he was taken by Muslim corsairs around the year 1545. In captivity he learned Arabic and traveled throughout portions of the Maghrib before returning to Spain early in the reign of Philip II. Settling in Granada, Mármol began to collect data for his first book, *Descripción general de Affrica*, the first part of which appeared in 1573. Shortly before that date a Spaniard from the province of Palencia, Diego de Torres, returned to Iberia after some ten years of travel throughout Morocco. In 1586 he published a detailed account of early sixteenth-century

Moroccan history. By far the most sophisticated of these end-of-the-century histories of Islam on the North African frontier was the study of Algiers by Diego de Haëdo. A captive of the Turks in Algiers between 1571 and 1581, the Benedictine monk put down on paper an accurate description of Ottoman politics and social organization for the province of Algiers that was published only in 1612. All these informative histories were simply brushed aside by the popularity of fictional descriptions of the Muslim frontier and by the state's abandonment of the war in the Mediterranean. Mármol had to publish the second part of his general description of Africa at his own expense in 1599, and the North African histories of Torres and Haëdo fell into obscurity. Even today there is no modern edition of these three accounts of sixteenth-century North Africa.[30]

The social differentiation of the frontier also destroyed the old literary language of the Muslim border in Spain. Since the Arabic of the Muslim conquerors had not driven the Romance dialects from the peninsula, Muslim writers had created a frontier literature for popular use that rendered Romance languages in the Arabic script. As the power of Muslim civilization waned, the importance of what the Arabic-speakers called *al-ʿAjamiyya* and the Spanish *Aljamía* increased as the main means by which Hispano-Muslims could polemicize against Christianity or communicate with their co-religionists on other matters. Whether or not Old Christians understood the special importance of the Arabic script in Islamic civilization—God's gift of the Koran in Arabic characters is the divine element in Islam roughly comparable to the role of Jesus Christ in Christianity—they strove mightily to repress the use of Arabic. This action of the Christians forced those who wished to write in *Aljamía* to do so secretly or to migrate to North Africa, where they could compose their works freely. Just as the expulsion of the Moriscos in 1609 ended the history of Islamic society in Spain, so also did it bring to a conclusion the history of *aljamiada* literature in the peninsula. During the seventeenth century works composed in Spanish but written in Arabic script were produced by Spanish exiles in North Africa. Yet there also the use of this frontier language soon eroded as the Hispano-Muslims gradually were absorbed into the Arabic cultural milieu of the Maghribian cities.[31]

Less rich than the Spanish output, the anti-Christian propaganda of Muslims inhabiting the fringes of the Ottoman empire in North Africa drifted away from the subjects of war and politics as the sixteenth century ended to emphasize the religious differences between the two sides of the frontier. For the Ottoman conquest, the *Gazavat-name of Hayreddin Barbarossa* was the classical means of exalting both state and religion through a rich celebration of the exploits of heroes who went to war on the frontier to defend and expand the House of Islam. At once an anti-Christian polemic and a fairly accurate frontier history, the memoirs of Hayreddin were written in simple Turkish for a popular audience and distributed throughout the empire. By the last quarter of the century, however, the adventures of the western corsairs dropped out of Turkish frontier histories until the historian Kâtib Çelebi, in an effort to stimulate interest in the navy, summarized the adventures of the Barbarossas in his late-seventeenth-century account of the maritime wars of the Ottomans.[32] But the expulsion of the Moriscos in 1609, like the Spanish expansion into North Africa, required a response from the defenders of the community. With large-scale warfare ruled out, the seventeenth-century Christian aggression against Islam generated instead an increase in anti-Christian polemics.

The elements of Muslim propaganda against Christianity are fairly well known: an attack on the divinity of Christ, an assault on the doctrine of the Trinity, a condemnation of Christian ritual, an account of the Christian corruption of the Scriptures, and a militant defense of Muḥammad's role as the Prophet.[33] Within this genre the Muslim convert ʿAbd Allāh al-Tarǧumān (Anselim Turmeda) composed a polemic in Arabic while he was in Tunisia during 1420. Although the diffusion of his manuscript, the *Tuḥfa*, is unknown for the fifteenth and early sixteenth centuries, it is clear that his refutation of Christianity was extensively recopied (in Arabic) and translated into Turkish at the turn of the seventeenth century.[34] Along with this propaganda assault on Christianity, designed to reinforce faith in North Africa, the Hispano-Muslim exiles composed anti-Christian poetry and Muslim apologetics in *Aljamía*. These tracts not only condemned Christian doctrine and the Inquisition but also eased the entry of the Hispano-Muslims into the Arabic culture of urban North Africa. Again, the hardened Muslim attitude toward the Christians acted as one more force formalizing the divisions between Islamic and Christian civilizations.[35]

Despite the paucity of information about Moroccan literature, some sense of the intellectual drift of the times can be grasped from the limited scope of Saʿdian histories. Bounded by the hostile Ottoman empire on the east and cut off from the former source of much of its intellectual inspiration—Spain—Saʿdian court culture emerged from a highly conservative religious environment that inhibited the production of profane works. The growth of political power nevertheless stimulated pride in the accomplishments of the dynasty. In the reign of al-Manṣūr (1578–1603), two important manuscripts not only recorded the history of the period but also dealt with the exterior world. Al-Fishtālī's panegyric of al-Manṣūr discussed the Saʿdian invasion of the Sudan and noted the influence of the Turks in Morocco, at-Tamgrūtī left a manuscript describing his mission to Istanbul at the end of Murad III's reign (d. 1595). But these two works were the only historical efforts that acknowledged the influence of the outside world on the country, and they both confined themselves to the boundaries of the Islamic community.

During the tumultuous seventeenth century, two more histories of the Saʿdian dynasty surfaced from among the far more numerous manuscripts on religious questions. An anonymous chronicle written in Fez by a man who probably represented the Hispano-Muslim exiles criticized the Saʿdian sultan ʿAbdallāh al-Ghalīb (1551–74) for permitting the Spanish occupation of Badis and for failing to aid the Moriscos during the revolt of 1568–70. Yet neither the breath of criticism nor the spirit of the unconventional was present in the other seventeenth-century history, the work of al-Ifrānī. Land of sufis, saints, and tribesmen, Morocco produced a small literate population far more interested in the lives of its local religious men or in the central questions of religious law than in the events of the outer world.[36] Both political decentralization and the loss of the cultural stimulus al-Andalus used to provide turned Morocco's intellectual life inward. Hence the energy of scholars went into preserving that blend of popular and Malikite religious tradition that distinguishes Morocco not only from Iberia but also from the rest of the Islamic world.[37]

Geographically closer to the heart of Turko-Muslim civilization, the cultural milieu of Tunisia differed from that of Morocco. Once established in Tunisia, the Ottomans sponsored the recovery of a more formal version of the great tradition than existed in Morocco. Yet what infused the work of the seventeenth-century ʿulamāʾ was not the creative spirit of the classical age but the authoritarian mentality of medieval Islam. Few manuscripts on profane subjects were produced; certainly Ottomans had no desire to support works in Arabic that might emphasize the alien character of their regime. Scholars poured their intellectual energies into an effort to find among the idealized images of the Muslim past some guide for the present. In this task the nature of the world beyond the boundaries of Islamic civilization was irrelevant.[38]

If an analysis of literature can place the mind in touch with the divisive temper of the frontier, the history of border architecture can give visual substance to the growth of cultural inflexibility. Long before the fifteenth century, the Gothic style of architecture, epitomized by the great cathedrals of Leon, Burgos, and Toledo, had evolved into a clearly stated symbol of the Christian society of the north. As the *reconquista* moved toward the south, Christian rulers carried this new style of religious architecture into Islamic territories. There the very size of the cathedrals left little doubt in the eyes of the beholder which of the two cultures would predominate. Surprisingly, however, Islamic art retained a position even in the monumental religious works of the conquerors. Although architects and stonecutters from Europe did shape the basic forms of the cathedrals and palaces of the Christian elite, the minor arts stayed largely in the hands of Muslim or Morisco craftsmen. There were two reasons for this. First, the abstract decorative art that the Muslims had raised to a high point of development remained popular despite its connection with the Islamic past. Second, many of the crafts that produced the bricks, sculptured wood, molded plaster, glazed tiles, metal ornaments, walls, ceilings, and floors remained in the hands of Muslims or Moriscos, who were willing to work for wages far less than those paid the master builders imported from northern Europe. But though both tradition and economics kept some part of Islamic art alive in the conquered regions, its future seemed dim. Everywhere the men who commissioned or built the new monuments pushed the Islamic heritage into the background or transposed its spirit into auxiliary elements that supported the religious mood of the Old Christians.[39]

A new stage in architectural development overtook Christian Spain in 1480, when the Catholic kings began to exert greater control over their realms. The architectural school appropriately named "Isabelline" combined the structures of the late Gothic era with the forms of the Italian Renaissance and with the decorative heritage of Islamic art. Although trained in Brussels, Juan Guas exemplified this eclectic nature of the Isabelline style, which blended the cultural forces of the time into buildings such as the Palacio del Infantado in Guadalejara or the chapel of San Gregorio in Valladolid.[40]

Balanced among three traditions, the Isabelline architecture advanced with the Catholic kings into Granada. Although Islam left many monuments in the southeastern portion of the peninsula, the main and most famous example of its late architectural glory was the royal palace complex of the Alhambra. When the Catholic kings entered the walls of the Naṣrid residence, they encountered a decorative art form that had reached its creative peak in the four-teenth century and an arrangement of imperial dwellings altogether foreign to the architecture of the European palace. Rather than organizing the grounds around the royal dwelling, the builders of the Alhambra set the Naṣrid chambers among courtyards and formal pleasure gardens arranged so that there was an alliance between the surrounding environment and the buildings. The modest size and exterior decoration of the pleasure palaces were intended not to praise the power and majesty of the builder but rather to insure the privacy of the interior. Equally, the intricate construction of the fragile courtyards and the elaborate use of molded plaster and colored tiles aimed to charm the eye of the guest rather than over-whelm him with the grandeur of the host's palace.[41]

Christian architects soon demonstrated that Granada's conquest would not give birth to any architectural compromise. Rather, the rulers of Spain commissioned buildings that announced the artistic incompatibility between the two civilizations. Three royal monu-ments, all in the city of Granada, give some sense of the symbolic clash that the final reconquest precipitated. Authorized on 13 Septem-ber 1504, the royal chapel that was to receive the remains of Ferdi-nand and Isabella was constructed in the pattern of the Gothic past. On the adjoining ground, originally the site of the city's main mosque, Isabella marked the spot for Granada's cathedral. Construc-tion of a large building, again in the Gothic mold, began in 1523. By 1528, however, the cathedral experienced a stylistic mutation at the hands of Diego de Silve. The outcome was a hybrid form whose lines moved away from the Gothic past and toward some sort of a compromise not with high Islamic culture, but with the Italian Renaissance. Erecting heavy walls covered with sculptured structures that gave the impression of a rough energy, Diego de Silve patterned the nave of the cathedral in the shape of a rotunda, thereby providing a direct contrast with the rectangular structure Muslims employed for the outline of mosques. But it was the palace of Charles V that pointed to the source of artistic inspiration for Spanish architects. Begun in 1526 by Pedro Machcusa, an Italian palace done purely in the Renaissance style was built next to the Alhambra.[42] This juxta-position of two strikingly different buildings yields a visual measure of the gap separating the Morisco society of Granada—which was compelled to pay for the palace—from the Old Christians.

To bring order into the controversies created by the cultural impact of Renaissance art upon Spain, Charles V organized royal works with greater care after 1530. But a slow and more tasteful transplanting of Italian motifs to Iberia did not satisfy the courtly class, who wished to develop an architectural symbol of Spain's imperial grandeur. Philip II met that demand with the construction of the grim Escorial, which then became a model for many other state structures. Dominating the surroundings with its massive size and forbidding gray exterior, the Escorial impresses upon the viewer the power of state and religion. Its towering walls everywhere stand in fearsome opposition to the spirit that moved the Naṣrid sultans during the construction of the Alhambra. Though glazed tiles, richly carved ceilings, and the tendency to soften harsh surfaces with patterned ornamentation did creep back into the provincial churches of Andalucia after 1560, the revival of Islamic motifs among the minor arts hardly challenged the national architecture of the late sixteenth century that brought to the old Muslim frontier the severe designs of the Seville exchange (1582–99) and the chancellería of Granada (1587).[43]

During the fifteenth century the Ottomans also encountered the symbolic problems that the variety of architectural styles and the competition with another civilization forced upon an expansive state. Having begun their urban history in Anatolia, where they occupied a position on the frontier of the Seljuk state of Konya, the Turkish march warriors erected their first religious buildings in a manner inspired by the practices of the Muslim east. When the Ottomans crossed into Europe and occupied Edirne, they began to create a style of architecture that was less dependent upon Anatolian traditions. During the reign of Murad II, the construction of the Three Gallied Mosque (Üç Şerefeli Camii, 1437–47) in Edirne presaged the development of an imperial style of architecture. Lengthening the minarets, adding on a courtyard surrounding a fountain, lightening the interior of the building, and increasing the size of the dome covering the prayer niche, Ottoman architects broke away from the pattern of mosque construction employed during the Seljuk period. The conquest of Istanbul in 1453, however, compelled the Turks to come to terms with a religious monument of extraordinary symbolic importance: the Hagia Sophia. Unlike the Spanish in Granada, the Turko-Muslims neither destroyed nor excluded the culture of

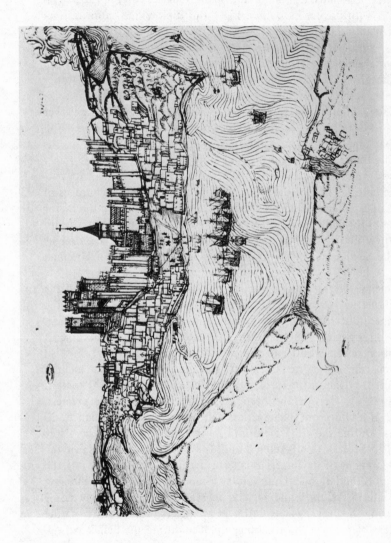

Fig. 8. The spectacular size of sixteenth-century Cadiz's cathedral and fortress symbolizes early modern Spain's appropriation of the frontier.

Orthodox Christianity from their monumental religious iconography; rather, they shaped the architectural accomplishments of Byzantium to their own needs, as the reconstructed plan of the conqueror's mosque—the Fatıh Camii (1463–71)—indicates. Maintaining the outer courtyard, the architect of the new mosque concentrated on the central dome while prolonging the space over the prayer niche with a half dome.[44]

Beginning with the creation of the Bayezit mosque in 1505, the classical age of Ottoman architecture reached its zenith in the latter half of the sixteenth century under the architect Sinan Paşa, who perfected a style of mosque architecture that was distinctly Ottoman. With the Şehzade mosque (1548), the great builder began to employ half domes and windows to satisfy the Turko-Muslim desire for a grand religious building that would have both a harmonious exterior and an interior lighter than that of the Hagia Sophia. With the completion of the Selimiye mosque in Edirne between 1570 and 1574, the Ottoman architect set the capstone on the classical religious architecture of the empire. Integrating the subsidiary buildings—almshouse, hospital, religious schools, and so on—into a unified plan in which the mosque was the principal structure, Sinan Paşa provided the Turkish rulers not only with a domed building whose span exceeded that of Hagia Sophia, but also with a religious edifice whose windows lit up an interior done in the firm colors of the Turkish style of Islamic decorative art. These creations of Sinan then set the pattern for future mosques—the Ahmediye or Blue Mosque (1609–17) and the Yeni Valide Camii (1651) in Istanbul—and became the architecture the sultans exported to their provinces.[45]

But the expansion of the Ottomans into the central Maghrib during the sixteenth century took the eastern dynasty into a land that already had a well-developed style of Islamic religious architecture. The grand mosque of Algiers, the main mosque of Tlemsen, and a smaller mosque at Nedromah represented this North African architectural tradition in Algeria. There square minarets, often decorated with a style of exterior brickwork going back to the Almoravid period, stood next to rectangular mosques whose peaked roofs were often covered with green tiles. The interiors of these buildings included the lobed arches, stalagtite wall decorations, and molded plaster that suggested the influence of the interior decorations of the Umayyad mosque at Cordoba.[46] Committed to the defense of Islam, the Ottoman conquerors maintained these old religious centers while adding their own places of worship.

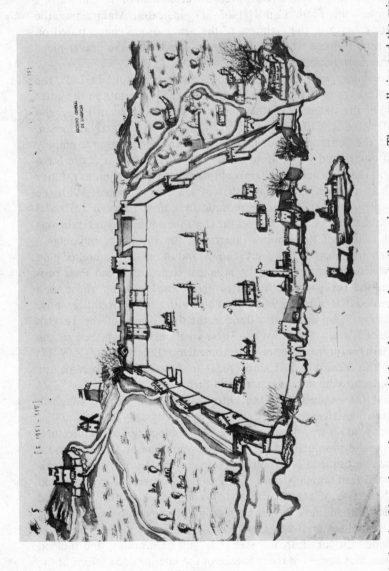

Fig. 9. A sketch of late-sixteenth-century Algiers drawn to locate the major mosques. The small size and the mixture of Ottoman and North African mosques marks the conservative form of Turkish imperialism.

Since the Ottoman religious architecture of North Africa has attracted little attention, it is difficult to discuss its influence upon the religious art of North Africa. Haëdo's detailed description of Algiers in 1580 argues strongly that the Ottomans did attempt to express their right to rule in North Africa by building mosques. Enough of these monuments of the Turkish period have survived to show how the influence of the east once again reached North Africa. The walls of the early-seventeenth-century Mosque of the Fisherman in Algiers, laid out not in a square but in the form of a Latin cross, support a great dome constructed from bricks in the Ottoman mode: the circle within the square. Similarly, the small mosque of Safir, built by a freed slave of Hayreddin Barbarossa, evokes images of the Anatolian plateau. The traces of Turkish architecture in Bône and Constantine and the cupola and tiles of the Zāwiya of Sidī ʿAbd ar-Raḥmān offer other reminders of a Turko-Muslim architecture that must have been considerably more developed than what remains visible today. However extensive the Ottoman mark in religious construction, its influence was related to the thinness of the Ottoman ruling class and the eastern sultanate's lack of concern for the North African border after 1580. West of Algiers the monumental art of the east rapidly gave way to older patterns.[47]

Isolated from the mainstream of political and artistic events, and conservative in intellectual and religious matters, Morocco adopted no new lines of development in architecture. As the building program of the Saʿdian sultan in Marrakesh indicated, the source of artistic inspiration was Hispano-Muslim.[48] When Spain eliminated the main source of talent for this religious architecture and the Ottomans blocked expansion to the east, the Moroccan elite in Marrakesh limited its horizons to what was known. Never going much beyond what the Merinids had accomplished in the fourteenth century, the religious architecture of Fez remained firmly conservative.[49] In Tetuan and Rabat Moriscos brought some architectural variety into the coastal cities of the western Maghrib, but the political disintegration of the Saʿdian state in the seventeenth century, the hostility between the Spanish Muslims and the older population, and the general reluctance to change checked whatever new ideas the Hispano-Muslims might have carried to Morocco.[50]

Moroccan architecture was another highly visible sign of a deepening division between the two Mediterranean civilizations. Artistic and linguistic impulses affecting the frontier indicated strongly that neither society could find much worthwhile in what the other had accomplished. Either through fantasy or through a refusal to study the ways of the unbeliever, the literate reduced their attempts to understand their neighbors. Similarly, the grand religious symbols that marked out the Ibero-African frontier displayed the acuteness of the divergence between the two civilizations. By the middle of the seventeenth century a long integration of great cultures was well on its way to being forgotten by both empires.

Ten: THE MEDITERRANEAN DIVIDED

*Man can never be reduced to one personality who can be summed up
in an acceptable simplification. This is everyone's pipe dream.*
Fernand Braudel, *Capitalism and Material Life, 1400–1800*

The long cohabitation of Muslims and Christians within the same
well-defined geographical arena became the basis for Fernand
Braudel's study of how Mediterranean peoples shared a common
history. But similarities between the experiences of these two
cultures should not encourage one to overlook the differences.
Even though the time was marked by such events as inflation,
population increase, disease, climatic change, and other manifestations of an underlying life rhythm that was culturally neutral, the
main theme of Mediterranean history during the sixteenth century
was the cumulative divergence of its two civilizations.

I have, however, not attempted to study the Mediterranean world
in its entirety; rather, I have concentrated upon a frontier that was a
historically important scene of cultural exchange and innovation,
in order to analyze how the rulers of the Habsburg and Ottoman
empires dealt with a common periphery. In the manner of an
economist employing marginal analysis, I have used the history of
this interaction of the two civilizations on the frontier itself to
support my argument about the course of Mediterranean history.

In the most general sense, both empires adopted strong defensive
postures that, at a time when state power reached new levels, reduced
the old zone of mixed cultures to a thin line between well-organized
societies. The attendant disappearance of cultural ambivalence along
the Ibero-African frontier was the border manifestation of a much
larger, unique divergence of Latin Christian and Turko-Muslim
civilizations.

For some, the emphasis placed upon the political history of this division will appear old-fashioned at a time when historians ought to go beneath the surface of events. I have ignored that caveat for three reasons. Mediterranean history during the early modern era is still approached from a European angle because Ottoman data remain largely inaccessible to most scholars. There is, moreover, a much deeper reason that warrants another jab at the already deflated reputation of the battle of Lepanto. In contrast to the history of Christendom, political achievement and the organization of Islamic society were born together. Muslims consequently have regarded accomplishment in war and politics as a manifestation of God's will. Victories like those won by Ottoman sultans had a great impact upon the strength of imperial institutions. Accordingly, both European and Ottoman historians need to be reminded that one of the elements in the history of decline is the powerful heritage of Ottoman political success: the persistence of the imperial ideal throughout the vast spaces of a decentralized empire.

Toward the end of the sixteenth century both Mediterranean empires withdrew from imperial warfare with a certain degree of honor. Paradoxically, the balance of naval power that lay behind this disengagement was accompanied by Europe's acquiring a decisive lead in naval technology. One of the enduring clichés for explaining the subsequent period of Ottoman decline underscores the importance of this event: "God gave the land to Muslims and the sea to the infidels."

Why did Islamic society, whose own contributions to the advance of naval technology were historically important, fail to innovate in this area? My answer is complex. First, by 1580 Europe had advanced qualitatively and quantitatively far beyond the experience of eastern Mediterranean mariners. Catching up would have required great exertion, and Ottomans displayed little interest in funding such an effort. Fleets were inordinately expensive and the galley still seemed to be an effective weapon within the Mediterranean. Why should the state experiment with oceanic conquests when it had difficulty exploiting a huge continental empire? Finally, the Ottomans governed a well-defined social and cultural order as arbitrators rather than as "oriental despots." Neither rulers nor subjects wished to adopt technologies or economies that would produce conflict within an imperial society composed of a multitude of nearly self-governing religious and ethnic communities. The vigorous state capitalism, extensive technological innovation, and extraordinary social mobility of early modern Europe exceeded the limits of the Islamic social order.

In any event, the failure of the Islamic community to participate in the maritime revolution of the early modern era marked a significant break with the history of Latin Christendom. As is well known, the sailing ship operated as an advanced communications system, diffusing ideas, techniques, and technology throughout Europe, and expanding the range and scale of Europe's commercial system. Though these changes in commerce and technology had no destructive impact upon the institutions of the Ottoman empire in the decades after 1580, they must be recognized as part of an external framework that later determined the special shape of both Turko-Muslim and Mediterranean decline. The surface consequences for the Ottomans are fairly well known: the empire's military establishment became land-bound and retrograde, while the commercial economy of Eurasian Islam shrank in comparison with the oceangoing trade of the West.

By far the most striking example of this structural divergence came about in the social arena. After having found their urban center in the fifteenth century, the Ottomans extended the boundaries of an imperial society to North Africa. With the help of new administrative techniques and military technology, the Turks overpowered the city-states of the Maghrib, drove the tribesmen away from urban centers, and superimposed an alien ruling class on local society. When expansion ceased, the power of the central administration weakened and the politics of the empire shifted toward a graded level of obedience between the center and the frontier. At no point in this history of political change did the Ottomans or the Saʿdians attempt to create a homogeneous society. The North African community was to remain, and wished to remain, organized into myriad ethnic, religious, and status groups. Ottomans applied their political and administrative talents to preserve the boundaries of these small human units; for maintaining such a social structure increased the subjects' dependence on the Ottomans as the only rulers capable of defending both the great tradition and the pluralistic character of the social order. Political decentralization and the migration of Spain's exiles merely strengthened the loyalty of the frontier's populations to a highly conservative society whose richly textured forms marked the periphery of the last and most powerful of Islamic civilization's bureaucratic empires.

Near the Strait of Gibraltar the edge of another empire with a strikingly different society approached the Ottoman frontier in

North Africa. Well before the rise of Turkish power in the Maghrib, social change on the peninsula had created a unique consciousness of unity among Old Christians—one that went beyond mere membership in a religious community. No better example of this yearning for a new order can be found than the efforts of the secular and ecclesiastical bureaucracies to impose the values and social practices of Old Christians on former Muslims. Although its actions were legitimized in terms of religion, the state wished to change more than the beliefs of its newly conquered populations. Loyalty to kin and attachment to village, religious community, and status group were to be downgraded in favor of membership in a more universal social order. If God made men and not lineages, as the cliché went, he also established the use of the Spanish language as one of the main requirements for entry into the larger community. Though not applied overnight, the persistent attempt of Spain's central administration to foster social and linguistic homogeneity among the populations of its southeastern periphery stood in sharp contrast to the internal policies of the Ottomans. For many of the Moriscos the cost of assimilation came too high. With a proficient demonstration of its willingness to tinker with the human order, the Habsburg government expelled the Hispano-Muslims and thereby drew the frontier of an emerging national society.

So the two civilizations followed distinctly different paths: the Ottoman was conservative and the Iberian radical; but the general result was the same in that the social differences between the two civilizations became more formal.

Similarly, this book advances the proposition that the systems of belief within Muslim North Africa and southeastern Spain neither eroded nor stood still during the sixteenth century. On the contrary, dynamic interaction between the two civilizations invigorated an attachment to exclusively defined religions just as it reinforced the social differences between the two great traditions. While saints, sufis, and scholars won the loyalty of Muslims, Spanish society pledged itself to the defense of a revived Roman Catholicism.

Both empires also produced an educated class that worked hard at creating an acceptable secular culture. Just as Ottomans defended an inherited religious tradition, they adopted a literary heritage infused with the spirit of conservatism, of a world already known. In Spain the growth of an early-modern lettered public stirred up problems entirely different from those of the Islamic world. Armed with the printing press, a national language, and a network of universities, the educated threatened religious doctrine. They gave birth to a tension in Latin Christian society that had no parallel in Ottoman lands, where the threat to established religion came not from the middle ranges of society but from the periphery. But it was in the area of secular literature that the divergence is best grasped. There the protean capacities of early modern Spanish authors created a national literature in stark contrast to the Islamic prose and poetry of the Ottoman court. Even the Ottoman language itself—a complex mixture of Turkish, Arabic, and Persian—underlined the strength of a cultural tradition that long before had definitively rejected a national identification and an easy access to knowledge.

After 1580 the Habsburg and Ottoman empires participated much less in the unified maritime culture that the sea encouraged. Rather, the history of their common frontier showed how each imperial center contributed to the formalization of a border structure that inhibited cultural diffusion. By the first decade of the seventeenth century, the two empires entered an era in which Mediterranean civilizations drifted apart under the influence of differing social and cultural forces. For the Ibero-African border, this separation further reduced the level of exchange and conflict between the two opposing societies, permitting the frontier to be "forgotten."

At the end of the eighteenth century a new collection of human and technological power destroyed the old cultural division of the Mediterranean world. Islamic and Western civilizations came together to begin a long period of conflict that produced no convergence of the two traditions. Thus the tranquility of the relations between Turko-Muslim and Western states during the centuries of stability cannot be taken as evidence of an emerging Mediterranean civilization. Nor can scholars describe the centuries of decline as an Islamic Dark Ages that prepared the way for the westernization or modernization of Islamic society. Powerful divisions remained. How to respect the strengths of profoundly different civilizations and to explain the cultural violence the intermixing of the two traditions produced are the central problems for an understanding of Mediterranean decline. In light of those requirements the history of the Ibero-African frontier, complete with all the tragic encounters resulting from multiple human identities, cannot be forgotten.

ABBREVIATIONS

AGS	Archivo General de Simancas
AHR	*American Historical Review*
AM	*Archives Marocaines*
BA	Başbakanlık Arşivi, Istanbul
BAE	*Biblioteca de autores españoles*
BM	British Museum, London
BN	Bibliothèque Nationale, Paris
BNM	Biblioteca Nacional de Madrid
BSOAS	*Bulletin of the School of Oriental and African Studies*
CODOIN	*Colección de documentos ineditos para la historia de España*, 112 vols. (Madrid, 1842–90)
Danişmend	Ismail Hami Danişmend, *Izahlı Osmanlı Tarihi Kronolojisi*, 2d ed., 5 vols. (Istanbul, 1971)
DOP	*Dumbarton Oaks Papers*
*EI*²	*The Encyclopedia of Islam*, new ed. (London, 1954–)
Es-Salâoui	Ahmed Ben Khalid en-Naçiri, *Kitab el-Istiqça Li Akhbar Doul el-Maghrib el-Aqça*, trans. Mohammed en-Naçiri, in *Archives marocaines*, vol. 24 (Paris, 1936)
Gómara	Francisco Lopez de Gómara, *Crónica de los Barbarojas*, in *Memorial histórico español*, vol. 6 (Madrid, 1853)
Hayreddin	"Gazavat-i Hayreddin Paşa," British Museum, Oriental Ms. no. 2798
İA	*İslâm ansiklopedisi*, Istanbul, 1940–
IBLA	*Institut des belles lettres arabes*

IJMES	*International Journal of Middle Eastern Studies*
JEH	*Journal of Economic History*
Kâtib Çelebi[2]	Kâtib Çelebi, *Tuhfet ül kibar fi Esfar ul Bihar* (Istanbul, 1911)
MD	Mühimme Defterleri
MEAH	*Miscelánea de estudios árabes y hebraicos*
RA	*Revue Africaine*
ROMM	*Revue d l'Occident musulman et de la Mediterranée*
SIHM	*Sources inédits de l'histoire du Maroc*
TKS	Topkapı Sarayı, Istanbul
TOEM	*Tarih-i Osmani Encümeni Mecmuası*, (Istanbul, 1908–18)

NOTE ON UNPUBLISHED SOURCES

The documentary core of this study is based upon archival research in the Baş Bakanlık Arşivi in Istanbul, Turkey, and the Archivo General de Simancas in Simancas, Spain.

To date, the most important material in the Turkish Archives available for the study of North African history comes from the Mühimme Defterleri [Registers of important affairs]. The importance of these materials is covered in Uriel Heyd, *Ottoman Documents on Palestine, 1552–1615* (Oxford, 1960). My system for citing these sources is as follows: archival number of the register (MD 23), page number followed by the order number (139:284), and the date attached to the order in the register (28 B 981/1573). To indicate months I have used the archival system: Muharram, M; Safer, S; Rebiyülevvel, RA; Rebiyülahır, R; Cemaziyelevvel, CA; Cemaziyelahır, C; Recep, B; Şaban, Ş; Ramazan, N; Şevval, L; Zilkade, ZA; Zilhicce, Z. Where the date is important, I have given the Christian equivalent according to the table in Faik Reşit Unat, *Hicrî Tarihleri Milâdî Tarihe Çevirme Kılavusu* (Ankara, 1959).

A brief description of the other registers and documents employed in this research is available in Midhat Sertoğlu, *Muhteva Bakımından Başvekâlet Arşivi* (Ankara, 1955). A survey of Ottoman archival sources in English is in S. J. Shaw, "Archival Sources for Ottoman History: The Archives of Turkey," *Journal of the American Oriental Society* 80 (1960): 1–12.

The Archivo General de Simancas is a major source for the history of both sixteenth-century North Africa and the Ottoman empire. A guide to the materials contained therein is Angel de la Plaza's *Guía del Investigador* (Valladolid, 1962). I have profited most from the following series:

1. Secretaría de Estado, especially the sections dealing with Costas de Africa y Levante and Expediciones marítimas a Levante y prevenciones de guerra.
2. Cámara de Castilla.
3. Guerra y Marina.
4. Contaduría Mayor de Cuentas.

NOTES

CHAPTER ONE

1. J. H. Hexter, "Fernand Braudel and the *Monde Braudellier* ...," *Journal of Modern History* 44, no. 4 (December, 1972): 480–539.

2. Fernand Braudel, *The Mediterranean and the Mediterranean World in the Age of Philip II*, trans. Siân Reynolds (New York, 1975), 2:892–903ff.

3. Ibid., 2:827, for example. Braudel, however, recognized the permanence of Mediterranean civilizations (ibid., 2:757–835).

4. Although a center-periphery analysis is applied here on a comparative basis, the article by Şerif Mardin, "Center-Periphery Relations: A Key to Turkish Politics?" *Daedalus* 102, no. 1 (winter 1973), pp. 169–90, is highly suggestive.

5. Xavier de Phantol, *Les fondements géographiques de l'histoire de l'Islam* (Paris, 1968), pp. 282–90..

6. Thomas F. Glick and Oriol Pi-Sunyer, "Acculturation as an Explanatory Concept in Spanish History," *Comparative Studies in Society and History* 2, no. 2 (April 1969): 136–54.

7. For other frontiers, see Dietrich Gerhard, "The Frontier in Comparative View," *Comparative Studies in Society and History* 1, no. 3 (1958–59): 205–29.

8. Elena Lourie, "A Society Organized for War: Medieval Spain," *Past and Present* 25 (1966): 54–76, is a good example of the military theme in Spanish history.

9. A recent addition to this scholarly controversy is Andrew S. Ehrenkreutz, "Another Orientalist's Remarks concerning the Pirenne Thesis," *Journal of the Economic and Social History of the Orient* 15, nos. 1–2 (June 1972): 94–104.

10. The best summary of the influence Islamic civilization exerted on Europe is still *The Legacy of Islam*, ed. Thomas Arnold and Alfred Guillaume (London, 1947), pp. 180–209 and passim.

11. On Wittek's theory concerning the origin of the Ottoman state, see Paul Wittek, *The Rise of the Ottoman Empire* (London, 1938). Castro's ideas are available in Américo Castro, *The Spaniards*, trans. Willard F. King and Selma Margaretten (Berkeley, 1971).

12. Although aware of the importance of the Maghribian border after 1571, Braudel, *The Mediterranean*, 2:1027–1142, follows the traditional path of European political history. For a criticism of this viewpoint based on Ottoman materials, see Andrew C. Hess, "The Battle of Lepanto and Its Place in Mediterranean History," *Past and Present* 57 (November 1972): 53–73. From a Maghribian perspective, Abdallah Laroui, *L'histoire du Maghreb: Un essai de synthèse* (Paris, 1970), pp. 9–17, 211–43, also criticizes the European-centered interpretations of North African history.

13. Queiros Velloso, *D. Sebastião, 1557–1578*, 3d ed. (Lisbon, 1945), pp. 337–420; and E. W. Bovill, *The Battle of Alcazar* (London, 1952).

14. Es-Salâoui, *Les Saadiens*, *AM* 34:143. An Ottoman author of the same generation as Es-Salâoui gave only a few lines to the battle of Alcazar. Mustafa Nuri Paşa, *Netaic-ül-vukuat* (Istanbul, 1877–1909), 1:121–22. One of the main reasons for the lack of interest Turkish historians have displayed in the history of Morocco is that the seventeenth-century Ottoman scholar, Kâtib Çelebi, *Tuhfet ül Kibar fi Esfar ul Bihar* (Istanbul, 1911), pp. 98–99, (hereafter cited as Kâtib Çelebi[2]), ends his history of Ottoman naval expansion four years before the battle of Alcazar with the reconquest of Tunis in 1574. Modern Turkish historians tend to follow Kâtib Çelebi's organization of North African history: Ismail Hakkı Uzunçarşılı, *Osmanlı Tarihi* (Ankara, 1954), 3:268–69; the Mustafa Cezar et al., *Mufassal Osmanlı Tarihi* (Istanbul, 1959), 3:1299–1302, where the authors, on the basis of archival sources, give the battle of Alcazar more space and importance.

15. See two classic studies, representing different points of view: Henry Charles Lea, *The Moriscos of Spain* (Philadelphia, 1901); and D. Pascual Boronat y Barrachina, *Los Moriscos españoles y su expulsión* (2 vols., Valencia, 1901).

16. Instead, Moroccan warriors invaded sub-Saharan Africa. E. W. Bovill, *The Golden Trade of the Moors*, 2d ed. (London, 1970), pp. 154–206.

17. Albert Mas, *Les Turcs dans la littérature espagnole du siècle d'or* (Paris, 1967), 2:469–72.

18. R. L. Playfair, *The Scourge of Christendom* (London, 1884), describes the corsairs in the manner of the medieval propagandists against Islam. The work of Alberto Tenenti, *Piracy and the Decline of Venice, 1580–1615*, trans. Janet and Brian Pullan (London, 1967), goes well beyond both propaganda and romance.

19. Braudel, *The Mediterranean*, 2:1186–1237; and his subsequent work, *Capitalism and Material Life, 1400–1800*, trans. Miriam Kochan (New York, 1973).

CHAPTER TWO

1. Andrew C. Hess, "Piri Reis and the Ottoman Response to the Voyages of Discovery," *Terrae Incognitae* 6 (1974): 19–37.

2. Jean Delumeau, *La civilisation de la Renaissance* (Paris, 1967), pp. 173–203 and passim. Here only those general movements that directly encouraged European expansion have been touched upon.

3. Vitorino Magalhães Godinho, *História económica e social da expansão portuguesa* (Lisbon, 1947), 1:129–30, arrived at a figure of 6,527,625 for the population of Morocco, which is clearly too high. Even half this number, however, would place Morocco among the well-populated regions of the Mediterranean world. Portugal's human weight in the sixteenth century is taken from Braudel, *The Mediterranean* 1:394–95.

4. Pierre Chaunu, *L'expansion européenne du xiiie au xve siècle* (Paris, 1969), pp. 106–10, 184–88.

5. Vitorino Magalhães Godinho, *A economia dos descobrimentos Henriquinos* (Lisbon, 1962), pp. 69–81, 109–27; and John L. Vogt, "Crusading and Commercial Elements in the Portuguese Capture of Ceuta (1415)," *Muslim World* 59, nos. 3–4 (July–October 1969): 287–99.

6. Frédéric Mauro, *Le Portugal et l'Atlantique au XVIIe siècle (1570–1670)* (Paris, 1960), pp. 28–52.

7. Piri Reis, *Kitab-ı Bahriye* (Istanbul, 1935), pp. 37–52.

8. Chaunu, *L'expansion européenne*, pp. 288–307.

9. C. R. Boxer, *The Portuguese Seaborne Empire, 1415–1825* (New York, 1969), pp. 4–17 and passim; and Vitorino Magalhães Godinho, *L'économie de l'empire portugais aux XVe et XVIe siècles* (Paris, 1969), pp. 181–88.

10. The connection between the goldfield of sub-Saharan Africa and the foundation of Mina was well known in the sixteenth century. Piri Reis, *Kitab*, pp. 31 and 34, and his early sixteenth-century map of the Atlantic show that the Ottomans had identified the source of the African gold and knew of the Portuguese activity in the Gulf of Guinea. Âfet Inan, in *The Oldest Map of America, Drawn by Piri Reis*, trans. Leman Yolaç (Ankara, 1954), pp. 28–34, has written a short history of the map. Godinho, *L'économie*, pp. 209–43 analyzes the history of the trading post on the basis of Portuguese sources.

11. Mauro, *Le Portugal*, pp. 13–27; Pierre Chaunu, *L'Amérique et les Amériques* (Paris, 1964), pp. 61–67, 88–93; Piri Reis, *Kitab*, pp. 34–47.

12. This is the implication of Carlo Cipolla's *Guns, Sails and Empires* (New York, 1966).

13. John Francis Guilmartin, Jr., *Gunpowder and Galleys* (London, 1974), pp. 163–66 and passim.

14. Ibid., pp. 194–220; and Cipolla, *Guns*, p. 81.

15. Pierre Chaunu, *Conquête et exploitation des nouveaux mondes* (Paris, 1969), pp. 277–90.

16. Danişmend, *Kronolojisi*, 2:330–31, 338–40, dates the Malta

campaign. The seasonal character of Mediterranean naval warfare was very old by the sixteenth century, as Braudel, *The Mediterranean*, 1:248–53, demonstrates.

17. Godinho, *Descobrimentos Henriquinos*, pp. 83–107, 129–50, portrays the history of the Portuguese imperial adventure as a struggle between terrestrial and maritime modes of expansion. Jean-Léon l'Africain, *Description de l'Afrique*, trans. A. Epaulard (Paris, 1956), 1:74–79, 92, 96, 109–10, 119–27, 160–61, 172–74, 251–58, 261–65, 268–71; and Robert Richard " Le commerce de Berbérie et l'organisation économique de l'empire portuguese aux xvᵉ et xviᵉ siècles," *Etudes sur l'histoire de portugais au Maroc* (Coimbra, 1955), pp. 81–144, document the establishment of the Portuguese factories from opposite sides of the frontier.

18. Andrés Bernáldez, *Memorias del reinado de los reyes católicos* (Madrid, 1962), pp. 103–7; Ibn Kemal, *Tevārih-i-Âl-i Osman, III Defter*, transcription by Şerafettin Turan (Ankara, 1954–57), 2:510–20; Piri Reis, *Kitab*, p. 445.

19. Catalonia's activity in North Africa is studied in great detail by Charles-Emmanuel Dufourcq, *L'Espagne catalane et le Maghrib aux XIIIᵉ et XIVᵉ siècles* (Paris, 1966), pp. 26–31, 267–68, 308–38, 511–76.

20. The problems the checkboard dispersion of Habsburg territories raised for the empire are the subject of Vitorino Magalhães Godinho, "A viragem mundial de 1517–1524 e o império português," in *Ensaios sobre história de Portugal* (Lisbon, 1968), 2:141–53.

21. Francisco-Felipo Olesa Muñido, *La organización naval de los estados mediterráneos y en especial de España durante los siglos XVI y XVII* (Madrid, 1968), 1:74–75, 119–22, 448–55.

22. The profoundly conservative maritime tradition the Ottomans acquired expressed itself in ship design, Kâtib Çelebi[2], pp. 151–53; in cartography, Svat Soucek, "The Ali Macar Reis Atlas and the Denizkitabı: Their Place in the Genre of Portolan Charts and Atlases," *Imago Mundi* 25 (1971): 17–27; and in nautical language, Henry and Renée Kahane and Andreas Tietze, *The Lingua Franca in the Levant* (Urbana, Ill., 1958), pp. 2–29.

23. Andrew C. Hess, "The Evolution of the Ottoman Seaborne Empire in the Age of the Oceanic Discoveries, 1453–1525," *AHR* 75, no. 7 (December 1970): 1892–1919.

24. Rachel Arié, *L'Espagne musulmane au temps des Naṣrides (1232–1492)* (Paris, 1973), pp. 230–38.

25. Ibid., pp. 238–60; and Lourie, "A Society Organized for War," pp. 54–76, for Christian tactics and armament in the prepowder era.

26. Arié, *L'Espagne musulmane*, pp. 261–62.

27. J. Vignón, *El ejército de los reyes católicos* (Madrid, 1968), pp. 14, 27, 42, 103, 124–25, 129–30, 190–91.

28. Miguel Ángel Ladero Quesada, *Castilla y la conquista del reino de Granada* (Valladolid, 1967), p. 159 and passim.
29. Ibid., pp. 117–28; and Vignón, *El ejército*, pp. 129–30.
30. Ladero Quesada, *Castilla y la conquista*, p. 126; and idem, *La hacienda real de Castilla en el siglo XV* (Seville, 1973), pp. 291–94, for the state expenses of Castile in 1488.
31. The decisive impact of powder weapons in the Portuguese invasion of Africa is noted in *Sources inédites de l'histoire du Maroc, première série; Dynastie sa'dienne, sous sèr. 5: Archives et bibliothèques de Portugal* (hereafter *SIHM*, Port.), ed. H. de Castries, R. Richard, and Chantal de la Véronne (Paris, 1934–53), 1:114–19, 226–28, 271–80; and R. Richard, "A propos de 'rebato'; Note sur la tactique militaire dans les places portugaises du Maroc," *Bulletin hispanique* 35 (1933): 448–53.
32. On the social structure of the tribesmen, see chap. 4. Ibn Khaldun, *The Muqaddimah*, trans. Franz Rosenthal, 2d ed., 3 vols. (Princeton, 1967), 2:3–200.
33. Charles-André Julien, *History of North Africa*, trans. John Petrie (London, 1972), pp. 138–217. On the shifting relationship between the tribes and settled governments, see Fredrik Barth, "A General Perspective on Nomad-Sedentary Relations in the Middle East," and Talal Asad, "The Beduin as a Military Force: Notes on Some Aspects of Power Relations between Nomads and Sedentaries in Historical Perspective," both in *The Desert and the Sown*, ed. Cynthia Nelson (Berkeley, Calif., 1973), pp. 11–21, 61–73.
34. Ibn Khaldoun, *Histoire des Berbères*, trans. Baron de Slaine, ed. P. Casanova (Paris, 1968–69), 2:316–18, 385–86, 463–66; 3:110–11, 119–22, 342–47, 414, 450–51; 4:297–300. Administrative details concerning the Almohad army are given in J. F. Hopkins, *Medieval Muslim Government in Barbary* (London, 1958), pp. 71–84, 85–111.
35. R. Brunschvig, *La Berbérie orientale sous les Ḥafṣids des origines à la fin du xve siècle* (Paris, 1940–47), 1:440–51; 2:75–98.
36. Dufourcq, *L'Espagne catalane*, pp. 101–6, 149–55, 283, 458–61, 487, 514–18, covers the use of Christian mercenaries in North Africa during the thirteenth and fourteenth centuries.
37. The figure is based upon the history of the Ḥafṣid army. Brunschvig, *La Berbérie*, 2:90.
38. On North African warfare, see Ibn Khaldun, *The Muqaddimah*, 2:73–89; and Brunschvig, *La Berbérie*, 2:75–98. G. S. Colin, "Bārūd-.-ii.-The Maghrib," in *EI²*, 1:1057–58, dates the arrival of powder weapons in Islamic North Africa at the beginning of the sixteenth century. For the resistance of the Maghribian warriors to the new weapons, see Luis del Mármol Carvajal, *Primera parte de la descripción general de Affrica . . .* (Granada, 1573), bk. 1, fols. 42^r–43^r; bk. 2, fols. 250^r, 266^v; bk. 3, fols. 13^r, 20^r; bk. 4, fols. 96^r–99^r; and Brunschvig, *La Berbérie*, 2:86–87.

39. A summary of this history is in Ladero Quesada, *La hacienda*, pp. 239–45.

40. A reason for the Iberian conquest of the Maghribian fisheries is given in Jean Despois, *L'Afrique du Nord* (Paris, 1969), pp. 458–64.

41. Ibn Khaldun, *The Muqaddimah*, 1:313.

42. Julius Klein, *The Mesta* (Cambridge, Mass., 1920), pp. 31–36, 49–63, and passim.

43. The *servicio* and *montazgo* amounted, in 1488–91, to approximately one-half the amount expended upon cannons in 1488–89. Ladero Quesada, *La hacienda*, p. 164.

44. Arié, *L'Espagne musulmane*, pp. 172–74; and Hess, "The Evolution of the Ottoman Seaborne Empire," pp. 1905–11.

CHAPTER THREE

1. Fernão Lopes, *Crónica de D. João I* (Porto, 1945–49), 1:40–43, 52–54, 348–49, 389–409.

2. António Sérgio, "Sobre a revolução de 1383–85," in *Ensaios* (Lisbon, 1971), 4:121–60.

3. Lopes, *João I*, 1:13–14, 98–103, 338–47, 419–24.

4. Ibid., 1:419–27; 2:4–9.

5. Diogo Ganes, "A relação dos descobrimentos da guinée das Ilhas," in Vitorino Magalhães Godinho, *Documentos sobre a expansão portuguesa* (Lisbon, 1924), 1:71; and Godinho, *L'économie*, pp. 131–57; where the monetary crisis that afflicted both the nobility and the crown is described.

6. Luis Suárez Fernández, *Relaciones entre Portugal y Castilla en la época del infante Don Enrique, 1393–1460* (Madrid, 1960), pp. 33–43, 169–81.

7. *Monumenta Henricina*, ed. Manuel Lopes de Almeda, et al. (Coimbra, 1960), 1: 25–26, 40–41, 178–86, 194–99, 207–14, are examples of papal bulls encouraging the Portuguese to participate in the crusade against Islam.

8. António Sérgio, "A conquista de Ceuta," in *Ensaios* (Lisbon, 1971), 1:253–73; Vogt, "Crusading and Commercial Elements," pp. 287–99.

9. Godinho, *Descobrimentos Henriquinos*, pp. 121–27.

10. *Monumenta Henricina*, 2:180–207, 224–29, 245–46; Gomes E. de Azurara, *The Chronicle of the Discovery and Conquest of Guinea*, trans. C. R. Beazley and Edgar Prestage (London, 1896–99), 1:10–17, 27–30; 2:280, reflect the values of the aristocratic party.

11. Abundantly documented in [Alvise da] Cadamosto, *The Voyages of Cadamosto*, trans. G. R. Crane (London, 1937), pp. 4–8, 11–14, 16–23, 35, 42–44; Duarte Pacheco Pereira, *Esmeraldo de situ Orbis, 1505–1508*, trans. George H. T. Kimble (London, 1937), pp. 36–37, 43–44, 46–50, 55–59, 70, 74–75, 85–89, 119–21; Godinho, *Descobrimentos Henriquinos*, pp. 109–27 and passim, and idem, *História económica*, 1:76–97, 112–26.

12. *Monumenta Henricina*, 1:342–48, reproduces the letter of John I (17 April 1411) that granted Prince Henry the Navigator his patrimony. João de Barros, *Da Asia* (Lisbon, 1778–88), déc. 1, bk. 1, chap. 4, pp. 23ff., is the best description of this independent phase of maritime expansion.

13. Duarte Leite, *História dos descobrimentos—Colectañea de esparsos* (Lisbon, 1959–62), 1:29–265, puts the work of Prince Henry within the framework of fifteenth-century history. See also Godinho, *Descobrimentos Heņriquinos*, pp. 129–50.

14. Godinho, *Documentos*, 1:95–106, 171–221.

15. Azurara, *The Chronicle of the Discovery*, 1:116–17; Vitorino Magalhães Godinho, *O "Mediterrâneo" saariano e as caravanos do ouro* (São Paulo, 1956), pp. 135–60; Manuel Nunes Dias, *O capitalismo monárquico português (1415–1549)* (Coimbra, 1963–64), 1:347–420, 2:189–202.

16. For the attack on Tangier, see Ruy de Pina, *Chrónica d'el rey D. Duarte*, in *Colecção de livros inéditos de história portugueza*, ed. José Corrêa de Serra (Lisbon, 1790–1824), 1, no. 2:103–11, 166–69, 182–84. On the political struggle that followed, see idem, *Chrónica d'el rey D. Affonso V*, in *Inéditos*, 1(3):332–34, 420–32.

17. Pina, *Affonso V*, in *Inéditos*, 1(3):452–54, 458–67, 480–83, 490–94, 501–12, 539.

18. Jaime Cortesão, *Os descobrimentos portugueses* (Lisbon, 1960), 1:233–44, deals with the impact of Afonso V's reign on the history of the Discoveries.

19. Pina, *Affonso V*, in *Inéditos*, 1(3): 541–64.

20. Antonio de la Torre y Luis Suárez Fernández, *Documentos sobre los relaciones con Portugal durante el reinado de los reyes católicos* (Valladolid, 1959), 1:245–84; Luis Suárez Fernandez, *Política international de Isabel la Católica* (Valladolid, 1965), 1:193–217.

21. Ruy de Pina, *Chrónica d'el rey D. João II*, in *Inéditos*, 2:5–17, 31–40, 42–64.

22. Ibid., 2:11–17; and Chaunu, *L'expansion européenne*, pp. 321–22.

23. Antonio H. de Oliveira Marques, *History of Portugal* (New York, 1972), 1:217–26.

24. Godinho, *L'économie*, pp. 209–11. The news of this transfer of gold spread from one end of the Mediterranean to the other. Hernando del Pulgar, *Crónica de los señores reyes católicos*, in *Biblioteca de autores españoles*, 70 (Madrid, 1878): 314–15; Marino Sanudo, *I Diarii*, ed. Nicolo Barozzi et al. (Venice, 1879–1903), 27:359; and Piri Reis, *Kitab*, p. 31.

25. Godinho, *L'économie*, pp. 211–18.

26. Ibid., pp. 537–47.

27. Ibid., pp. 698–709.

28. Ibid., pp. 829–35.

29. Damião de Góis, *Crónica do felicíssimo rei D. Manuel* (Coimbra, 1949–54), 1:14–33.

30. The military superiority of Portuguese garrisons in North Africa is described in *Chronique de Santa Cruz du Cap de Gué*, trans. Pierre de Cenival (Paris, 1934), pp. 20–159; and David Lopes, *História de Arzila* (Coimbra, 1924), pp. 63–73, 145–46, 204–8, 269–70.

31. Richard, "Le commerce," *Etudes*, pp. 81–114; Ibid., "A propos de 'rebate,'" pp. 345–55.

32. Fréderic Mauro, *Le Portugal et l'Atlantique au xviie siècle (1570–1670)* (Paris, 1960), pp. 183–219.

33. Diego Hurtado de Mendoza, *Guerra de Granada* (Madrid, 1970), p. 105.

34. Ladero Quesada, *Castilla y la conquista*, pp. 101–212.

35. Stephen Haliczer, "Modernization and Revolution in the Crown of Castile, 1475–1520," an unpublished paper delivered at the 1975 meeting of the American Historical Association, Chicago, notes the structural reasons for the violence of the times.

36. Fernando de Zafra to the Catholic kings, Granada, 25 April 1493 (?), 11:88–92; 27 April 1493, 11:484–86; 28 July 1493, 51:67–71; 14 January 1494, 51:72–74; 12 February 1494, 51:78–83; all in *Colección de documentos inéditos para la historia de España*, 112 vols. (Madrid, 1842–90), hereafter referred to as *CODOIN*.

37. J. M. Doussinague, *La política internacional de Fernando el Católico* (Madrid, 1944), pp. 521–24.

38. Ibid., pp. 76–78.

39. *El Tumbo de los reyes católicos del concejo de Sevilla*, ed. R. Carande and J. de M. Carriazo (Seville, 1929–68), 1:62–64, 252–54; 2:312–14, 331–32, 344–50.

40. Bernáldez, *Memorias*, pp. 343–53, 367–76.

41. Suárez Fernández, *Política International*, 5:79–80, 217–19; Bernáldez, *Memorias*, pp. 380–81.

42. Ibid., pp. 395–99.

43. Ibid., pp. 511–14, 539–42; and Doussinague, *Fernando el Católico*, pp. 154–67.

44. Bernáldez, *Memorias*, pp. 490–92; Doussinague, *Fernando el Católico*, pp. 128–53, 136–37.

45. Bernáldez, *Memorias*, p. 548; and Don Martín de los Heros, *Historia del Conde Pedro Navarro* in *CODOIN*, 25:102–13.

46. Bernáldez, *Memorias*, pp. 548–53.

47. *Cartas del Cardinal Don Fray Francisco Jiménez de Cisneros*, ed. Diego Lopez de Ayala (Madrid, 1867), pp. 50–58; and Martín de los Heros, *Historia del Conde Pedro Navarro*, pp. 115–30.

48. Pedro Navarro to Perez de Almazán, 6 January 1510, *CODOIN*, 25:456–59; Bernáldez, *Memorias*, pp. 558–63; and Doussinague, *Fernando el Católico*, pp. 327–43.

49. Doussinague, *Fernando el Católico*, pp. 208, 614–16.
50. Suárez Fernández, *Política internacional*, 3:414–15.
51. AGS, *Diversos de Castilla*, leg. 9, 31 May 1493, fol. 3.
52. Ibid., 13 August 1516, fol. 6.
53. AGS, *Estado*, leg. 477, 1553, no fol. no., Charles V to Philip.
54. AGS, *Contadurías generales*, leg. 3060, "Relación de los maravedis que...."
55. Chaunu, *L'Amérique*, pp. 78–99.
56. Francisco López de Gómara, *Crónica de los Barbarrojas* in *Memorial histórico español*, (Madrid, 1853), 6:335–36; Fray Diego de Haëdo, *Topografía e historia general de Argel* (Madrid, 1927), 1:288; and Ruth Pike, *Enterprise and Adventure* (Ithaca, N.Y., 1966), pp. 100–143 and passim.
57. Francisco López de Gómara, *Annals of the Emperor Charles V*, trans. R. B. Merriman (Oxford, 1912), pp. 44–67.
58. Paul Ruff, *La domination espagnole à Oran* (Paris, 1900), pp. 6–11, 28–32, 165–72.

CHAPTER FOUR

1. Jean-Léon L'Africain, *Description*, 1:235–41, 323–25, 378–88.
2. Brunschvig, *La Berbérie*, 1:283–359.
3. Ibid., 2:88–94, 98–113, 286–351; Ernest Gellner, *Saints of the Atlas* (Chicago, 1969), pp. 7–12; Emile Dermenghem, *Le culte des saints*, 5th ed. (Paris, 1954), pp. 121–34, 154–61, and passim.
4. E. E. Evans-Pritchard, *The Sanusi of Cyrenaica* (Oxford, 1948), pp. 29–61 and passim; Gellner, *Saints*, pp. 41–43; and C. C. Stewart, *Islam and Social Order in Mauritania* (Oxford, 1973), pp. 2–9.
5. For a definition of the *liff* and the role it played in the history of Berber society in southern Morocco, see Robert Montagne, *Les Berbères et le Makhzen* (Paris, 1930), pp. 55–100, 182–216; and the criticism of Montagne by David M. Hart, "Clan, Lineage, Local Community and the Feud in a Rifian Tribe," in *Peoples and Cultures of the Middle East: An Anthropological Reader*, ed. Louise E. Sweet (New York, 1970), 1:3–75.
6. Montagne, *Les Berbères*, pp. 48–51, 82–87: August Cour, *L'établissement des dynasties des Chérifs au Maroc et leur rivalité avec les Turcs de la régence d'Alger (1509–1830)* (Paris, 1904), pp. 13–17, 43–44; Gellner, *Saints*, pp. 7–12. The "emotional" life of sixteenth-century Islam in North Africa is best approached in Ibn ⁽Askar, *Daouhat An-Nâchir*, AM 19 (1913): 37–39, 48–54, 79–83, and passim.
7. Ibn Khaldun, *Muqaddimah*, 1:261–86 and passim, for the role of group feeling in the rise and fall of dynasties, and 1:327–36, for the place of frontiers in this history of states.
8. Es-Salâoui, *Les Mérinides*, AM 33 (1934): 473–505. Jamil M. Abun-Nasr, *A History of the Maghrib* (Cambridge, 1971), pp. 202–4, interprets these events.

9. Es-Salâoui, *Les Mérinides*, pp. 505–6; Abun-Nasr, *A History*, pp. 204–5; Robert Richard, "Moulay Ibrahim Caid de Chechaouen," in *Etudes*, pp. 261–80.

10. Es-Salâoui, *Les Mérinides*, p. 506.

11. M. Ben Cheneb, "al-Djazūlī," *EI²*, 2:527–28, gives a short history of the Djazūlī/Jazūlī movement in Morocco.

12. Montagne, *Les Berbères*, pp. 3–23.

13. *SIHM*, Port., 2/1 (letter to Manuel I, 30 July 1517), pp. 129–31, concerning a raid on a Sharīfian caravan that carried gold.

14. Jean-Léon l'Africain, *Description*, 1:87–95.

15. The Saᶜdians were probably on their way to becoming the leaders of a party that could command the tribes of the Anti Atlas through a manipulation of the *liff* of the Igezzoulen. Montagne, *Les Berbères*, pp. 193–95, 201–5.

16. Muhammad al-Ufrānī, or Ifrānī, *Nozhet al Hâdi: Histoire de la dynastie saadienne au Maroc, 1511–1670*, ed. and trans. O. Houdas (Paris, 1888–89), 1:20–23, is the basic source Ottoman chroniclers may have followed. Müneccimbaşı, *Sahaᵓif al-ahbar*, trans. Ahmed Nedim Efendi (Istanbul, 1868), 3:257–58; and Hezarfen Hüseyn b. Cafer, "Tenkih-i tevarih-i mülük," TKS Library, R. 1180, fol. 49ᵃ. A modern political interpretation is in Roger Le Tourneau, *Les débuts de la dynastie Saᶜdienne* (Algiers, 1954), pp. 1–29.

17. Ibn ᶜAskar, *Daouhat*, pp. 160–61; Es-Salâoui, *Les Saadiens*, p. 24.

18. *SIHM*, Port., 1 (5 November 1510), pp. 255–58; Port., 2 (2 January 1517), pp. 54–56; Es-Salâoui, *Les Saadiens*, pp. 24–25.

19. M. Ed. Michaux-Bellaire, "L'organisation des finances au Maroc," *AM* 11 (1907): 194–95; *SIHM*, Port., 1 (Estevão Rodriques Berrio to Manuel I, 19 May 1514), pp. 552–58.

20. *Chronique de Santa-Cruz*, p. 24; Edmond Fagnan, *Estraits inédits relatifs au Maghreb* (Algiers, 1924), pp. 338–41; *SIHM*, Port., 1 (11 September 1514), pp. 611–18.

21. al-Ifrānī, *Nozhet*, p. 33; Es-Salâoui, *Les Saadiens*, pp. 19–20.

22. Es-Salâoui, *Les Saadiens*, pp. 20–22.

23. al-Ifrānī, *Nozhet*, p. 39; Le Tourneau, *Les débuts*, pp. 35–37; August Cour, *La dynastie des Beni Waṭṭas (1420–1554)* (Constantine, 1920), pp. 150–67.

24. Fagnan, *Extraits*, pp. 363–64; *SIHM*, Port., 2/2 (9 June 1530), pp. 527–30.

25. *SIHM*, Port., 3 (31 July 1536), pp. 44–45; Cour, *Beni Waṭṭas*, pp. 161–63.

26. *SIHM*, Port., 2/2 (the Bishop of Lamego's reply to the King, 7 October 1534), pp. 656–61.

27. Mármol, 1, fols. 41ʳ–43ʳ; 3, fol. 13ʳ; 4, fols. 96ᵛ–97ᵛ; *Chronique de Santa-Cruz*, pp. 25–27, 49–51; Diego de Torres, *Relación del origen y sucesso de los Xarifes* (Seville, 1586), pp. 17–19, 147–48, 288.

28. *SIHM*, Port., 1 (15 June 1500), pp. 51–56.

29. *SIHM*, Port., 2 (2 January 1517), pp. 54–56.

30. *SIHM*, Port., 2/2 (15 September 1529), pp. 482–87.

31. *SIHM*, Port., 3 (September 1539), pp. 22–23; Port., 4 (26 July 1544), pp. 133–34.

32. For the relation between powder weapons and foreigners in the Saᶜdian army, see Mármol, *Affrica*, 1, fols. 250ʳ, 253ᵛ, 266ᵛ; 3, fol. 20ʳ; 4 fol. 97ᵛ.

33. Ibid., 2, fols. 254ᵛ–55ʳ; *SIHM*, Port., 1 (August 1515), *La Mamora*, pp. 695–706; *SIHM*, Port., 2/2 (1534), pp. 633–36; Port., 3 (1536), pp. 59–64 (1541), pp. 390–94.

34. *Chronique de Santa-Cruz*, pp. 72–73 and passim.

35. Godinho, *L'économie*, pp. 218–23.

36. Torres, *Relación*, pp. 112–14; Es-Salâoui, *Les Saadiens*, pp. 30–35.

37. Mármol, *Affrica*, 2, fol. 254ʳ.

38. Es-Salâoui, *Les Saadiens*, pp. 35–40.

39. Müneccimbaşı, *Sahaᵓif*, 3:258. The Saᶜdians did try to build a small naval force. *SIHM*, Spain, 1 (23 August 1549), pp. 337–40; *SIHM*, Port., 4 (16 September 1550), pp. 399–404.

40. al-Ifrānī, *Nozhet*, p. 55; Cour, *L'établissement*, pp. 74–86.

41. Cours, *L'établissement*, pp. 87–90.

42. Feridun Bey, *Münşaᵓat as Salatin* (Istanbul, 1858), 1:475.

43. BA, Fekete, 110, 1/46, December 1528.

44. Torres, *Relación*, pp. 205–8.

45. al-Ifrānī, *Nozhet*, pp. 77–79.

46. Cour, *Beni Waṭṭas*, pp. 186–91.

47. al-Ifrānī, *Nozhet*, pp. 79–81; Müneccimbaşı, *Sahaᵓif*, 3:260.

48. Fez remained a source of political subversion for the Saᶜdians. Torres, *Relación*, pp. 418–27.

49. Ibn ᶜAskar, *Daouhat*, pp. 91–92, 214–15; Es-Salâoui, *Les Saadiens*, pp. 41–42, 45–46; Cour, *Beni Waṭṭas*, pp. 192–210.

50. al-Ifrānī, *Nozhet*, pp. 88–90.

51. Hess, "Evolution of the Ottoman Seaborne Empire," pp. 1892–1919.

52. Halil Inalcık, *The Ottoman Empire* (New York, 1973), pp. 55–58 and passim.

53. V. J. Parry, "Bārūd.iv. The Ottoman Empire," *EI²*, 1:1061–66.

54. Tursun Bey, Tarih-i Ebul Feth, ed. Mehmet Arif, *TOEM*, 5–6/26–28 (Istanbul, 1914–16): 138; Andrew C. Hess, "The Ottoman Conquest of Egypt (1517) and the Beginning of the Sixteenth Century World War," *IJMES* 4, no. 1 (January 1973): 55–76; and Kenneth M. Setton, "Pope Leo X and the Turkish Peril," in *Proceedings of the American Philosophical Society* 113, no. 6 (December 1969): 367–424.

55. Suárez Fernández, *Política internacional*, 1:249, 250–53; 2:14–15, 52–55, 146–49; 3:25; 4:22.

56. Efdaleddin, "Bir Vesikayı Müellim," in *TOEM* 4 (Istanbul, 1910): 201–22. An English translation of a later appeal was done by James T. Monroe, "A Curious Morisco Appeal to the Ottoman Empire," *Al-Andalus* 31 (1966): 281–303. Mustafa Cenabi, "Tarih-i Cenabi," National Library of Vienna, Ms. 853, fol. 335, places the arrival of the Naşrid ambassadors in the eastern Mediterranean in the year A.H. 892/ A.D. 1486–87. The reaction of the Mamluks is examined by Arié, *L'Espagne musulmane,* pp. 145–46.

57. Kemalpaşazade, "Tevarih-i âl-i ʿOsman," VIII Defter, Millet Kütûbhanesi, Ali Emîrî, no. 32, fols. 64ʳ–66ʳ; Hans Albrecht von Burski, *Kemal Reis: Ein Beitrag zur Geschichte der türkischen Flotte* (Bonn, 1928), pp. 1–25; and Ismet Parmaksızoğlu, "Kemal Reis," 1, 6, pp. 566–69.

58. Piri Reis, *Kitab,* pp. 11, 635–41 (Bougie).

59. The primary source for the corsair migration is the unedited holy war account of Hayreddin Barbarossa, the *Gazavat-i Hayreddin Paşa.* Most modern authors have relied upon a French paraphrase of an eighteenth-century Arabic translation of the Ottoman manuscript: Sander-Rang and F. Denis, *Foundation de le régence d'Alger: Histoire des Barberousse* (Paris, 1837). A. Gallotta, "Le Gazavāt di Hayreddin Barbarossa," *Studi Magrebini* 3 (1920): 79–160, dates and connects the various versions of Hayreddin's work to the original manuscript.

60. "Gazavat-i Hayreddin Paşa," BM, or. no. 2798, fols. 5ʳ, 6ᵛ, 7ʳ, and 12ʳ, where Hayreddin's brother, Oruç/ʿArudj, is reported to have understood a European language (Greek?). For the Latin Christian version of the origins of the family of corsairs from which Barbarossa came, see Francisco Lopez de Gómara, *Crónica de los Barbarojas,* in *Memorial histórico español* (Madrid, 1853), 6:350–53. Hayreddin, fol. 12ʳ.

61. Svat Soucek, "The Rise of the Barbarossas in North Africa," *Archivum Ottomanicum* 3 (1971): 238–50, places the arrival of the Barbarossa brothers in North Africa during the year 1513.

62. Hayreddin, fols. 27ᵛ–28ʳ; Gómara, p. 361.

63. Hayreddin, fols. 39ᵛ–40ʳ.

64. Ibid., fols. 24ʳ–24ᵛ, 40ʳ, where Hayreddin claims to have distributed a portion of the corsair booty to the religious leaders in Tunis.

65. Ibid., fols. 29ᵛ–30ᵛ, where Hayreddin underlines the desperate situation of the Hispano-Muslims: "And the Unbelievers took young women with children and gave them to Christians—that is they could not be married to Muslims. Their desire was to cut out the Islamic population from their society."

66. Most sources link the Hispano-Muslim exiles with the corsairs. Müneccimbaşı, *Sahaʾif,* 3:260–61; Haëdo, *Topografia,* 1:50–52; al-ʿIfrānī, *Nozhet,* p. 99; Fagnan, *Extraits,* pp. 390–91; and Fernand Braudel, "Les Espagnoles et l'Afrique du Nord de 1492 à 1577," *RA* 69 (1928): 184–234, 351–428, for a general view of the question.

67. Hayreddin, fols. 41ᵛ–43ʳ; Gómara, p. 365; Aḥmad Tawfīḳ al-Madanī, *Ḥarb al-Thalāthimiᵓa sana beyn al-Jazāᵓır wa Isbāniyā* [300 years of war between Algeria and Spain] (Algiers, n.d.), pp. 172–74.

68. Piri Reis, *Kitab*, p. 642.

69. Hayreddin, fols. 45ᵛ–46ᵛ; Gómara, pp. 366–68; ᶜAbd al-Ḥamīd Shamhū, *Dukhūl al-Atrāk al ᶜUthmāniyyin ilā Jazāᵓir* (Algiers, 1972), pp. 71–72.

70. Hayreddin, fols. 49ʳ–50ᵛ, where the figures for the fleet and army of Diego de Vera are exaggerated; Gómara, pp. 368–71; Shamhū, *Dukhūl*, pp. 73–76.

71. Hayreddin, fols. 54ᵛ–56ʳ; Gómara, pp. 370–75; J. J. L. Bargès, *Complément de l'histoire des Beni Zeiyan* (Paris, 1887), pp. 427–33.

72. Hayreddin, fol. 47ᵛ.

73. Giancarlo Sorgia, *La politica nord-africana di Carlo V* (Padova, 1963), p. 15.

74. Hayreddin, fols. 60ᵛ–61ᵛ; Gómara, pp. 374–79.

75. Hayreddin, fols. 61ʳ–61ᵛ.

76. Hayreddin, fols. 75ʳ–76ᵛ; Ibrahim Artuk, *Kanunî Sultaṇ Süleyman Adına Basılan Sikkeler* (Ankara, 1972), pp. 29–30, where the earliest coin struck in Ottoman Algeria in the name of Süleymen is dated A.H. 927/A.D. 1520–21. From the Istanbul side, "Tarih-i-Al-i-Osman," TKS Library, R. 1099, fols. 148ᵇ–49ᵇ, dates the first contacts between Hayreddin and the Ottoman sultan from the reign of Selim the Grim (d. 1520).

77. Hayreddin, fols. 78ʳ–79ᵛ; Hasan ibn Yusuf Ahıskalı, "Tarih-i Cezayir veya Tehzib et Tevarih," TKS, R 1775/76, fols. 41ᵛ–42ʳ.

78. Prudencio de Sandoval, *Historia del emperador Carlos V* in *BAE*, 80/1 (Madrid, 1955): 138; Cesáreo Fernández Duro, *Armada española* (Madrid, 1895), 1:127–29.

79. Hayreddin, fols. 88ᵛ–89ᵛ; Ahıskalı, "Tarih," fol. 41ᵛ.

80. Hayreddin, fol. 93ʳ; Gómara, pp. 382–85.

81. Hayreddin, fol. 102ᵛ, where the reasons for abandoning the city were given as the shortage of men and money; Gómara, p. 384, gives hunger as a major cause of the Ottoman retreat.

82. Sandoval, *Historia*, 1:141, 158–62, 233–36, 251; Duro, *Armada*, 1:31.

83. Duro, *Armada*, 1:153; Sorgia, *La politica nord-africana*, pp. 30–31.

84. The Ottomans distributed food from their prizes to the local population. Hayreddin, fols. 104ᵛ–105ʳ.

85. Ibid., fols. 107ʳ–108ʳ, where the refusal of Ibn al-Ḳāḍī to accept the Hispano-Muslim exiles is mentioned.

86. Ibid., fols. 107ᵛ, 115ᵛ–116ʳ, 117ᵛ; Gómara, pp. 390–91.

87. Haëdo, *Topografía*, pp. 117–23.

88. Hayreddin, fols. 122ᵛ–127ʳ; and Louis Berbrugger, *Le pégnon d'Alger* (Algiers, 1860), pp. 5–105.

89. Hayreddin, fols. 129^v–130^v; Gómara, pp. 397–99.
90. Hayreddin, fols. 118^v–122^r; Ruff, *Domination*, pp. 19–20.
91. Sorgia, *La politica nord-africana*, pp. 35–38.
92. The earliest evidence of the Ottoman tax system in Algeria is BA, MD 2 63:563, 4, 5, 6; 210:1899 (963–4/1556–7). How the Ottomans organized conquered provinces is described by Halil Inalcık, "Ottoman Methods of Conquest," *Studia Islamica* 2 (1954): 103–29.
93. Hayreddin, fols. 175^r–177^v.

CHAPTER FIVE

1. Lutfi Paşa, *Tevarih-i Ali Osman* (Istanbul, 1922), pp. 343–45; and Francisco de Laiglesia, *Estudios históricos (1515–1555)* (Madrid, 1908), pp. 93–162. For Kemankeş Ahmet Paşa, see Danişmend, 2:152–53, 5:180.
2. Hayreddin, fols. 177^v–79^v, 191^r; Celalzade Mustafa Çelebi, "Tabakat-ul-memalik ve deracat-ul-mesalik," Istanbul University Library, TY 5997, fols. 264^v–66^r; Gómara, pp. 405–12.
3. Hayreddin, fols. 203^v–4^v, where Hayreddin mounted sails on the cannon carriages. Gómara, pp. 413–14; *CODOIN*, 2:381–92.
4. Charles V's reasons for the campaign and the arrangements he made with the Ḥafṣid sultan are given in "Historia y Conquista de Túnez," BNM, Ms. 19441, fols .111^v–17^r; a modern study of Spanish activities in sixteenth-century Tunisia is Pablo Álvarez Rubiano, "La política imperial española y su relación con los Hafsides tunecianes— Nuevos datos para su estudio," *Hispania* 3 (1941): 32–36.
5. Matrakçı Nasuh, "Dastan-ı Sultan Süleyman," TKS Library R 1286, fols. 281^b–83^b, describes Hayreddin's defeat. Roger B. Merriman, *The Rise of the Spanish Empire in the Old World and the New* (New York, 1918–34), vol. 3, *The Emperor*, pp. 310–18, gives the details of the Spanish action.
6. Sandoval, *Historia*, 2:554–55, 559–61; and *CODOIN*, vol. 1, *Relación de lo que sucedió en la conquista de Tunez y La Goleta*, pp. 159–207. The conditions of the tributary agreement are analyzed in Sorgia, *La politica nord-africana*, pp. 74–76, and restated with some additions in AGS, E 476, no fol. no., January 1551; and in El-Madanī, *Ḥarb*, pp. 228–34.
7. Hayreddin, fol. 179^r; Lutfi Paşa, *Tevarih*, p. 356; Kâtib Çelebi², p. 45; and Merriman, *The Emperor*, 3:321–24.
8. Gómara, pp. 431–37; Sorgia, *La politica nord-africana*, pp. 99–123, and documents 1–7, pp. 155–75. An eighteenth-century Ottoman account is in Ahıskalı, "Tarih," fols. 50^r–50^v.
9. According to Ottoman chroniclers, the French requested the assistance. Hezarfen, "Tenkih," fol. 131^r; for the campaign see Kâtib Çelebi², p. 68; Gómara, pp. 437–38; and Jean Deny and Jane Laroche, "L'expédition en Provence de l'armée de mer du Sultan Suleyman sous

le commandement de l'amiral Hayreddin Pacha, dit Barberousse (1543–1544)," *Turcica* 1 (1969): 161–211.

10. Merriman, *The Emperor*, 3:340–41.

11. AGS, E 474, no fol. no., Algiers (15 C 956/10 July 1549), written in *diwānī*. Diplomatic documents and scripts for the Ottoman empire are described in J. Reychmann and A. Zafaczkowski, "Diplomatic. iv. Ottoman Empire," *EI*², 1:313–16.

12. Haëdo, *Topografía*, pp. 274–94; and Ruff, pp. 76–131.

13. Suárez Fernández, *Política international*, 4:24–27; 5:74–78; Luis del Mármol Cavarajal, *L'Afrique de Marmol*, trans. Nicolas Perrot d'Ablancourt (Paris, 1667), 2:572; Ibn Ghalbūn, *Taʾrikh Ṭarāblus al Gharb* (Cairo, 1930), pp. 92–94.

14. Kâtib Çelebi², pp. 67–68; Ali Reza Seyfi, *Turgut Reis* (Istanbul, 1899), pp. 3–62.

15. Aziz Samih Ilter, *Şimali Afrikada Türkler* [*The Turks in North Africa*] (Istanbul, 1937), 2:187–94.

16. Nicolas de Nicolay, *The Navigations...*, trans. T. Washington (London, 1585), pp. 19ᵛ–26ᵛ.

17. Mármol, *L'Afrique*, 2:572; Ilter, *Şimali*, 2:194–96.

18. Haëdo, *Topografía*, pp. 299–301.

19. AGS, E 479, fols. 123–24, dated 1555, where Count Alcaudète advocated the formation of a grand anti-Turkish coalition between the Sharīf, the anti-Ottoman faction in Tlemsen, and the Ḥafṣid sultan of Tunis. See also Suárez, "Historia," fol. 93ʳ; Cour, *L'éstablissement*, pp. 119–23; and Chantal de la Veronne, "Política de España, de Marruecos y de los Turcos en los reinos de Fez y Tremecen a mediados del siglo XVI," *MEAH* (1954), pp. 87–95.

20. Haëdo, *Topografía*, pp. 306–9; Ilter, *Şimali*, 1:128–34.

21. Haëdo, *Topografía*, pp. 310–13; Kâtib Çelebi², p. 72.

22. Haëdo, *Topografía*, pp. 314–19. MD 7 20:67 (8 S 975/August 1567) records a dispute between the Janissaries and the ᶜ*Azabs*, the fighting men who manned the corsair ships. For the use of this term, see Mehmet Zeki Pakalın, *Tarih deyimleri ve terimleri sözlüğü* [*A dictionary of historical expressions and terms*] (Istanbul, 1946), 1:128–31, Haëdo, *Topografía*, p. 344, confirms that such a clash took place in 1567.

23. Ibid., pp. 288, 333.

24. Kâtib Çelebi², p. 72.

25. Ibid.

26. Duro, *Armada española*, 2:10–22; Kâtib Çelebi², pp. 72–73.

27. Pierre Chaunu, *L'Espagne de Charles Quint* (Paris, 1973), 2:397–442.

28. Şerafeddin Turan, *Kanuninin oğlu şehzade Bayezid vakᶜası* [*Prince Bayezit's revolt*] (Ankara, 1961), pp. 11–52 and passim.

29. MD 208:578 (4 RA 967/1559); MD 3 223–24:626 (16 *RA* 967/1559).

30. An exhaustive treatment of the Gerba campaign from Christian sources is given by Charles Monchicourt, *L'expédition espagnole de 1560* (Paris, 1913).

31. Ogier Ghiselin de Busbecq, *The Turkish Letters* . . . , trans. C. T. Forster and F. H. B. Daniell (London, 1881), 1:318–28; Kâtib Çelebi[2], pp. 73–74.

32. Monchicourt, *L'expédition*, pp. 135–36; Ernest Charrière, *Negociations de la France dans le Levant* (Paris, 1840–60), 2:629–32.

33. Cour, *L'établissement*, pp. 134–35.

34. Haëdo, *Topografía*, pp. 333–38.

35. Duro, *Armada española*, 2:49–56; Suárez, "Historia," fols. 39^{r}–42^{v}.

36. "Relación del sucesso de la jornada del Rio Tetuán," BNM, Ms. 1750, fol. 260^{v}; Duro, *Armada española*, 2:56–73; Cour, *L'établissement*, p. 137.

37. MD 6 266:565 (25 CA 972/December 1564); Mustafa Selaniki, *Tarih-i Selaniki* (Istanbul, 1864), p. 7.

38. MD 6 451:972 (7 N 972/8 April 1565).

39. MD 3 223–4:626 (16 RA 967/December 1559); Ibn Abī Dīnār al-Ḳayrawānī, *Histoire de l'Afrique*, trans. E. Pellissier and Rémusat, in *Exploration scientifique de l'Algérie* (Paris, 1845), 8:283–88.

40. MD 5 94:215 (12 S 973/September 1565).

41. Şerafettin Turan, "Rodos'un Zaptından Malta Muhasarasına," [From the conquest of Rhodes to the siege of Malta], in *Kanunî Armağanı* Ankara, 1970), pp. 47–117.

42. Geoffrey Parker, *The Army of Flanders and the Spanish Road* (Cambridge, 1972), pp. 3–21; and Guilmartin, *Gunpowder and Galleys*, pp. 253–73.

43. Paul David Lagomarsino, "Court Factions and the Formation of Spanish Policy towards the Netherlands (1159–67)," diss., Cambridge University, 1974.

44. Selaniki, *Tarih*, pp. 64–68, 72–73, 76–77.

45. Ibrahim Peçevi, *Tarih-i Peçevi* (Istanbul, 1867), 1:476–77, 484–85; and "Cilt-i Evvel min tarih-i al-i Osman," TKS Library, R 1099, fols. 179^{a}–181^{a}.

46. Safvet Bey, "Bir Osmanlı Filosunun Sumatra Seferi," [The Sumatra campaign of an Ottoman fleet], *TOEM*, 10:604–14; C. R. Boxer, "A Note on Portuguese Reactions to the Revival of the Red Sea Spice Trade and the Rise of Acheh, 1540–1600," *Journal of Southeast Asian History* 10, no. 3 (December 1969): 415–28.

47. C. Max Kortepeter, *Ottoman Imperialism during the Reformation: Europe and the Caucasus* (New York, 1972), pp. 26–32.

48. Selaniki, *Tarih*, p. 100; Peçevi, *Tarih*, p. 486; and George Hill, *A History of Cyprus* (Cambridge, 1948–52), 3:878–949.

49. MD 7 889:2439 (12 CA 976/November 1568); Torres, *Relación*, pp. 482–85.

50. MD 7 898:2460 (18 CA 976/November 1568); 899:2461; 899:2462 (all the same date); and 906:2481 (22 CA 976/November 1568). Spanish sources confirm these actions: AGS, E 485, no fol. no., "Relación del Alférez Diego de Esquilla de Cosas de Berbería," 1574–76?

51. MD 907:2484 (22 CA 976/November 1568).

52. Cour, *L'établissement*, pp. 137–40.

53. K. Garrad, "The Original Memorial of Don Francisco Nuñez Muley," *Atlante* 2 (1954): 199–226.

54. Idem, "La industria Sedera Granadina en el siglo XVI y su conexión con el Levantamiento de las Alpujarras (1568–1571)," *MEAH* (1956), pp. 73–98.

55. L. P. Harvey, "A Morisco Reader of Jean Lemaire de Belges," *Al-Andalus* 28 (1963): 231–36, gives evidence of the Hispano-Muslim interest in the progress of the Turkish empire.

56. Andrew C. Hess, "The Moriscos: An Ottoman Fifth Column in Sixteenth Century Spain," *AHR* 74, no. 1 (October 1968): 1–25.

57. Suárez, "Historia," fols. 161ʳ, 165ʳ–66ʳ; Hezarfen, "Tenkih," fol. 134ʳ.

58. Diego Hurtado de Mendoza, *Guerra de Granada* (Madrid, 1970), pp. 109–15, 142, 221, 252–53, 269, 280, 290–306, 313–18, 327, 334, 362–63.

59. Ibid., p. 236; and Hess, "Moriscos," p. 16.

60. The financial contribution of Ottoman Egypt is given in Stanford J. Shaw, *The Financial and Administrative Organization and Development of Ottoman Egypt, 1517–1798* (Princeton, 1962), pp. 283–85. How geography molded the course of Ottoman expansion is the subject of D. E. Pitcher, *An Historical Geography of the Ottoman Empire* (Leiden, 1972), pp. 100–123 and maps 20–23.

61. Hess, "Lepanto," pp. 53–62.

62. Quoted in ibid., p. 54.

63. Murad III, "Murad Salisin Hatti Hümayunları," TKS Lib. R 702/1943 fols. 3ʳ⁻ᵛ; Halil Inalcık, "L'empire ottoman," in *Les peuples de l'Europe du sud-est et leur rôle dans l'histoire* (Sofia, 1969), 3:97; and Ömer Lutfi Barkan, "The Price Revolution of the Sixteenth Century: A Turning Point in the Economic History of the Near East," trans. Justin McCarthy, *IJMES* 6, no. 1 (January 1975): 17

64. MD 24 13:33 (16 ZA 981); 30:90 (212 A 981); 88:235 (14 Z 981), all February to March of 1574.

65. MD 27 38:100 (20 B 983/1575) is one order calling for the punishment of *Sipahis* who failed to show up for the 1574 campaign to reconquer Tunis.

66. Hess, "Lepanto," pp. 63–64.

67. Juan Reglá, "La epoca de los tres primeros Austrias," in *Historia de España y America, social y económica*, ed. J. Vicen Vives (Barcelona, 1972), pp. 157–58.

68. Ilter, *Şimali*, 1:154; Paul Masson, *Histoire des établissements et du commerce français dans l'Afrique Barbaresque* (*1560–1793*) (Paris, 1903), pp. 1–14, 55–57.

69. MD 15 27:234 (4 S 979/July 1571); MD 23 121:244 (19 B 981/ November 1573); 139:284 (same date).

70. MD 22 214:418 (14 R 981/13 August 1573).

71. MD 12 325:665 (3 S 979/27 June 1571).

72. MD 18 15:25 (27 N 979/8 February 1572); Torres, *Relación*, pp. 482–85.

73. MD 18 13:24 (27 N 979/8 February 1572).

74. MD 22 332:656 (15 CA 981/12 September 1573).

75. Hess, "Moriscos," pp. 17–25; and Peter Dressendörfer, *Islam unter der Inquisition* (Wiesbaden, 1971), pp. 128–30.

76. MD 24 59:166 (5 Z 981/March 1574).

77. Alphonse Rousseau, *History of the Conquest of Tunis and of the Goletta by the Ottomans, AH 981/AD 1573*, trans. J. T. Carletti (London, 1883), p. 28; Hasan Beyzade Ahmet Paşa, "Tarih-i Hasan Beyzade," TKS Library, Ms. B 207/745, fols. 292ᵇ–93ᵃ.

78. Parker, *The Army*, pp. 235–36.

79. AGS E 1515, fol. 217, letters from Constantinople, 19 February 1575; E 1334, fol. 35, 25 April 1575, Guzmán de Silva to Philip II, where it was reported that the Ottomans would invade Morocco by land because it was too far west to be attacked by sea. The more formal accounts are in Müneccimbaşı, *Saha²if*, 3:271–72; and Haëdo, *Topografia* pp. 367–68.

80. Cour, *L'établissement*, pp. 140–42.

81. MD 3 204–5 (13 R 984/10 July 1576).

82. MD 30 208–9:489 (11 RA 985/29 May 1577).

83. Velloso, *Don Sebastião*, pp. 89–123, 189–219, 259–92.

84. MD 30 208–9:489 (11 RA 985/29 May 1577); MD 35 189:475 (2 B 986/4 September 1578).

85. Cour, *L'établissement*, pp. 142–43.

86. The decision to make peace with the Ottomans may have been made just after the Ottoman-Venetian peace treaty of 7 March 1573. In AGS E 485, no fol. no., dated 5 May 1573, where the terms of a proposed peace treaty with the Turks are set down. The arrival of Martin Diego de Acuña in Istanbul is noted in AGS, E 1336, fol. 20, Guzmán de Silva to Philip II, 20 April 1577; for the Ottoman data, see Hess, "Lepanto," pp. 67–68.

87. Mauro, *Le Portugal et l'Atlantique*, pp. 147–234; and Philip D. Curtin, *The Atlantic Slave Trade: A Census* (London, 1969), pp. 95–126.

88. AGS, E 1335, fol. 60, 23 May 1576.

89. AGS, E 1335, fol. 53, 8 July 1576.

90. Bovill, *Alcazar*, pp. 12–165; Es-Salâoui, *Les Saadiens*, pp. 112–46.

91. Peçevi, *Tarih*, 2:36–37; Lazaro Soranzo, *The Ottoman of Lazaro*

Soranzo (London, 1603), pp. 41ᵃ–45ᵇ, lists the strategic reasons why the Ottomans decided to invade Persia.

92. J. H. Mordtman and V. L. Ménage, "Ferīdūn Bey," *EI*², 2:881–82.

93. Kortepeter, *Imperialism*, pp. 42–83.

94. Bekir Kütükoğlu, *Osmanlı Safevî Siyasi Münasebetleri 1578–1590 (Ottoman-Safavid Political Relations)* (Istanbul, 1957), pp. 1–19 and passim.

95. Negotiations on the Spanish side were bedeviled by the degree of political influence the Ottomans were to have in Morocco and by whether or not the Knights of Saint John could be controlled. AGS, E 1080, fol. 28, letters of Juan Margliani, March to April 1579; and E 1079, fol. 236, 12 December 1579. For the documents the two empires exchanged, see Hess, "Lepanto," pp. 68–73; and S. A. Skilliter, "The Hispano-Ottoman Armistice of 1581," in *Iran and Islam*, ed. C. E. Bosworth (Edinburgh, 1971), pp. 491–515.

96. Hess, "Lepanto," pp. 70–73.

CHAPTER SIX

1. Fernand Braudel and Ruggiero Romano, *Navires et marchandises à l'entrée du port de Livourne, 1547–1611* (Paris, 1951), pp. 49–63. For the union between the Atlantic privateers and their Maghribian counterparts, Andrew Barker, *A True and Certaine Report of the Beginning, Proceedings, Overthrowes, and now present Estate of Captaine Ward and Danseker* . . . (London, 1609), pp. 1–27, is one among many accounts.

2. Joaquium Veríssimo Serrão, *O reinado de D. António Prior do Crato* (Coimbra, 1956), 1:1–107, 267–316, and passim.

3. MD 39 196:409 (9 M 988/February 1580); MD 42 82:344 (G B 989/August 1581).

4. MD 40 63:143 (12 S 987/4 October 1579); MD 42 84:347 and 86:352 (B 989/August 1581). For a Moroccan report on this exchange, see Abou-l-Hasen . . . Et-Tamgrūtī, *En-Nafhat el-Miskiya Fi-s-Sifaret Et-Tourkiya, 1581–1591* [The report on the mission to Turkey, 1581–1591], trans. Henry De Castries (Paris, 1929). AGS E 1339, fol. 68, 27 July 1581, contains a list of the gifts to the Ottoman sultan. Hezārfen, "Tenḳīḥ," fol. 50ᵃ, gives a figure of 200,000 florins for the tribute.

5. AGS E 1337, fol. 91, Cristóbal de Salazar to Philip II, Venice, 8 July 1580, on the false letters; and Darío Cabanelas Rodríquez, "Proyecto de alianza entre los sultanes de Marruecos y Turquía contra Felipe II," *MEAH* 6 (1957): 57–75.

6. AGS E 1337, fol. 69, Christóbal de Salazar to Philip II, Venice, 27 May 1580.

7. The French, for example, encouraged Don Antonio to approach the Ottomans for aid. Serrão, *O reinado*, 1:173–74; Charrière, *Negociations*, 3:939.

8. Soranzo, *The Ottoman*, fol. 42a, lists the eight frontiers: Persia, Fez, Malta, Spain, Venice, Italy, Poland, and Austria.

9. Ibid., fols. 43ʳ⁻ᵛ.

10. Ibid., fols. 44ʳ⁻46ʳ.

11. AGS E 1338, fol. 85, Venice, 21 May 1580, is one of many reports that make the connection between the shortage of money, the war in Persia, and the decline of the Ottoman fleet. It was, however, Cardinal Granvelle who drew what turned out to be the right conclusions. AGS E 1527, fols. 100, 119, 131, Cardinal Granvelle to Philip II, 4 January to 17 October 1582.

12. MD 58 80:230 (17 CA 993/May 1585) and Darío Cabanelas Rodríquez, "Proyecto de ᶜUluǧ ᶜAli para la conquista de Orán 1583," in *Etudes d'orientalisme dédiées à la mémoire de Lévi-Provençal* (Paris, 1962), 1:69–78.

13. Akdes Nimet Kurat, *Türk-İngiliz Münasebetlerinin Başlangıcı ve Gelişmesi (1553–1610)* [The foundation and development of Anglo-Ottoman relations] (Ankara, 1953), pp. 118–75.

14. Ibid., pp. 120–25; AGS E 1340, fols. 25⁻28, Cristóbal de Salazar to Philip II, Venice, 7–14 May 1583.

15. Selaniki, *Tarih*, p. 209.

16. Ahmet Refik, *Türkler ve Kraliçe Elizabet* (Istanbul, 1932), pp. 16–29, doc. 11.

17. Kurat, *Türk-İngiliz*, pp. 125–39.

18. This time in Valencia, Kurat, *Türk-İngiliz*, p. 152.

19. Mustafa Selaniki, "Tarih-i Selaniki," Nur-u-ᶜOsmaniye Library, Ms. 2685/3132, fol. 277ᵛ.

20. Selaniki, *Tarih*, pp. 278–79.

21. Kâtib Çelebi², pp. 99–100. Murad III, "Hatti Hümayun," fols. 2ʳ–3ʳ; and BM, Ms. Nero BXI, fols. 1ʳ–16ʳ, describe the poor condition of the Ottoman navy.

22. Peçevi, *Tarih*, 2:128–29, 131–33.

23. Inalcık, *The Ottoman Empire*, pp. 41–52; Bernard Lewis, *The Emergence of Modern Turkey* (New York, 1961).

24. Klause Röhrborn, *Untersuchungen zur Geschichte osmanischen verwaltungs Geschichte* (Berlin, 1973), pp. 22–26; Metin Ibrahim Kunt, "Ethnic Regional (Cins) Solidarity in the Seventeenth Century Ottoman Establishment," *IJMES* 5, no. 3 (June 1974): 233–39; and Kortepeter, *Ottoman Imperialism*, pp. 213–24.

25. Mustafa Akdağ, *Celâlî Isyanları, 1550–1603* (Ankara, 1963), pp. 13–58, 109–14, and passim.

26. Inalcık, *The Ottoman Empire*, pp. 47–50.

27. Röhrborn, *Untersuchungen*, pp. 64–96.

28. Inalcık, *The Ottoman Empire*, pp. 179–80.

29. Kâtib Çelebi, *The Balance of Truth*, trans. G. L. Lewis (London, 1957), pp. 22–30.

30. Braudel, *The Mediterranean*, 1:517–42; Barkan, "Price Revolution," pp. 3–28.

31. MD 30 180:422, 180:423, 199:471, 183:430, 223:517, 223:518, 228:531, 228:532, all in the spring of 1577. These same problems appeared slightly later in the eastern regions of the Ottoman empire. Gengiz Orhonlu, *Telhisler* (*1597–1607*) [Summaries of vizierial correspondence] (Istanbul, 1970), pp. 38–44.

32. Haëdo, *Topografía*, pp. 396–401; Inalcık, *The Ottoman Empire*, p. 49.

33. MD 43 148:265 (G C 988/July 1580).

34. Mübahat S. Kütükoğlu, *Osmanlı-İngiliz Iktisâdi Münâsebetleri* (*1580–1838*) [Ottoman-English economic relations] (Ankara, 1974), pp. 11–16; Halil Inalcık, "Imtiyāzāt," *EI²*, 3:1179–89.

35. MD 60 201:472 (17 S 994/February 1586). Godfrey Fisher, *Barbary Legend* (Oxford, 1957), pp. 111–24, discusses the problems the Levant Company encountered in North Africa.

36. MD 61 30:85 (14 B 994/July 1586); MD 62 14:43 (14 RA 995/February 1587).

37. MD 62 190:428 (4 RA 996/February 1588).

38. MD 70 210:413 (19 C 1001/March 1593).

39. MD 70 212:416–17 (19 C 1001/March 1593).

40. MD 73 452:998 (11 L 1003/June 1595); MD 73 574:253 (18 L 1003/June 1595); and Hüseyn b. Cafer Hezarfenn, "Telhis ul Beyan fi Kavanin-i al-i Osman," BN, Ms. Turc 40, fols. 61ᵃ–62ᵇ.

41. Pierre Boyer, "Introduction à une histoire intérieure de la Régence d'Alger," *Revue historique* 235 (1966): 297–316.

42. Idem, "Espagne et Kuko, les négociations de 1598 et 1610," *ROMM* 8, no. 2 (1970): 25–40.

43. MD 43 162:292 (19 C 988/July 1580).

44. MD 39 212–17:432–39 (12 M 988/February 1580); MD 50 237: 618–20 (19 M 992/February 1584); *MD* 53 149:434 (27 Ş 992/September 1584); MD 58 187:491 (25 C 993/June 1585).

45. MD 58 189:495 (25 C 993/June 1585).

46. MD 64 106:289, 111:301–3, 126:329, 127:332 (11 L to Ş 996/ September to December 1587).

47. The absorption of the old urban elite is recorded in MD 24 59:166 (5 Z 981/1574); MD 28 231:548 (24 CA 984/1576); MD 50 237-618 (19 M 992/1584); and Aḥmad Ibn Abī al-Ḍiyāf, *Itḥāf ʾahl al-Zamān* (Tunis, 1963), 2:26.

48. Ilter, *Şimali Afrikada*, 2:136–38; Jamil M. Abun-Nasr, "The Beylicate in Seventeenth-Century Tunisia," *IJMES* 6, no. 1 (January 1975): 70–72.

49. MD 39 215:436 (12 M 988/February 1580).

50. MD 62 15:45, 127:282–83, 127–28:284–85, 140–41:308–9 (L 995/September 1587).

51. MD 64 182:468 (Z 996/October 1588).

52. AGS E 1090, fol. 124, Naples, 18 September 1589.

53. MD 64 179:464 (15 ZA 996/October 1588).

54. Ilter, Şimali Afrikada, 2:215–17.

55. Mustafa ibn Ahmet ᶜÂli, "Künh ül-Ahbar," Nur-u-Osmaniye Lib., Ms. 3409, fols. 399ᵇ–401ᵇ; and Suraiya Faroqhi, "Der Aufstand des Yaḥyā ibn Yaḥyā as-Suwaydi," Der Islam 47 (1971): 67–92.

56. Saᶜdian military organization was, however, influenced by Ottoman practices. Muḥammad al-Fishtālī, Manāhil al-Ṣafā fī Akhbār al-Mulūk al-Shurafā, ed. ᶜAbdallāh Gannūn (Tetuan, 1964), pp. 161–66.

57. T. S. Willan, Studies in Elizabethan Foreign Trade (New York, 1968), pp. 92–332.

58. E. W. Bovill, The Golden Trade of the Moors, 2d ed. (New York, 1970), pp. 1–154.

59. B. G. Martin, "Maî Idrîs of Bornu and the Ottoman Turks, 1576–78," IJMES 4, no. 3 (1972): 470–90.

60. Henry de Castries, "La Conquête du Soudan par el Mansour (1591)," Hespéris 3, no. 4 (1923): 433–88.

61. Ibid., 3:437–43.

62. al-Ifrānī, Nozhet, pp. 160–62.

63. ᶜAbd al-Raḥmān ibn ᶜAbdallāh al-Saᶜdī, Tarikh es-Soudan, trans. O. Houdas (Paris, 1964), pp. 215–19, 277, 317–19.

64. Bovill, The Golden Trade, pp. 154–206.

65. Es-Salâoui, Les Saadiens, pp. 201–2, 302–29.

66. Aḥmad ibn Khālid an-Nāṣirī al-Slāwī, Kitāb al-Istiḳṣā li akhbār duwal al-Maghrib al-Aḳṣā (Casablanca, 1955), 6:30–34.

67. Ibid., pp. 24–25, 50–52; Moḥammad Hajjī, al-Zāwiya al-Dalāʾiya (Rabat, 1964), pp. 143–49, 156–57.

68. Abun-Nasr, A History, pp. 216–24.

69. AGS E 1090, fol. 51, 24 May 1589; E 1948, fol. 109, Valladolid, 21 December 1604; and E 1354, fol. 172, 1 November 1610.

70. MD 42 85–86:350–51 (G B 989/August 1581); AGS L 1527 fol. 119, 22 June 1582, where Cardinal Granvelle predicted the failure of this invasion.

71. AGS E 1540, fol. 134, Naples, 10 September 1589.

72. Carlos Rodrigues Joulia Saint-Cyr, Felipe III y el rey de Cuco (Madrid, 1954), pp. 17–77, and documents, pp. 83–94.

73. AGS E 1950, fols. 189–91, Madrid, 1618; and Pierre Boyer, L'évolution de l'Algérie médiane (Paris, 1960), pp. 11–77, on the Ottoman methods for controlling the tribes.

74. AGS, Guerra Antigua, 126/32 Fez, 12 May 1582; SIHM, France, 2:114–16, Madrid, May 1584.

75. AGS, E 1948, fol. 117, 10 October 1606; and AGS E 495, "Papel sobre la empresa de Zale (Salé)," 1614.

76. Parker, The Army, pp. 231–68.

77. Kenneth Brown, "An Urban View of Moroccan History, Salé, 1000–1800," *Hespéris Tamuda* 12 (1971): 46–63; Muḥammad Dāwūd, *Tārīkh Tiṭwān* (Tetuan, 1959), 2:181–82; Roger Le Tourneau, *Fès avant le Protectorat* (Paris, 1949), pp. 79–94.

78. J. D. Latham, "Towards a Study of Andalucian Immigration and Its Place in Tunisian History," *Cahiers de Tunisie* 5 (1957): 203–52.

79. Kurat, *Türk-İngiliz*, pp. 173–75; I. H. Uzunçarşılı, *Osmanlı Tarihi*, 2d ed. (Ankara, 1964), 2:194.

80. Bernard Lewis, "Corsairs in Iceland," *ROMM* 15–16 (1973): 139–44.

81. MD 38 125:254 (8 RA 987/May 1579); MD 42 82:344 (G B 989/August 1581).

82. MD 53 88:241 (24 C 992/July 1584), MD 48 107:294 (17 CA 993/May 1585).

83. Selaniki, "Tarıh-ı Selaniki," fol. 158ʳ.

84. Guilmartin, *Gunpowder*, pp. 7–15.

85. Kâtib Çelebi², pp. 106–7; Kortepeter, *Ottoman Imperialism*, p. 105 and passim.

86. Haëdo, *Topografía*, pp. 386–94.

87. Danişmend, 5:184–203, lists the admirals and gives a short description of their backgrounds.

88. Halil Inalcık, "Capital Formation in the Ottoman Empire," *JEH* 29, no. 1 (1969): 94–140.

89. Alberto Tenenti, *Piracy and the Decline of Venice, 1580–1615*, trans. Janet and Brian Pullman (London, 1967), pp. 16–86, and passim.

90. The most profitable prizes were vessels plying the trade route to Egypt. Kâtib Çelebi, *Fezleke* (Istanbul, 1869), 1:330–31.

91. AGS, E 1948, fols. 3 (4 June 1531); 5 (5 April 1599); 35 (1601); 40–41 (28 March 1602), all *Consulta de Estado*, Madrid.

92. Salvatore Bono, *I corsari barbareschi* (Torino, 1964), pp. 267–349.

93. Brian Pullan, "Editor's Introduction," in *Crisis and Change in the Venetian Economy in the Sixteenth and Seventeenth Centuries*, ed. Brian Pullan (London, 1968), pp. 1–21, and passim; and Topkapı Sarayı Arşivi, D 7687, which lists the losses the Venetians suffered at the hands of corsairs from the Maghrib between 1612 and 1638. The scribe estimated the damage to be 5,000,000 kuruş, with the average ship and cargo being worth approximately 100,000 kuruş.

CHAPTER SEVEN

1. Jerónimo Münzer, *Viaje por España y Portugal*, trans. Julio Puyal in *Boletín de la Real Academia de la Historia* 84 (1924): 78–96.

2. Robert Ignatius Burns, *Islam under the Crusaders* (Princeton, N.J., 1973), pp. 155–83 and passim; Tulio Halperín Donghi, "Recouvrements de civilisation: Les morisques du royaume de Valence au xviᵉ siècle," *Annales* 11 (1956): 154–82.

3. Ladero Quesada, *Los mudéjares*, pp. 15–26; Arié, *L'Espagne musulmane*, pp. 307–14; and L. P. Wright, "The Military Orders in Sixteenth and Seventeenth-Century Spanish Society: The Institutional Embodiment of a Historical Tradition," *Past and Present* 43 (May 1969): 34–70.

4. Braudel, *The Mediterranean*, 2:780–802; Henri Lapeyre, *Géographie de l'Espagne morisque* (Paris, 1960), pp. 3–6, 117–33, 203–13.

5. See Albert A. Sicroff, *Les controverses des statuts de "pureté de sang" en Espagne du XVe au XVIIe siècle* (Paris, 1960), pp. 32–35; Stephen Haliczer, "The Castilian Urban Patriciate and the Jewish Expulsion of 1480–92," *AHR* 78, no. 1 (February 1973): 35–58.

6. Luis del Mármol Carvajal, *Historia del rebelión y castigo de los moriscos del reino de Granada*, in *BAE*, 24 (Madrid, 1858): 127, 135, 153–59; and *Fragmento de la época sobre noticias de los reyes nazaritas capitulación de Granada y emigración de los Andaluces a Marruecos*, trans. Afredo Bustani and Carlos Quirós (Larache, 1940), pp. 49–50. Ladero Quesada, *Los mudéjares*, pp. 58–61, summarizes the information available on the role of the Muslims who cooperated with the Christian regime in Granada.

7. Henry Kamen, *The Spanish Inquisition* (New York, 1965).

8. Ladero Quesada, *Los mudéjares*, pp. 2, 20–22.

9. Ibid., pp. 20–25; Arié, *L'Espagne musulmane*, pp. 307–14; and Lapeyre, *Géographie*, p. 27. Note, however, that in rural areas like Valencia, where Muslims predominated, they often lived under semi-independent conditions that did not resemble an urban ghetto. Burns, *Islam under the Crusaders*, pp. 144–45.

10. Ladero Quesada, *Los mudéjares*, pp. 25–26, 245–46 (doc. 97), 315–16 (doc. 144); idem, *Castilla y la Conquista*, pp. 16–17.

11. Ladero Quesada, *Los mudéjares*, pp. 30–39, 106–10 (doc. 14), *Capitulación de Comares*.

12. Ibid., pp. 39–43, 130–33 (doc. 28); pp. 157–59 (doc. 44); and *Fragmento*, pp. 41–42.

13. Ladero Quesada, *Los mudéjares*, pp. 44–49, 172–82 (doc. 50); Muḥammad ʿAbdallāh ʿInān, *Nihāyat al-Andalus* (Cairo, 1958), p. 233.

14. Ladero Quesada, *Los mudéjares*, pp. 34–36, 41–43, 51; and *Fragmento*, pp. 41–42, 48–50.

15. Ladero Quesada, *Los mudéjares*, pp. 203–4 (doc. 62).

16. Ibid., pp. 62–63.

17. Mendoza, *Guerra de Granada*, pp. 99–101; and Erika Spivakovsky, *Son of the Alhambra* (Austin, 1970), pp. 3–27.

18. Mármol, *Rebelión*, *pp*. 151–53, 159. Ladero Quesada, *Los mudéjares*, pp. 59, 64–65, 70–71.

19. Mármol, *Rebelión*, pp. 151–53; and Ladero Quesada, *Los mudéjares*, pp. 64–65.

20. Ladero Quesada, "La Repoblación del Reino de Granada anterior al año 1500," *Hispania* 28, no. 110 (1968): 489–563.

21. Both these measures violated the capitulation for Granada and, if contested, would throw the Muslims into Christian courts. Ladero Quesada, *Los mudéjares*, p. 228 (doc. 83).

22. One of the major violations of the capitulations in the period before 1499 was the levying of new taxes—*servicios*; ibid., pp. 57–58, 210 (doc. 69).

23. Mármol, *Rebelión*, pp. 153–55.

24. Ladero Quesada, *Los mudéjares*, pp. 66–82 (doc. 232–36).

25. Darío Cabanelas Rodríguez gives the names of these men in his introduction to Antonio Gallego y Burín and Alfonso Gámir Sandoval, *Los Moriscos del reino de Granada* (Granada, 1968), pp. 19–20.

26. Mármol, *Rebelión*, pp. 155–57; Julio Caro Baroja, *Los Moriscos del reino de Granada* (Madrid, 1957), pp. 14–20.

27. *Fragmento*, pp. 52, 57; James T. Monroe, "A Curious Morisco Appeal to the Ottoman Empire," *Al-Andalus* 21 (1966): 281–303.

28. Mármol, *Rebelión*, pp. 157–59; Mendoza, *Guerra*, pp. 103–8.

29. Monroe, "A Curious Appeal," pp. 281–303. Another effort in verse to involve the Ottomans has been published by Efdaleddin, "Bir Vesika-ı Müellim," pp. 201–22.

30. Monroe, "A Curious Appeal," pp. 295–300. Caro Baroja, *Los Moriscos*, pp. 35–53.

31. N. J. Coulson, *A History of Islamic Law* (Edinburgh, 1964), pp. 9–20 and passim; and idem, *Succession in the Muslim Family* (Cambridge, 1971), pp. 10–51. J. P. Le Flem, "Les Morisques du nord-ouest de l'Espagne en 1594, d'après un recensement de l'Inquisition de Valladolid," *Mélanges de la casa de Velázquez* (Madrid, 1967), pp. 223–44, discusses the relation between endogamic marriage patterns and the survival of Islam under Christian rule.

32. Gallotta, "Le Gazavāt di Ḥayreddin Barbarossa," pp. 79–132.

33. Hayreddin, fols. 29ᵇ–30ᵇ.

34. Ibid., fols. 172ᵇ–174ᵃ.

35. Ibid., fols. 29ᵇ–30ᵇ.

36. Gallego y Burín, *Los Moriscos del reino de Granada*, pp. 170–82 (docs. 8–17).

37. Ibid., pp. 182–84 (doc. 18).

38. Garrad, "The Original Memorial," pp. 199–226; Henry Charles Lea, *The Moriscos of Spain* (Philadelphia, 1901), pp. 57–60.

39. Elliott, *Imperial Spain*, pp. 148–56.

40. Lea, *The Moriscos*, pp. 62–67.

41. Ibid., pp. 67–95.

42. Chaunu, *L'Espagne de Charles Quint*, 1:77–98, 125–32; 2:365–95.

43. Compare Mármol, *Rebelión*, pp. 157–62, with Mendoza, *Guerra*, pp. 103–7.

44. Caro Baroja, *Los Moriscos*, pp. 12–25; K. Garrad, "La Inquisición y los Moriscos granadinos, 1526–1580," *Bulletin Hispanique* 67 (1965):

63–77; and Juan Reglá, *Estudios sobre los Moriscos* (Valencia, 1964), pp. 164–66.

45. Caro Baroja, *Los Moriscos*, pp. 67–99.

46. Gallejo y Burín, *Los Moriscos del reino de Granada*, pp. 25–31 and passim.

47. Caro Baroja, *Los Moriscos*, pp. 141–51.

48. Haëdo, *Topografía*, pp. 50–52; and Hayreddin, fols. 73[a–b], 84[b]–108[a], are contemporary accounts of the ties between the Moriscos and the Muslims in North Africa. Evidence of the Morisco interest in the rise of Ottoman power is discussed by L. P. Harvey, "A Morisco Reader of Jean Lemaire de Belges?" *Al-Andalus*, 28, no. 1 (1963): 231–36. For the Old Christian view of the Morisco, see Caro Baroja, *Los Moriscos*, pp. 101–39. The international dimension of the Morisco threat, and especially its connection with Protestantism, is examined by Reglá, *Estudios*, pp. 139–50; and Louis Cardaillac, "Morisques et Protestants," *Al-Andalus* 36, no. 1 (1971): 29–61.

49. Caro Baroja, *Los Moriscos*, pp. 119–24.

50. Gallego y Burín, *Los Moriscos del reino de Granada*, pp. 62–64, and passim.

51. Caro Baroja, *Los Moriscos*, pp. 101–18; and Dressendörfer, *Islam unter der Inquisition*, pp. 153–62.

52. Mármol, *Rebelión*, pp. 169–74; and AGS, Cámara de Castilla, L 2152, fol. 39.

53. AGS, Cámara de Castilla, L 2172, no fol. no., 12 March 1572; Caro Baroja, *Los Moriscos*, pp. 181–87.

54. Gallego y Burín, *Los Moriscos del Reino de Granada*, pp. 20, 170–71 (docs. 7–8).

55. Caro Baroja, *Los Moriscos*, pp. 159–69.

56. Mármol, *Rebelión*, pp. 157, 160, 166, 173; Duro, *Armada española*, 1:45–46; Reglá, *Estudios*, pp. 139–49; Hess, "Moriscos," pp. 1–13.

57. Garrad, "La industria sedera," pp. 73–98.

58. Mármol, *Rebelión*, pp. 160–63; Mendoza, *Guerra*, p. 108; and Caro Baroja, *Los Moriscos*, pp. 148–54.

59. Mendoza, *Guerra*, p. 243 and passim.

60. AGS, Cámara de Castilla, L 2154, fol. 168, letter to Philip II from the audiencia of Granada, 22 June 1570; L 2161, fol. 125, letter to the king from María Rodríguez Ginda, 4 August 1571; L 2188, no fol. no., 23 October 1569; L 2182, no fol. no., 26 January 1581; and L 2172, no fol. no., letter to the king from the audiencia of Granada, 20 April 1572; and Caro Baroja, *Los Moriscos*, pp. 173–80.

61. Lea, *The Moriscos*, pp. 236–68; and Caro Baroja, *Los Moriscos*, pp. 173–208, give the details. The spirit of intolerance permeates the letters of Granada's administrators AGS, Cámara de Castilla, L 2152, fol. 267, letter from the audiencia of Granada to the king, 2 October 1571, calling for "la justicia de sangre sin remisión ni misericordia"; but

see also L 2152, fol. 195, letter from the archbishop of Granada, 30 August 1569, demanding an end to the excessive violence.

62. AGS, Cámara, de Castilla, L 2153, fols. 9–84, 18 February 1570 to 14 March 1570.

63. Bernard Vincent, "L'expulsion des Moriscos du royaume de Granada et leur répartition en Castille (1570–71)," in *Mélanges de la Casa de Velázquez*, 6 (1970): 211–40.

64. AGS, Cámara de Castilla, L 2168, no fol. no., November 1572; L 2172, no fol. no., 16 March 1572.

65. AGS, Cámara de Castilla, L 2168, no fol. no., memorial from Granada to the king, 2 January 1572; L 2157, fol. 236, president of the audiencia of Granada to the king, 8 April 1571; L 2162, fol. 1.

66. Instructions for the repopulation of Granada with Old Christians are in AGS, Cámara de Castilla, L 2166, fol. 3, 28 February 1571; L 2161, fol. 51, 15 October 1571.

67. AGS, Cámara de Castilla, L 2168, no fol. no., report from Burgos, winter 1572; L 1271, no fol. no., report on the repopulation of Granada, 2 September 1572; and L 2179, no fol. no., letter from the president of the audiencia of Granada to the king, 10 September 1576.

68. AGS, Cámara de Castilla, L 2182, no fol. no., 31 January 1580, reports a total of 8,601 free and enslaved Moriscos living in Granada. The largest concentrations of New Christians were in Granada and its environs, 3,851, and Malaga, 1,274. See also Lapeyre, *Géographie*, pp. 117–43.

69. AGS, Cámara de Castilla, L 2153, fol. 73, letter from Don Juan to the king, 12 March 1570; and L 2161, fol. 51, 15 October 1571.

70. On this much-debated question, see Juan Reglá, "La expulsión de los Moriscos y sus consecuencias," *Hispania* 13, nos 51–52 (1953): 215–67, 402–79.

71. Lea, *The Moriscos*, pp. 97–125.

72. Ibid., pp. 161–71.

73. Reglá, *Estudios*, pp. 44–54.

74. AGS, Cámara de Castilla, L 2173, no fol. no., copy of instructions from the archbishop of Cordoba for the administration of Moriscos, 15 January 1573.

75. AGS, Cámara de Castilla, L 2181, no fol. no., Baeza, February 1579; L 2181, no fol. no., Granada, 4 April 1579; L 2181, no fol. no., Malaga, 20 September 1578; and Antonio Domínguez Ortiz, "Los Moriscos granadinos antes de su definitiva expulsión," *MEAH* 12, no. 1 (1963–64): 113–28.

76. Reglá, *Estudios*, pp. 26–60; María Soledad Carrasco Urgoiti, *El problema Morisco en Aragón al comienzo del reino de Felipe II* (Madrid, 1969), pp. 11–44; and James Casey, "Moriscos and the Depopulation of Valencia," *Past and Present* 50 (February 1971): 19–40.

77. Thomas Kendrick, *Saint James in Spain* (London, 1960), pp. 70–85, 109–15, 138–42, 206, 212; Darío Cabanelas Rodríguez, *El Morisco*

244   NOTES TO PAGES 154–58

granadino Alonso del Castillo (Madrid, 1965), pp. 177–236; and Monroe, *Islam and the Arabs*, pp. 7–15, 109. For a Muslim description of these events, see Clelia Sarnelli Cerqua, "Al-Maġarī in Andalusia," in *Studi Magrebini* 3 (Naples, 1970): 161–84.

78. Pascual Baronat y Barrachina, *Los Moriscos españoles y su expulsión* (Valencia, 1901), 1:291–94, 300–305.

79. Pierre Chaunu, "Minorités et conjuncture: L'expulsion des Morèsques en 1609," *Revue historique* 225, no. 1 (January, March 1961): 81–98, and Reglá, *Estudios*, pp. 153–76, deal with the economic causes for the expulsion. Braudel, *The Mediterranean*, 2:796, argues that the basic reason for the expulsion of the Moriscos was their refusal to accept western civilization.

80. Lapeyre, *Géographie*, pp. 203–13.

81. María Soledad Carrasco Urgoiti, *El Moro de Granada en la literatura* (Madrid, 1956), pp. 20–48.

CHAPTER EIGHT

1. Charles-André Julien, *History of North Africa*, trans. John Petrie, ed. C. C. Stewart (New York, 1970), p. 343, concludes, however, that "the Turks nevertheless failed to impart any fresh impetus to the age-old Maghrib."

2. Halil Inalcık, "Suleiman the Lawgiver and Ottoman Law," *Archivum Ottomanicum* 1 (1969): 105–38. An example of the sultan's concern for the just treatment of his subjects in Algeria is MD 7 897:2456 (17 C 976/7 December 1568).

3. Quoted in Norman Itzkowitz, *Ottoman Empire and Islamic Tradition* (New York, 1972), pp. 87–89.

4. Hess, "Conquest of Egypt," pp. 55–76, and MDZ 3 204–5 (13 R 984/10 July 1576), where the Algerian governor, Ramazan Paşa, reports that the Ottoman candidate ʿAbd al-Malik was administering Morocco like Egypt; this underscores how the administrative organization of Egypt served as a model for the rest of Ottoman North Africa. See also Hezarfen, "Telhis," fols. 55ᵇ–56ᵃ.

5. Inalcık, *The Ottoman Empire*, pp. 104–10; and Haëdo, *Topografía*, pp. 204–12, describe the Ottoman provincial system and the men who ruled it.

6. MD 43 125:226 (27 CA 988/10 July 1580); and Inalcık, *The Ottoman Empire*, pp. 61–88.

7. Haëdo, *Topografía*, pp. 51–52, 58. One notable exception was Hasan Paşa, the son of Hayreddin Barbarossa. Roger Le Tourneau and Cengiz Orhonlu, "Hasan Paşa," *EI²*, 3:251–52. In later centuries this prohibition was not observed; nevertheless the Ottoman provinces continued to exclude the sons of slaves, usually by enrolling them in military organizations in other provinces such as Syria. Abdul Karim Rafeq, "The local forces in Syria in the seventeenth and eighteenth

centuries," in *War, Technology and Society in the Middle East*, ed. V. J. Parry and M. E. Yapp (London, 1975), pp. 286–87.

8. Haëdo, *Topografía*, pp. 56–58, 60–62, 98–103, 168–81; and Koçu Bey, *Risale-i Koçu Bey* (Istanbul, 1861), pp. 15–16, where the mixture of the subject class into the Janissary corps was counted as a major reason for Ottoman decline. This lack of respect for the hereditary principle never ceased to amaze Christians. Mas, *Les Turcs*, 2:178–85, 333.

9. Haëdo, *Topografía*, pp. 204–12.

10. Inalcık, "Ottoman Methods of Conquest," pp. 103–29; idem, *Ottoman Policy and Administration in Cyprus after the Conquest* (Ankara, 1969), pp. 5–23.

11. Haëdo, *Topografía*, pp. 46–51; and MD 79 23:58 (4 RA 1019/27 May 1610), where the sultan revoked some of these conquest concessions.

12. Inalcık, "Ottoman Methods of Conquest," pp. 103–29; and M. A. Cook, *Population Pressure in Rural Anatolia, 1450–1600* (Oxford, 1972), pp. 46–81, describe how the *tahrir* was performed. These cadastral surveys were regularly conducted in Ottoman North Africa. MD 28 42:103 (25 B 984/18 October 1576), for example, orders the governor of Tunisia to finish the *tahrir* for that province.

13. MD 30 228:531 (13 RA 985/1577); Haëdo, *Topografía*, pp. 58–60; Andrew C. Hess, "Firearms and the Decline of Ibn Khaldun's Military Elite," *Archivum Ottomanicum* 5 (1972): 173–201; and Inalcık, *The Ottoman Empire*, pp. 104–18.

14. Stanford J. Shaw, "The Land Law of Ottoman Egypt (960/1553): A contribution to the study of landholding in the early years of Ottoman rule in Egypt," *Der Islam* 38, nos 1–2 (October 1962): 109.

15. MD 36 108:312 (8 M 987/8 March 1579) contains instructions on the granting of private property: *mülk*.

16. Haëdo, *Topografía*, pp. 103–11.

17. MD 48 44:127 (27 B 990/17 August 1582); MD 73 574:1254 (18 L 1003/26 June 1595).

18. Haëdo, *Topografía*, pp. 60–79, 204–12.

19. Inalcık, *The Ottoman Empire*, pp. 41–52.

20. MD 43 148:265 (G C 988/14 July 1580); MD 39 215:436 (12 M 988/1 March 1580).

21. Hezarfen, "Telhis," fols. 33b–34a, 55b–56a, describes the application of the salary system in the Arab provinces.

22. MD 2 63:564 (9 C 963/10 April 1556); MD 24 91–92:1246 (14 Z 981/6 April 1574); MD 30 197:467 (5 RA 985/23 May 1577); and Ilter, *Şimali Afrikada*, 2:126–28.

23. Haëdo, *Topografía*, pp. 298–301; AGS, E 1950, fol. 189, Roderigo Pardo, "Relación de Algers," 1611(?).

24. Hess "Firearms," pp. 173–201

25. Haëdo, *Topografía*, pp. 46–51; Suárez, "Historia del Maestro," fols. 51ʳ–52ʳ, 165ʳ–168ʳ; and Ali Riza Paşa, *Mir°at al-Cezayir*, Ottoman trans., Ali Şevki (Istanbul, 1876), pp. 39–43.

26. Boyer, *Algérie médiane*, pp. 20–25, 42–54. Although he summarizes the tribal policies of the Turkish government for a later period, the techniques were the same over time and space. For the Bedouin in Palestine, see Uriel Heyd, *Ottoman Documents on Palestine, 1552–1615* (Oxford, 1960), pp. 90–116; for Ottoman tactics against the Berber rebellion in Algeria of 1603–8, see Saint-Cyr, *Felipe III y el rey de Cuco*, pp. 49–77.

27. Haëdo, *Topografía*, pp. 56–58, 60–62, Suárez, "Historia del maestre," fols. 167ʳ–176ʳ.

28. Kahane and Tietze, *The Lingua Franca*, pp. 20–45.

29. Jean-Léon l'Africain, *Description*, 2:467; Piri Reis, *Bahriye*, p. 634.

30. Haëdo, *Topografía*, p. 46; and compare with the population increase in Mardin, also conquered by the Turks early in the sixteenth century. Nejat Göyünç, *XVI Yüzyılda Mardin Sancağı* (Istanbul, 1969), pp. 101–6.

31. Et-Tamgrouti, *En-Nafhat*, pp. 75–78.

32. Compare Pike, *Enterprise*, pp. 25–26, and Haëdo, *Topografía*, pp. 28–43.

33. MD 22 186:359 (28 RA 981/28 July 1573).

34. Haëdo, *Topografía*, pp. 28–31; and AGS, *Mapas y Dibujos y Planas*, 19/149–50, 1603, 8/164–65, ca. 1600, for the city and 18/143–45, ca 1619, for the surrounding fortifications.

35. Compare Pike, *Enterprise*, pp. 25–35, 130–35; Haëdo, *Topografía*, pp. 43–46; and Riza, *Mir°at*, pp. 30–31, 39, 44–46.

36. *Les mosques en Algerie*, publication of the Algerian Ministry of Information (Madrid, 1970), pp. 46–55 and passim.

37. AGS, Mapas y Dibujos y Planas, 19/151; Haëdo, *Topografía*, pp. 103–4, 191–99; and Ömer L. Barkan, *Süleymaniye Cami ve Imareti Inşaatı (1550–1557)* (Ankara, 1972), 1:47–64, for the development of the mosque complex.

38. Haëdo, *Topografía*, pp. 191–99; Pike, *Enterprise*, pp. 26–27.

39. MD 210:1899 (8 RA 964/8 January 1557) lists the staff from the highest to lowest rank of the governor, Salih Paşa.

40. Riza, *Mir°at*, pp. 28–31, 45–49; Haëdo, *Topografía*, pp. 204–12. The police duty of the Janissary corps in Algiers is mentioned in MD 7 20:67 (8 S 975/14 August 1567). The place of the *mizwār* and *muḥtasib* in North African administration is discussed by Hopkins, *Medieval Muslim Government*, pp. 94–96, 125–26.

41. Haëdo, *Topografía*, pp. 60–62, 204–12; Riza, *Mir°at*, p. 44.

42. Mas, *Les Turcs*, 2:297.

43. MD 22 339:671 (15 CA 981/12 September 1573); and Haëdo, *Topografía*, pp. 150–68, 204–12.

44. MD 21 267:639 (16 Z 980/19 April 1573), where they are referred to as *ayan* and *ümera*. Ira M. Lapidus, *Muslim Cities in the Later Middle Ages* (Cambridge, Mass., 1967), pp. 116–42; *The Islamic City*, ed. A. H. Hourani and S. M. Stern (Oxford, 1969), pp. 16–20; and Le Tourneau, *Fès avant le Protectorat*, pp. 481–95, discuss the position of the notables in the Muslim city.

45. Riza, *Mir²at*, pp. 44–50; Haëdo, *Topografía*, 46–62, 93–97, 204–12.

46. MD 21 267:639 (16 ZA 980/1572); MD 47 185:436 (1 C 990/1582); MD 58 189:496 (25 C 993/1585).

47. Haëdo, *Topografía*, pp. 210–12; MD 43 162:292 (19 C 988/August 1580).

48. Haëdo, *Topografía*, pp. 51–79, where the word "Turk" is used loosely for anyone who came from Ottoman territories.

49. Ibid., pp. 52–56; George Sandys, *A Relation of a Journey Begun An. Dom. 1610* (London, 1615), pp. 166–69, 358–60; Père Dan, *Histoire de la Barbarie et de ses corsaires* (Paris, 1637), pp. 78, 110, 170–75, 210, 273–77.

50. RD 225 79 (28 R 980/7 September 1572).

51. Herzarfen, "Telhis," fol. 62ᵃ.

52. Compare Haëdo, *Topografía*, pp. 46–51, 93–97; and Pike, *Aristocrats*, pp. 99–109.

53. Haëdo, *Topografía*, pp. 46–51, 93–103; Riza, *Mir²at*, pp. 28–30; and Pike, *Aristocrats*, pp. 130–36. The place of the guild in sixteenth-century Ottoman history is the subject of Gabriel Baer, "The Administrative, Economic, and Social Functions of Turkish Guilds," *IJMES* 1, no. 1 (January 1970): 28–50.

54. Riza, *Mir²at*, p. 46.

55. Ibn Khaldun, *Muqaddimah*, 2:302–3.

56. Haëdo, *Topografía*, pp. 46–51; and Pierre Bourdieu, *The Algerians*, trans. Alan C. M. Ross (Boston, 1962), pp. 1–118.

57. Miguel de Epalza, "Moriscos et Andalous en Tunisie au XVIIᵉ siècle," in *Etudes sur les Moriscos andalous en Tunisie*, ed. M. de Epalza and R. Petit (Madrid, 1973), pp. 150–86, and the other articles in the volume.

58. Haëdo, *Topografía*, pp. 46–51; Dan, *Histoire de Barbarie*, pp. 89–90.

59. Ibid., pp. 111–14; Emanuel d'Aranda, *The History of Algiers and Its Slavery . . .*, trans. John Davis (London, 1666), pp. 49–50; and M. Eisenbeth, "Les Juifs en Algérie et en Tunisie à l'époque turque (1516–1830)," *Revue africaine* 96 (1952): 114–87, 343–84.

60. Haëdo, *Topografía*, pp. 79–97, 204–12; and Francis Knight, *A Relation of Seven Years Slaverie under the Turks of Argeire* (London, 1640), pp. 44–45.

61. Bono, *I corsari*, pp. 4–12, 217–66, 267–399.

62. Haëdo, *Topografía*, pp. 46–51, 98–103.

63. Haëdo, *Topografía*, pp. 150–68; Mármol, *L'Afrique de Marmol*, 2:412; and Coulson, *Succession*, pp. 10–51.

64. Haëdo, *Topografía*, pp. 118–35.

65. Ibid., pp. 135–42.

66. Ibid., pp. 150–68, 181–84.

67. al-Ifrānī, *Nozhet*, pp. 237–56; Fagnan, *Extraits*, pp. 376–77; *SIHM*, Port., 3 (12 December 1540): 308; Gaston Deverdun, *Marrakech des origines à 1912* (Rabat, 1959–66), 1:349–436.

68. Torres, *Relación*, pp. 147–48, 158–59, 288, 475–81, 487, 491; Deverdun, *Marrakech*, 1:440–46.

69. Hopkins, *Medieval Muslim Government*, pp. 1–19 and passim; Michaux-Bellaire, "L'organisation," pp. 171–251; and idem, "Les impôts marocains," *AM* 1 (1904): 56–96.

70. Fagnan, *Extraits*, pp. 378–79, Es Salâoui, *Les Saadiens*, pp. 47–49, and Brahim Harakat, "Le Makhzen Saadien," *ROMM* 15–16 (2ᵉ sem., 1973): 43–59.

71. Fagnan, *Extraits*, pp. 379, 387; and August Cour, "Djaysh. iii. Muslim West 2. Djīsh," *EI²*, 2:509–11; Gellner, *Saints*, pp. 2–65; and *Arabs and Berbers*, ed. Ernest Gellner and Charles Micaud (London, 1972), pp. 11–20 and passim.

72. Mohammed El Menouni, "Apparition à l'époque mérinide et Ouattaside des éléments constitutifs du sentiment national marocain," *Hespéris Tamuda* 9, no. 2 (1968): 119–227; and Mohammed Hajji "L'idée de nation au Maroc aux XVIᵉ et XVIIᵉ siècles," *Hespéris Tamuda* 9, no. 1 (1968): 109–21.

73. Deverdun, *Marrakech*, 1:1–24, 358–423; and vol. 2, pl. 16. For the relation of Marrakesh to other Muslim cities of its time, see Roger Le Tourneau, *Fez in the Age of the Marinides*, trans. Besse Alberta Clement (Norman, Okla., 1961); and George Marçais, "La conception des villes dans l'Islam," *Revue d'Alger* 2 (1954–55): 517–33.

74. Deverdun, *Marrakech*, 1:358–62.

75. Ibid., 1:363–67.

76. Ibid., 1:367–79; and Pike, *Aristocrats*, pp. 140–41.

77. Deverdun, *Marrakech*, 1:380–416.

78. Torres, *Relación*, p. 469; Deverdun, *Marrakech*, 1:417–46.

79. Deverdun, *Marrakech*, 1:446–48.

80. Ibid., 1:455–62.

81. Henri Terrasse, "Note sur les contacts artistiques entre le Maroc et le Portugal du XVᵉ au XVIIᵉ siècle," in *Mélanges d'études luso-marocaines dédiés à la mémoire de David Lopes et Pierre de Cenival* (Lisbon, 1945), pp. 401–17.

CHAPTER NINE

1. *The Legacy of Islam*, ed. Thomas Arnold and Alfred Guillaume Oxford, 1931), pp. 12, 198, and passim.

2. AGS E, L 1948, fol. 155, 11 January 1611.

3. Immanuel Wallerstein, *The Modern World System* (New York, 1974), pp. 225-97.

4. Inalcık, "Capital Formation in the Ottoman Empire," pp. 97-140.

5. Lewis V. Thomas, *A Study of Naima*, ed. Norman Itzkowitz (New York, 1972), pp. 144-45.

6. For the importance of Egypt to the Ottomans, see Stanford J. Shaw, *The Budget of Ottoman Egypt, 1005-1006/1596-1597* (Paris, 1968), pp. 18, 120, 204-5.

7. Pike, *Aristocrats*, pp. 21-30 and passim.

8. Willan, *Studies*, pp. 92-296.

9. Rafael A. Guevara Bazan, "Muslim Immigration to Spanish America," *Muslim World* 56, no. 3 (July 1966): 173-87; idem, "Some Notes for a History of the Relations between Latin America, the Arabs and Islam," *Muslim World* 61, no. 4 (October 1971): 284-92.

10. Jean-Léon L'Africain, *Description*, 1:9, 43, 62-65, 75-76, 83, 160-69; 2:324-25, 329, 334, 348-51, 364-68, 369-71, 382-85; Haëdo, *Topografía*, pp. 93-97; Torres, *Relación*, pp. 469-70; Mármol, *L'Afrique*, 2:332-33, 412; Knight, *A Relation*, pp. 44-45; and H. J. Fisher, "The Central Sahara and Sudan," in *The Cambridge History of Africa* (Cambridge, 1975), 4:84-91, 97-105.

11. Andrew C. Hess, "Piri Reis and the Ottoman Response to the Voyages of Discovery," *Terrae Incognitae* 6 (1974): 19-37. For a Byzantine parallel, see Hélène Ahrweiler, *Byzance et la mer* (Paris, 1966), pp. 41, 389-95.

12. An introduction to Ottoman geography is given by Fr. Taeschner, "Djughrāfiyā. vi. The Ottoman Geographers," *EI*², 2:587-90. Abdülhak Adnan Adıvar, *Osmanlı Türklerinde Ilim* (Istanbul, 1943), pp. 55-79, gives further detail. For Ottoman interest in the New World, I have relied upon V. L. Ménage, "The Map of Hajji Ahmed and Its Makers," *BSOAS* 21 (1958): 291-314; Svat Soucek, "The ʿAli Macar Reis Atlas and the Deniz Kitabı: Their Place in the Genre of Portolan Charts and Atlas," *Imago Mundi* 25 (1971): 17-27; and T. D. Goodrich, "Sixteenth Century Ottoman Americana" (diss., Columbia University, 1969).

13. Kâtib Çelebi, *Tuhfet*, p. 3; and for the Arab ignorance of Europe, see Ibrahim Abu-Lughod, *Arab Rediscovery of Europe* (Princeton, 1963), pp. 11-27, 67.

14. Inalcık, *The Ottoman Empire*, p. 174.

15. Alessio Bombaci, *Histoire de la littérature turque*, trans. I. Melikoff (Paris, 1968), pp. 265-311.

16. Walter G. Andrews, "A Critical-Interpretive Approach to the Ottoman Turkish Ġazel," *IJMES* 4, no 1 (January 1973): 97-99.

17. J. H. Mordtmann and H. W. Duda, "Ewliyā Çelebī," *EI*², 2:717-20.

18. Inalcık, *The Ottoman Empire*, pp. 179–85; Haëdo, *Topografía*, pp. 150–68.

19. This is the point Kâtib Çelebi, *The Balance of Truth*, trans. G. L. Lewis (London, 1957), pp. 89–90, wished to make in his chapter on innovation.

20. Richard L. Kagan, "Universities in Castile, 1500–1700," *Past and Present* 49 (November 1970): 44–71: Mas, *Les Turcs*, 1:211–12.

21. Robert Schwoebel, *The Shadow of the Crescent: The Renaissance Image of the Turk (1453–1517)* (New York, 1967), pp. 202–26; and Mas, *Les Turcs*, 1:19–136; 2:296–97.

22. Louis Cardaillac, "Morisques et protestants," pp. 29–61.

23. For example, "Historia y conquista de Túnez," BNM, Ms. 19441, fols 47ʳ–62ʳ and passim.

24. Mas, *Les Turcs*, 2:25–29, 178–85; Jean Deny, "Les pseudo-prophéties concernant les Turcs au XVIᵉ siècle," *Revue des études islamiques* 10, no. 2 (1936): 202–5.

25. Mas, *Les Turcs*, 2:207–29.

26. Ibid., 1:160 and passim.

27. The tenacious survival of these negative opinions about Islam has been studied by Norman Daniel, *Islam and the West* (Edinburgh, 1966), especially pp. 271–307; and idem, *Islam Europe and Empire* (Edinburgh, 1966). The Spanish manifestation of this movement in the Golden Age is treated in detail by Mas, *Les Turcs*, 2:231–353 and passim. For other less intense reflections of the same movement in Europe, see Clarence Dana Rouillard, *The Turk in French History, Thought, and Literature (1520–1660)* (Paris, 1938), pp. 77–110, 379–408; and Samuel C. Chew, *The Crescent and the Rose* (New York, 1937), pp. 130–33, 251–52, 495–549

28. Monroe, *Islam and the Arabs*, pp. 7–15, sums up the modern judgment on Miguel de Luna's history, which was translated into English as *The History of the Conquest of Spain by the Moors* (London, 1687). Carrasco Urgoiti, *El Moro de Granada*, pp. 20–48, analyzes the use of the Moors in Spanish literature.

29. Mas, *Les Turcs*, 2:357–451.

30. On Mármol and Torres, see the brief description of Monroe, *Islam and the Arabs*, pp. 13–20. There is no satisfactory study of Haëdo's position in Spanish literature on Islam. The image of Africa that did emerge in seventeenth-century European literature was that of Black Africa. Walter Rodney, "Africa in Europe and the Americas," in *Cambridge History of Africa*, 4:578–79.

31. The best introduction to *aljamiada* literature is L. P. Harvey's "Aljamía," *EI²*, 1:404–5. An example of how the process of arabization for the Hispano-Muslim exiles in Tunisia began is given by Henri Pieri, "L'accueil par des Tunisiens aux Morisques expulsés d'Espagne: Un témoignage morisque," *IBLA* 31, no. 121 (1968): 63–70.

32. The change can be seen in Agah Sırrı Levend's *Gazavât-Nâmeler ve Mihaloğlu Ali Bey'in Gazavât-Namesi* (Ankara, 1956), pp. 70–105.

33. Miguel de Epalza, "Notes pour une histoire des polémiques anti-chrétiennes dans l'occident musulman," *Arabica* 18 (1971): 99–107.

34. Idem, *La Tuḥfa, autobiografía y polémica islámica contra el Cristianismo de ᶜAbdallāh al-Tarȳumān (fray Anselmo Turmeda)*, in *Atti della Accademia Nazionale dei Lincei*, ser. 8, 15 (Rome, 1971): 40–49 and passim.

35. Harvey, "Aljamía," p. 405; and see also Juan Panella, "Littérature morisque en espagnol à Tunis," in *Etudes*, pp. 187–98.

36. E. Lévi-Provençal, *Les historiens des Chorfa* (Paris, 1922), pp. 2–11, 87–140.

37. Jacques Berque, *Al-Yousi* (Paris, 1958), pp. 51–66, 69–82, and passim, is an essay on the seventeenth-century culture of Morocco that stresses its individuality without denying its connection to the East. A less analytic examination of Moroccan literary themes in the seventeenth century is Mohammed Lakhdar, *La vie littéraire au Maroc sous la dynastie ᶜAlawide (1075–1311/1664–1894)* (Rabat, 1971), pp. 15–43, 53–61.

38. Ahmed Abdesselem, *Les historiens tunisiens de XVIIe, XVIIIe, et XIXe siècles* (Tunis, 1973), pp. 21–58.

39. Henri Terrasse, *Islam d'Espagne* (Paris, 1958), pp. 233–60, 265–68.

40. G. Kubler and M. Soria, *Art and Architecture in Spain and Portugal* (London, 1959), pp. 1–2.

41. Terrasse, *Islam d'Espagne*, pp. 202–32.

42. Valeriano Bocal, *Historia del Arte en España* (Madrid, 1972), pp. 114–32.

43. Kubler, *Art and Architecture*, pp. 13–20.

44. Oktay Aslanapa, *Turkish Art and Architecture* (New York, 1971), pp. 65–81, 92–187; and Aptullah Kuran, *The Mosque in Early Ottoman Architecture* (Chicago, 1968), pp. 15–27, 30–70, 177–81, 202–13. The old compromise between Byzantine and Islamic architecture and its continuance into the Ottoman period is the subject of Halil Inalcık, "The Policy of Mehmed II toward the Greek Population of Istanbul and the Byzantine Buildings of the City," *DOP* 23–24 (1969–70): 253–308. A summary of previous interaction between Byzantine and Islamic art is given by Oleg Grabar, "Islamic Art and Byzantium," *DOP* 18 (1964): 73–78 and 87–88.

45. Aslanapa, *Turkish Art*, pp. 217–28.

46. The most comprehensive treatment of Muslim architecture of the West for the Turko-Muslim era is George Marçais's *L'architecture musulmane d'Occident* (Paris, 1954), pp. 183–260, 267–301.

47. Marçais, *L'architecture musulmane d'Occident*, pp. 426–54; and *Les mosques en Algerie*, pp. 46–67. The Turkish influence on the architecture of Tunis was complicated by the late Ottoman conquest, the strength of Tunisia's own old tradition, and the absorption of a large

number of Hispano-Muslims. Marçais, *L'architecture musulmane d'Occident*, pp. 464–94. Sixteenth-century Turkish architecture in Tripoli is the subject of Ali Saim Ülgen, "Trablusgarpta Turgut Reis Mimarî Manzumesi," *Vakıflar Dergisi* 5 (Ankara, 1962): 87–92.

48. Deverdun, *Marrakech*, 1:367–418.

49. Marçais, *L'architecture musulmane d'Occident*, pp. 384–422.

50. J. D. Latham, "Towns and Cities of Barbary: The Andalusian Influence," *Islamic Quarterly* 16 (1973): 189–204.

GLOSSARY

Ağa The term means chief or commander. In Ottoman North Africa it was employed most often to name the commander of the Janissary corps: Ağa of the Janissaries.

Akçe Asper. The silver coin of account in the Ottoman empire.

Aljamía In its early modern sense the term refers to a Hispanic Romance language written not in Latin characters, but in Arabic script. Heavily influenced by Arabisms, the literature in this "frontier language" is known as *aljamiada*.

Bey The Ottoman title employed to describe the ruler of a district, usually a *sanjak*.

Celâlî Anatolian rebels of the late sixteenth century.

Cezayir-i Arab Cezayir-i Garb was used more commonly in Ottoman documents. Both terms refer to the province of Algeria.

Çavuş An official of the palace who was often sent to the provinces to convey orders or to conduct an inspection. This office also existed at the provincial level.

Converso In its strictest sense, Jews who had converted to Christianity.

Defterdar The official in charge of the treasury. Just as the central administration had its *defterdar*, so did each of the provinces.

Dey The common meaning in Turkish is maternal uncle. After 1591 it became the honorific title for the local rulers of Ottoman North Africa.

Divan The provincial council or the central organ of Ottoman government at the provincial level.

Emir In Ottoman terminology, the title of emir was often used synonymously with bey. Occasionally it was applied to officials of a higher rank. The term emir does not approach the stature of the title sultan.

Hidalgos The lower portion of the Spanish nobility. Socially and

253

politically ambitious, this element of society epitomized the values of Early Modern Spain.

İmâret A complex of public buildings and institutions supported by religious trusts.

Janissary corps Armed with firearms, this standing infantry corps was recruited from outside North African society.

Kadi The judge who administered both the holy law of Islam and the secular laws promulgated by sultans.

Kaid Commander. A title used loosely in Ottoman North Africa and Morocco for the rulers of areas smaller than a district.

Kanun A secular law or set of laws issued by sultans. These regulations are not part of the holy law of Islam.

Kapudan The complete term is Kapudan Paşa or Kapudan-i derya. It is the title given to the grand admiral of the Ottoman fleet.

Kul Slave, but in the military and political sense of its use in Islamic civilization: a man educated by the state for the purpose of serving the sultanate.

Kuloğulları Sons of slaves. The offspring of slaves, who were excluded from all but minor positions in the Ottoman government.

Liffs Also known as *saffs*. Intertribal alliances that characterize the tribal structure of North African society.

Madrasa Medrese in Ottoman Turkish. An institute of Muslim education where the literary versions of Islam are taught.

Mahalla The Ottoman's annual campaign to collect taxes from their North African subjects.

Mahdi The guided one who will come to deliver Muslims from oppression and to restore mankind to righteousness. This name is usually taken by Muslim revolutionaries.

Marabouts The North African title for popular, as opposed to orthodox, religious leaders, who through their saintly behavior were believed to be close to God.

Mizwār Chief policeman in the Ottoman cities of North Africa.

Moriscos The Hispano-Muslims residing in Spain who were officially declared Christians between 1502 and 1526.

Mudéjares The Hispano-Muslims who remained in Spain and retained their religion and customs under the protection of Christian kings.

Muḥtasib Custodian of public morality.

Presidio The fortified outposts Spain maintained along the coast of North Africa.

Reaya The taxpaying subjects of the Ottoman empire as distinct from the ruling class.

Salyane The system of administration in the provinces by which all the servants of the state were paid salaries and the surplus left in the provincial treasury was sent to Istanbul.

Sanjak The chief administrative unit of the Ottoman empire, governed by a sanjak beyi.

Sharif The title taken by men who claimed a distinguished position in society because of their descent from illustrious ancestors, especially the family of the Prophet.

Shayka A shallow-draft riverboat used in the Black Sea.

Shaykh Senior Muslim elder in the Ottoman cities of North Africa.

Shiʿism The nonmajoritarian sects of Islam that start from the proposition that Ali, the fourth caliph, was the legitimate successor to the Prophet.

Sipahi Cavalryman. Or a cavalryman holding a *timar* (q.v.) in the provinces in return for military service.

Sufism The mystical as opposed to the legalistic version of Islam.

Sunnism The legalistic or orthodox brand of Islam followed by the majority of Muslims.

Tahrir A land survey for the purposes of collecting taxes.

Taragins The terms applied in the city of Algiers to those Hispano-Muslims who emigrated from provinces other than Granada.

Timar A nonhereditary grant of the right to collect legal taxes in return for military service. The annual value of this "fief" was less than twenty thousand aspers.

Ulema/ʿulamāʾ The doctors of Muslim canon law, tradition, and theology. They were often employed by the Ottoman government to handle legal and administrative problems.

Vizier A minister of the sultan and a member of the imperial council.

BIBLIOGRAPHICAL ESSAY

Historians who wish to deal with frontiers soon find themselves struggling with an unusual mixture of sources. The events that determine the location of the frontier often range over a wide geographic area—here the Mediterranean world. Always a zone where the authority of the state is weak, the edges of empires rarely provide the central administration with a clear and chronologically arranged flow of data. One finds this reflected time and again in court chronicles, where only an occasional battle moves the writer to shed some light on border life. Frontiers formed between two civilizations must also reflect the cultural differences that separate the two traditions. Thus the western Mediterranean border of the sixteenth century produced Ottoman and Spanish records that vary widely in quality and content. Some manuscripts and books are fundamental works; others contribute little to this study. Some documents yield only specific information; others reveal the operations of richly textured societies.

It follows that a bibliography listing one source after another in numerous languages would be misleading. Hence the object of this bibliographical essay is to single out a few works in which one will find either a concentrated amount of information on a specific topic or at the very least an introduction to one of the many historical problems under examination.

Frontier historians usually begin with Owen Lattimore's *Inner Asian Frontiers of China*, 2d ed. (New York, 1940) and his *Studies in Frontier History* (London, 1962). For the sixteenth-century history of Mediterranean frontiers, the fundamental work of Fernand Braudel, *The Mediterranean and the Mediterranean World in the Age of Philip II*, trans. Siân Reynolds, 2 vols. (New York, 1973), sets the stage. The relation between cultural borders and geography in the Mediterranean environment is at the heart of Xavier de Phantol's *Les fondements géographiques de l'histoire de l'Islam* (Paris, 1968). A number of important monographs

257

stress the role of the frontier in Turko-Muslim history. Speros Vryonis, Jr., *The Decline of Medieval Hellenism in Asia Minor and the Process of Islamization from the Eleventh through the Fifteenth Century* (Los Angeles, 1971), and Paul Wittek, *DasFürstentum Mentesche: Studien zur Geschichte Westkleinasiens im 13.–15. Jahrhunderts* (Istanbul, 1934), cover the pre-Ottoman period. The classic studies of Ottoman origins are frontier histories: Paul Wittek, *The Rise of the Ottoman Empire* (London, 1938), and Fuad Köprülü, *Les origines de l'empire ottoman* (Paris, 1935). For Europe's border with the Turks, W. H. McNeill, *Europe's Steppe Frontier, 1500–1800* (Chicago, 1964), and C. Max Kortepeter, *Ottoman Imperialism during the Reformation: Europe and the Caucasus* (New York, 1972), provide essential information. Europe's cultural entanglement with Islamic civilization on the western Mediterranean frontier is a major subject in Thomas Arnold and Alfred Guillaume, eds., *The Legacy of Islam*, 2d ed., ed. J. Schact and C. E. Bosworth (London, 1974). The emergence of Modern Spain on the Hispano-Muslim border is the theme of Américo Castro's *The Spaniards*, trans. Willard F. King and Selma Margaretten (Berkeley, 1971). The use of the frontier as a guide to Spanish history is developed by Thomas F. Glick and Oriol Pi-Sunyer, "Acculturation as an Explanatory Concept in Spanish History," *Comparative Studies in Society and History* 2, no. 2 (April 1969): 136–54. Although not directly concerned with the Islamic world, Immanuel Wallerstein's *The Modern World-System* (New York, 1974) begins to deal with frontier history on a global scale for the early modern period.

The rise of Portuguese seapower as part of the fifteenth-century military revolution has been studied many times. C. R. Boxer, *The Portuguese Seaborne Empire, 1415–1825* (New York, 1969), is an excellent summary of this complex event. Portugal's economic interest in North Africa and her subsequent creation of a commercial maritime empire is exhaustively studied in Vitorino Magalhães Godinho, *L'économie de l'empire portugais aux xvᵉ et xviᵉ siècles* (Paris, 1969). A sense of the military life on the Portuguese border during the early modern era can be gained through the articles of Robert Richard, some of which are collected in his *Etudes sur l'histoire de Portugais au Maroc* (Coimbra, 1955). Finally, the most accessible source of primary information concerning the Portuguese in North Africa remains *Sources inédits de l'histoire du Maroc, première sèrie, Dynastie saᶜdienne, sous sèr. 5: Archives et bibliothèques de Portugal*, ed. H. de Castries, R. Richard, and Chantal de la Véronne, 5 vols. (Paris, 1934–53).

Iberia on the march along its Mediterranean flanks is not well known. Elena Lourie, "A Society Organized for War, Medieval Spain," *Past and Present* 25 (1966): 54–76, summarizes the history of the period before the arrival of gunpowder. Charles-Emmanuel Dufourcq, *L'Espagne catalane et le Maghrib aux xiiiᵉ et xivᵉ siècles* (Paris, 1966), studies how medieval Catalonia translated her naval and military superiority into North African imperialism.

Spain's participation in the early modern military revolution and its consequence for Naṣrid Granada are themes in Rachel Arié, *L'Espagne musulmane au temps des Naṣrides (1232–1492)* (Paris, 1973); and Miguel Angel Ladero Quesada, *Castilla y la conquista del reino de Granada* (Valladolid, 1967). The rise of a new army and navy in the powder era is studied by J. Vigón, *El ejército de los reyes católicos* (Madrid, 1968), and Francisco Felipo Olesa Muñido, *La organización naval de los estados mediterráneos y en especial de España durante los siglos XVI y XVII*, 2 vols. (Madrid, 1968). How Spain translated her military power into an occupation of the North African coast was recorded by the chronicler Andrés Bernáldez, *Memorias del reinado de los reyes católicos* (Madrid, 1962). Details of the Maghribian conquests are also to be found throughout the vast collection of documents published in *Colección de documentos inéditos para la historia de España*, 112 vols. (Madrid, 1842–95).

A rich source of information on the military culture of North Africa during the period preceding the powder age is Ibn Khaldun's *The Muqaddimah*, trans. Franz Rosenthal 2d ed., 3 vols. (Princeton, 1967). One can also learn a great deal about Muslim warfare from Ibn Khaldoun, *Histoire des Berbères*, trans. Baron de Slaine, ed. P. Casanova, 4 vols. (Paris, 1968–69). R. Brunschvig, *La Berbérie orientale sous les Ḥafṣids des origines à la fin du xvᵉ siècle*, 2 vols. (Paris, 1940–47), describes the modes of North African warfare on the eve of the Spanish invasion. At the turn of the sixteenth century, Jean-Léon l'Africain, *Description de l'Afrique*, trans. A. Epaulard, 2 vols. (Paris, 1956); and Luis del Mármol Carvajal, *Primera parte de la descripción general de Affrica . . .* (Granada, 1573), are primary sources of information for the early impact of firearms on Maghribian society. On the sea, Carlo Cipolla, *Guns, Sails and Empires* (New York, 1966); and Andrew C. Hess, "The Evolution of the Ottoman Seaborne Empire in the Age of the Oceanic Discoveries, 1453–1525," *American Historical Review*, 75, no. 7 (December, 1970), pp. 1892–1919, chart two different responses to an age of naval expansion.

Four chroniclers have left a record of the relation between the history of the North African frontier and the evolution of Portuguese politics: Fernão Lopes, *Crónica de D. João I*, ed. A. Braamcamp Freire and H. Sérgio, 2 vols. (Porto, 1945–49); Ruy de Pina, *Chrónica d'el rey D. Affonso V*, *Chrónica d'el rey D. Duarte*, and *Chrónica d'el rey D. João II*, all in *Colecçâo de libros inéditos de história portugueza*, ed. José Corrêa de Serra, vols 1 and 2 (Lisbon, 1790–1824); Damião de Góis, *Crónica do felicissimo rei D. Manuel*, 4 vols., (Coimbra, 1949–54); and João de Barros, *Da Asia*, 8 vols. (Lisbon, 1778–88). On the rise of Portuguese commercial imperialism along the Atlantic coast of Africa, Vitorino Magalhães Godinho, *O "Mediterrãneo" Saariano e as caravanos do ouro* (São Paulo, 1956); and Manuel Nunes Dias, *O capitalismo mon-árquico Português (1415–1549)*, 2 vols. (Coimbra, 1963–64) are excellent studies.

Two collections of state papers document the widening ambitions of the Catholic kings along the Atlantic border: Luis Suárez Fernández, *Política International de Isabel la Católica*, 5 vols. (Valladolid, 1965–   ) and Antonio de la Torre and Luis Suárez Fernández, *Documentos sobre los relaciones con Portugal durante el reinado de los reyes católicos*, 2 vols. (Valladolid, 1959). For Spain's limited advance into Mediterranean North Africa the chroniclers, Hernando de Pulgar, *Crónica de los senores reyes católicos*, in *BAE*, vol. 70 (Madrid, 1878). Francisco López de Gómara, *Annals of the Emperor Charles V*, trans. R. B. Merri-man (Oxford, 1912), and Prudencio de Sandoval, *Historia del Emperador Carlos V*, in *BAE*, vol. 80 (Madrid, 1955), provide the basic political details. Among the modern histories dealing with Spain's Ibero-African border, J. M. Doussinague, *La política internacional de Fernando el Católico* (Madrid, 1944) and Paul Ruff, *La domination espagnole à Oran* (Paris, 1900) describe the North African frontier as a bastion against Islam, while Ruth Pike, *Enterprise and Adventure* (Ithaca, 1966) shows why the conquests in the New World attracted attention away from the less-rewarding Maghribian border.

The autonomy of North Africa's history as a part of either the Mediterranean or the Islamic world is the main theme of Jamil M. Abun-Nasr, *A History of the Maghrib* (Cambridge, 1971); Abdallah Laroui, *L'histoire du Maghreb: Un essai de synthèse* (Paris, 1970); and Charles-André Julien, *History of North Africa*, trans. John Petrie, ed. C. C. Stewart (London, 1970).

How the Saᶜdians established their state remains largely speculative; there are few sources from the foundation era. Aside from the docu-ments contained in *SIHM*, the standard accounts for the rise of the Saᶜdian dynasty are Muhammad al-Ufrānī or Ifrānī, *Nozhet al-Hâdi: Histoire de la dynastie saadienne au Maroc, 1511–1670*, ed., trans. O. Houdos, 2 vols. (Paris, 1888–89); Diego de Torres, *Relación del origen y sucesso de los Xarifes* (Seville, 1586); and Edward Fagnan, trans., *Extraits inédits au Maghreb* (Algiers, 1924). This last work contains portions of a chronicle by Jannabī that were translated from a poor text. A better edition is G. S. Colin, ed., *Chronique anonyme de la dynastie saᶜdienne* (Rabat, 1934). A fresh source for the history of the Saᶜdians is Müneccimbaşı, *Sahaʾif alʾahbar*, trans. Ahmed Nedim Efendi (Ottoman), 3 vols. (Istanbul, 1868). In the modern period Ahmed Ben Khalid En-Naçiri Es-Salâoui, *Kitab el-Istiqça Li-Akhbar Doul el maghrib el-Aqça "Les Saadiens,"* trans. Mohammed en-Naçiri, *Archives Marocaines*, vol. 34 (Paris, 1936), reproduces most of the material available in the Arabic sources. There are two analytical studies of Saᶜdian origins: August Cour, *L'établissement des dynasties des chérifs au Maroc et leur rivalité avec les Turcs de la régence d'Alger (1509–1830)* (Paris, 1904), and Roger Le Tourneau, *Les débuts de la dynastie saᶜdienne* (Algiers, 1954). The place of the Saᶜdians in Moroccan history is accessible in Henri Terrasse, *Histoire du Maroc,* 2 vols. (Casablanca, 1949–50).

Ottoman expansion into North Africa is connected with the growth of the Turko-Muslim navy and the conquest of Egypt. The best source for the first reconnaissance of the Ottomans in the western Mediterranean basin is Piri Reis, *Kitab-ı Bahriye* [The book of sea lore] (Istanbul, 1935). Hans Albrecht von Burski, *Kemal Reis: Ein Beitrag zur Geschichte der türkischen Flotte* (Bonn, 1928), has studied the life of the Ottoman who commanded the first expedition. This work, however, should be supplemented by Ismet Parmaksızoğlu, "Kemal Reis," *Islam Ansiklopedisi,* 6 (Istanbul, 1940–): 566–69. The second wave of Ottoman naval activity in North Africa begins with the arrival of the Barbarossas. Hayreddin Barbarossa's own account, "Gazavat-i Hayreddin Paşa," British Museum, Or. Ms. no. 2798, is the basic source. There are several versions of this manuscript. A. Gallotta, "Le Gazavāt di Hayreddin Barbarossa," *Studi Magrebini* 3 (1970): 79–160, traced the history of this frontier epic. Francisco Lopez de Gómara, who may have had access to a copy of Barbarossa's manuscript, produced in *Crónica de los Barbarojas,* in *Memorial histórico español,* vol. 6 (Madrid, 1853), a history of the Ottoman corsairs that parallels the corsair's own account. Modern histories of the Barbarossa era are ᶜAbd al-Ḥamīd, *Dukhūl al-Atrāk al ᶜUthmaniyyin ilā Jazaᵓir* [The Entry of the Ottoman Turks into Algeria] (Algiers, 1972), and Svat Soucek, "The Rise of the Barbarossas in North Africa," *Archivum Ottomanicum* 3 (1971): 238–50.

Political and military aspects of the imperial conflict between the Ottomans and the Habsburgs are described in R. B. Merriman's *The Rise of the Spanish Empire in the Old World and the New,* 4 vols. (New York, 1918–34); Leopold von Ranke's *The Ottoman and Spanish Empires in the Sixteenth and Seventeenth Centuries,* trans. W. K. Kelley (London, 1843); and, for Philip II's reign, Fernand Braudel's *The Mediterranean World.* Two excellent studies of the competing empires are John Elliott, *Imperial Spain, 1469–1716* (London, 1963); and Halil Inalcık, *The Ottoman Empire: The Classical Age, 1300–1600* (New York, 1973). The course of imperial warfare along the North African border was traced by two contemporary Spanish historians: Luis del Mármol Carvajal, *L'Afrique de Marmol,* trans. Nicolas Perrot d'Ablancourt, 2 vols. (Paris, 1667); and Fray Diego de Haëdo, *Topografía e historia general de Argel,* 3 vols. (Madrid, 1927). On the Ottoman side, the modern history of Aziz Samih Ilter, *Şimali Afrikada Türkler* [The Turks in North Africa], 2 vols. (Istanbul, 1937), summarizes much of the information available in the vizierial notebooks concerning North African matters. A history of the Ottoman activity in Spain during the Morisco revolt of 1568–70 is contained in Diego Hurtado de Mendoza,

Guerra de Granada (Madrid, 1970). How the Morisco uprising fit into the framework of Ottoman imperialism is analyzed by Andrew C. Hess, "The Moriscos: An Ottoman Fifth Column in Sixteenth Century Spain, *AHR* 74, no. 1 (October 1968): 1–25.

Braudel, *The Mediterranean World*, provides a general economic background for the end of imperial warfare. Portugal's drift toward disaster is described by Queiros Vélloso, *D. Sebastião, 1557–1578*, 3d ed. (Lisbon, 1945); and E. W. Bovill, *The Battle of Alcazar* (London, 1952). Paul David Lagomarsino, "Court Factions and the Formation of Spanish Policy towards the Netherlands 1559–67," diss., Cambridge University, 1974; and Geoffrey Parker, *The Army of Flanders and the Spanish Road* (Cambridge, 1972), study the conditions within Philip II's reign that led to the decision to favor the northern rather than the Mediterranean frontier. For the Ottoman empire, Bekir Kütükoğlu, *Osmanlı Safevi Siyasi Münasebetleri, 1578–1590* [Ottoman Safavid relations, 1578–1590] (Istanbul, 1957), gives the political reasons for the Ottoman decision to go to war with Persia. John Francis Guilmartin, Jr., *Gunpowder and Galleys* (London, 1974) shows how the costs of galley warfare encouraged both empires to abandon the Mediterranean conflict. Finally, the conditions of the disengagement are described by Andrew C. Hess, "The Battle of Lepanto and Its Place in Mediterranean History," *Past and Present* 57 (November 1972): 53–73; and S. A. Skilliter, "The Hispano-Ottoman Armistice of 1581," in *Iran and Islam*, ed. C. E. Bosworth (Edinburgh, 1971).

How the Ottomans lost control over their frontiers awaits a historian of Ottoman decline. Bernard Lewis, "Ottoman Observers of Ottoman Decline," *Islamic Studies* 1 (1962): 71–87, shows how the Turko-Muslim elite viewed the problems of the state at the turn of the seventeenth century. Ömer Lutfi Barkan, "The Price Revolution of the Sixteenth Century: A Turning Point in the Economic History of the Near East," trans. Justin McCarthy, *IJMES* 6, no. 2 (January 1975): 3–28, offers an explanation that emphasizes the devastating impact of the price revolution on the economic stability of the Near Eastern empire.

Political decentralization became the main manifestation of Ottoman decline in North Africa. Ilter, *Şimali Afrikada*, exposes this process on the basis of Ottoman archival documents. His work can be supplemented by Haëdo, *Topografía*, for Algeria; Jamil M. Abun-Nasr, "The Beylicate in Seventeenth Century Tunisia," *IJMES* 6, no. 1 (January 1975): 70–93, for Tunisia; and Suraiya Faroqhi, "Der Aufstand des Yaḥyā ibn Yaḥyā as-Suwaydi," *Der Islam* 47 (1971): 67–92. Morocco's somewhat different history can be approached through the chapter on the Sharifian empire, 1553–1830, in Julian, *North Africa*. For the Saᶜdian invasion of the Sudan, E. W. Bovill's *The Golden Trade of the Moors*, 2d ed. (New York, 1970), gives the basic details. On the relations between the Saᶜdians and the Turks at the end of the sixteenth century, the travel account of Abou-l-

Hasen ... Et-Tamgrūtī, *Kitab An-Nafḥa al-Miskiya Fī s-Sifara at-Turkiya 1581–1591* [Relation d'une ambassade marocaine en Turquie (1589–1591)], trans. Henry De Castries (Paris, 1929), is a primary source. Muḥammad Hajjī, *Al-Zāwiya al-Dalā'iya* [The Zawiya of Dila] (Rabat, 1964), shows how Moroccan society retained its cohesion at the end of the Saᶜdian era.

During the period of decline corsair warfare replaced the great galley conflicts of the mid-sixteenth century. Kâtib Çelebi, *Tuhfet ül kıbar fi Esfar ul Bihar* (Istanbul, 1911), is the primary Ottoman source. There is a partial English translation of this work, Hajji Khalifeh, *The History of the Maritime Wars of the Turks*, trans. James Mitchell (London, 1831), that does carry the story of the Ottoman navy beyond the age of expansion. Modern histories of the corsairs vary widely in quality. Salvatore Bono, *I corsari barbareschi* (Torino, 1964), contains a good deal of information on the Catholic missions in North Africa. Godfrey Fisher, *Barbary Legend* (Oxford, 1957), demonstrates on the basis of English documents that there was more to the North African regencies than the desire to raid Christian vessels. Finally, Alberto Tenenti, *Piracy and the Decline of Venice, 1580–1615*, trans. and ed. Janet and Brian Pullan (London, 1968), sets the Barbary corsairs within the framework of late sixteenth-century Mediterranean history.

Relations between Muslims and Christians in Spain before the reconquest of Granada are best approached through Robert Ignatius Burns, *Islam under the Crusaders* (Princeton, 1973); and Miguel Angel Ladero Quesada, *Los Mudéjares de Castilla en tiempos de Isabel I* (Valladolid, 1969). Two sources for the history of the Moors of Granada are Luis del Mármol Carvajal, *Historia del Rebelión y Castigo de los Moriscos de reino de Granada*, in *BAE*, vol. 24 (Madrid, 1858), and Mendoza, *Guerra de Granada*. Evidence on the attempts of the church to change the social customs of the Moriscos is given in Antonio Gallego y Burín and Alfonso Gámir Sandoval, *Los Moriscos del reino de Granada* (Granada, 1968). The best study of the social conflict between the Moriscos and Old Christians in Granada is Julio Caro Baroja, *Los Moriscos de reino de Granada* (Madrid, 1957). Juan Reglá, *Estudios sobre los Moriscos* (Valencia, 1964), deals with the history of Hispano-Muslims outside Granada. Henri Lapeyre, *Géographie de l'Espagne morisque* (Paris, 1959), is a detailed survey of the Morisco population before, and during the time of, the final expulsion of 1609–14. Muḥammad ᶜAbdallāh ᶜInān, *Nihāyat al-Andalus* [The end of Muslim Spain] (Cairo, 1958), is a general history of the entire topic that emphasizes the illegality of Christian Spain's treatment of the Hispano-Muslims.

An introduction to the urban history of the Ottoman empire is Robert Mantran's *Istanbul dans la second moitié du XVIIᵉ siècle* (Paris, 1962). On the North African border, Haëdo, *Topografía*; Mármol *Descripción*; and Père Dan, *Histoire de la Barbarie et de ses corsaires*

(Paris, 1637), document the Ottoman embellishment of the Maghrib's cities. So also do Muḥammad ibn Abī Dīnār al-Ḳairawānī, *Histoire de l'Afrique*, trans. E. Pellissier et Rémusat, vol. 3 of *Exploration scientifique de l'Algérie* (Paris, 1845); Ali Riza Paşa, *Mirᵓat al-Cezayir* [A view of Algeria], trans. Ali Şevki (Ottoman), (Istanbul, 1876); and Ibn G̲h̲albūn, *Tāᵓrik̲h̲ Ṭarāblus al-G̲h̲arb* [A history of Tripolitania] (Cairo, 1930), comment on the recovery under Ottoman rule of Orthodox Islam. For Morocco, Roger Le Tourneau's *Fès avant le Protectorat* (Casablanca, 1949) gives a good description of Morocco's urban institutions. The chapters on the Saᶜdian era in Gaston Deverdun's *Merrakech des origines à 1912*, 2 vols. (Rabat, 1959–66), are particularly valuable for understanding the cultural impact of this sultanate upon Morocco. The final settlement of the Moriscos in North Africa and their contribution to a revived Islamic society can be gathered from Muḥammad Dāwūd, *Tārik̲h̲ Tiṭwān*, 18 vols. (Tetuan, 1959–70); Miguel de Epalza and R. Petit, eds., *Etudes sur les Moriscos andalous en Tunisie* (Madrid, 1973); and Kenneth Brown, "An Urban View of Moroccan History, Salé, 1000–1800," *Hespéris-Tamuda* 12 (1971): 46–63.

The growing cultural discontinuity expressed itself in a number of literary forms. An excellent study of the changing image of the Turk in Spanish literature is Albert Mas, *Les Turcs dans la littérature espagnole du siècle d'or*, 2 vols. (Paris, 1967). Spain's waning interest in Islamic history, until the modern period, is studied by James T. Monroe, *Islam and the Arabs in Spanish Scholarship* (Leiden, 1970). A sense of the introverted character of Ottoman culture at the turn of the seventeenth century can be grasped from the works of Kâtib Çelebi, *The Balance of Truth*, trans. G. L. Lewis (London, 1957); and Alessio Bombaci, *Histoire de la littérature turque*, trans. I. Melikoff (Paris, 1968).

Frontier manifestations in North Africa of this same event start with anti-Christian polemics: Miguel de Epalza, "Notes pour une histoire des polémiques anti-chrétiennes dans l'occident musulman," *Arabica* 18 (1971): 99–107. L. P. Harvey, "Aljamía," *EI*², 1:404–5, summarizes what is known about the declining role of this frontier language. Ahmed Abdesselem, *Les historiens tunisiens des xviiᵉ, xviiiᵉ, et xixᵉ siècles* (Tunis, 1973) describes the conservative cultural milieu of the most cosmopolitan region of North Africa. Morocco's inward retreat is discussed by E. Lévi-Provençal, *Les historiens des Chorfa* (Paris, 1923); and Mohammed Lakhdar, *La vie littéraire au Maroc sous la dynastie ᶜAlawide, 1075–1311/1664–1894* (Rabat, 1971). Jacques Berque, *Al-Yousi* (Paris, 1958) captures the essence of Moroccan cultural values in his history of a seventeenth-century religious figure.

Henri Terrasse, *Islam d'Espagne* (Paris, 1958), shows how the history of religious symbols on the Hispano-Muslim frontier reflected the increasing difference between Islamic and Latin Christian civilizations. G. Kubler and M. Soria, *Art and Architecture in Spain and Portugal*

(London, 1959), traces the arrival of early modern Spanish architecture in southeastern Spain. An introduction to the history of Ottoman architecture can be found in Oktay Aslanapa, *Turkish Art and Architecture* (New York, 1971). Ottoman architecture in North Africa has not been the subject of any systematic study. George Marçais, *L'Architecture musulmane d'Occident* (Paris, 1954), provides some information. Ali Saim Ülgen, "Trablusgarpta Turgut Reis Mimarî Manzumesi," *Vakıflar Dergisi*, 5 (Ankara, 1962): 87–92, shows how the patterns of Ottoman religious construction had spread to Tripolitania. *Les mosques en Algerie* (Madrid, 1970), contains some information on Ottoman buildings in North Africa. Deverdun, *Merrakech*, and Le Tourneau, *Fès*, provide observations about the retention of Hispano-Muslim forms in the religious art and architecture of Morocco long after Islamic civilization was driven from Spain.

INDEX